Happy 90th Birthday Doug!

D1558273

TWIN PORTS
BY TROLLEY

Also Published by the University of Minnesota Press

Twin Cities by Trolley: The Streetcar Era in Minneapolis and St. Paul

John W. Diers and Aaron Isaacs

TWIN PORTS BY TROLLEY

THE STREETCAR ERA IN DULUTH–SUPERIOR

AARON ISAACS

University of Minnesota Press
Minneapolis • London

Illustrations in this book appear courtesy of the Minnesota Streetcar Museum unless otherwise credited. See **www.trolleyride.org** for more information.

Published by the University of Minnesota Press
111 Third Avenue South, Suite 290
Minneapolis, MN 55401–2520
http://www.upress.umn.edu

Book design by bedesign, inc.

Library of Congress Cataloging-in-Publication Data
Isaacs, Aaron, author.
Twin ports by trolley : the streetcar era in Duluth–Superior / Aaron Isaacs.
Includes bibliographical references and index.
ISBN 978-0-8166-7308-7 (hc : alk. paper)
1. Street railroads—Minnesota—Duluth—History. 2. Street railroads—Wisconsin—Superior—History. 3. Street railroads—Rolling stock—Minnesota—Duluth—History. 4. Street railroads—Rolling stock—Wisconsin—Superior—History. 5. Duluth (Minn.)—History. 6. Superior (Wis.)—History. I. Title.
TF725.D85I83 2014
388.4'609776771—dc23
2014011997

Printed in Canada on acid-free paper

The University of Minnesota is an equal-opportunity educator and employer.

20 19 18 17 16 15 14   10 9 8 7 6 5 4 3 2 1

CONTENTS

There is no mistaking this scene for anywhere but Duluth in the
1890s. A locally manufactured whaleback lake steamer and barge
are docked amid spring ice. Climbing the Central Hillside is the 7th
Avenue West Incline, in its original incarnation. A pair of counter-
weighted, garage-sized cars shuttle up and down between Superior

PREFACE

There is no other American city quite like Duluth. An international seaport in the middle of the continent, Duluth is draped over a steep hillside featuring some of the highest hills in Minnesota. The Zenith City is extremely oblong, stretching twenty-five miles along Lake Superior, the harbor, and the St. Louis River, yet it is only three miles wide in most places. An industrial powerhouse during its heyday, atop the ridge the north woods begin well within the city limits.

East of downtown, its neighborhoods look out over Lake Superior. This portion of Duluth is wooded and residential, with much high-quality housing. With its connections to mining, steel making, lumber, railroads, and shipbuilding, Duluth boasted a moneyed and managerial class out of proportion to its population of roughly 100,000. The London Road neighborhood features miles of mansions, their backyards sloping down to the lakeshore.

The Central Hillside, above and just to the west of downtown, is the steepest, with more modest houses and apartments clinging to the rocks. The working-class West End and West Duluth, heavily populated by immigrants, face the harbor, which is lined with industry and docks, including the famous ore docks. In addition to the traditional development pattern radiating out from downtown, Duluth has neighborhoods such as Woodland, Lakeside, and Duluth Heights that began as far-flung suburban real estate developments. Few neighborhoods are more unusual than Park Point, one block wide and three miles long, strung out along the sandbar separating the lake from the harbor. Duluth's city limits expanded to incorporate all these suburbs in the 1890s.

Streetcar days in Duluth—The big yellow car on the East 8th Street line has just turned from 9th Street onto 7th Avenue East. As soon as the ladies finish boarding, it will begin easing down the steep hill toward downtown, 400 feet below. 1937.

Duluth–Superior has an excellent harbor, the largest on the Great Lakes. Shipping has secured the city's economy for more than 140 years. First came logging and the export of lumber from Minnesota's huge pine forests to cities and farms across the country. Grain followed, as farms replaced grasslands in western Minnesota and the Dakotas. Then in 1884 North America's largest high-grade iron ore deposit was discovered only one hundred miles to the north and west, and the city boomed. From open-pit mines iron ore moved by rail to Duluth for shipment in lake boats to the steel mills in Chicago, Michigan, Ohio, and Pennsylvania. Eventually, U.S. Steel built a mill on the south side of the city. It spawned the company town of Morgan Park with its unusual concrete-block architecture and construction. The communities of Gary and New Duluth grew up nearby to support the mill.

With all this activity, Duluth became a magnet for railroads. In fact, the Northern Pacific, the nation's second transcontinental, struck out for the Pacific coast from Carlton, twenty miles southwest of Duluth, rather

As flat as Duluth is hilly, Superior is centered on Tower Avenue. Why the corner of Tower and Belknap Avenue is so busy on this day is unclear, but the streetcars are waiting to carry everyone home. Ca. 1920. Courtesy of the Douglas County Historical Society.

than from the more populous Twin Cities. Eventually, the Twin Ports of Duluth–Superior were served by thirteen main lines run by eight railroad companies.

Duluth's sister city across the harbor, Superior, Wisconsin, occupies a large triangle of land bordered on the northeast by Lake Superior and on the northwest by the harbor and the St. Louis River. It is as flat as Duluth is hilly. Duluth has always been the dominant twin; in 1930 Duluth's population of 101,000 compared to Superior's peak of 46,000.

Because of its less-challenging topography, Superior had more railroad activity. It was honeycombed with rail lines and yards, which reduced the residential districts to a series of islands and peninsulas, centered on the commercial spine of Tower Avenue. Superior originally developed along the east end of the harbor, facing Lake Superior. This is the neighborhood now known as the East End. Development there was anchored by the construction of ore docks on the lakeshore.

Superior's center shifted to what was then called West Superior as the entire harbor front developed and the rail network was completed. Tower Avenue became the new downtown. Unlike Duluth, Superior has little upscale housing. Most of the residential development is working-class. The outlier neighborhoods of South Superior and Allouez clustered around a rail junction and an ore dock, respectively.

The Duluth Street Railway (DSR) and its predecessor and successor companies tied these neighborhoods and businesses together with a transit system that was the second largest in Minnesota. It had strong connections to the mighty Twin City Rapid Transit Company (TCRT) and its founder, Thomas Lowry. Incorporated in 1881, DSR began operations in 1883. By 1890, it owned 4.5 miles of line, 15 horsecars, and 178 mules. Lowry joined its board of directors in 1886 with a 20 percent interest. In 1890 he arranged for financing from Eastern banks to convert the system to electric power and construct an incline railway. Thereafter, in a series of corporate moves, the DSR, with the backing of TCRT interests, subsequently acquired the Superior Rapid Transit Railway Company. It also purchased four independent streetcar lines, one on Park Point and three built in the 1890s to serve suburban real estate developments. All of the respective companies were united under the corporate umbrella of the Duluth–Superior Traction Company. Due to corporate reorganizations over time, there were name changes, but for purposes of this book the company will be called Duluth Street Railway (DSR).

Financially, the Duluth–Superior system was never strong, and its decline followed the well-worn path of other street railways. Geography and increasing automobile and unregulated jitney competition combined to work against it. Duluth's population was spread thinly along the twenty-five miles of waterfront, requiring long lines to bring riders into the downtown business district. Serving this sprawling, low-density city was a major challenge for a street railway system that also had to contend with some of the coldest and snowiest weather in the country. Duluth had approximately 1,700 persons per square mile, and Superior had 1,200, compared to 7,600 in Minneapolis and 5,600 in St. Paul at the time.

Because of Duluth's larger population and economic power, its transit system was stronger than Superior's. A 1925 ridership report showed 4000 passengers entering downtown Duluth during the peak morning hour versus 600 entering downtown Superior. The Duluth system required 94 streetcars during the morning rush hour, while Superior needed only 16 cars. DSR's peak year was 1919, when it carried thirty-eight million riders, operated 5,538,000 car miles, and employed 670 people.

After that, it was all downhill. Economizing became necessary as ridership declined. Company management realized that on some of its marginally profitable lines, its standard cars were too big, too heavy, and too costly to operate, so it acquired a number of smaller, more economical cars. It began converting its streetcars to one-man operation, eliminating conductors. It wasn't enough. The Great Depression hit the Twin Ports hard, and the company entered receivership in 1930. It was reorganized as the Duluth Superior Transit Company. Bus substitutions followed. Interestingly, Duluth opted for trolley buses (buses running on electrical power from the trolley overhead wires) on its heaviest lines mainly because so much of its electrical distribution system was not fully depreciated. Superior's streetcars disappeared in 1935, and Duluth's followed in 1939. The trolley buses remained until 1957. Today the system is publicly owned and operated by the Duluth Transit Authority.

Students of economics will find nothing unusual in the history of the Duluth system. Like most street railways, it was undercapitalized and overbuilt. The system was well managed and, for a time, revenues were able to cover operating expenses, but there was never enough income to handle long-term debt. As costs went up, revenues declined. The pattern continued through bus conversion until eventual public ownership.

Although the focus of this book is the Twin Ports' streetcar system, the development of buses is also covered. While the main narrative ends in 1939, the electric trolley buses ran until 1957 and deserve a postscript. As a bus–streetcar hybrid, they are a curiosity to the public, and like streetcars, they depended for power on overhead wires, so their entire tenure is included in this book.

Streetcars may not have been a financial success in their later years, but they helped build Duluth–Superior and were essential to the daily lives of more than two generations of residents. Remembered with nostalgia, streetcars are woven into the history of the cities and their residents. The purpose of this book is to revive those streetcar memories and tell the story of a fine public transportation system and how it served its community. To that end, the reader will see extensive quoted passages from company memos, employee newsletters, and newspapers of the time. This was done to capture the style and feel of the period from the perspective of those who were there.

This book follows the 2007 publication of *Twin Cities by Trolley,* the illustrated history of streetcars in Minneapolis and St. Paul. The Twin City Rapid Transit Company had a strong influence on the Duluth–Superior system.

This book is heavily dependent on the previous work of transit historians and museum collections in Minnesota and Wisconsin. The late Wayne C. Olsen, a founder of the Lake Superior Railroad Museum, gathered many photographs and files of the Duluth–Superior streetcar system. Before his death, he donated the Duluth portion of his collection to the Northeast Minnesota Historical Center, which is located at the University of Minnesota Duluth. The Center also acquired corporate records from the transit company, making it a primary resource for this book. Curator Patricia Maus was extremely helpful to the author and generously made the collection available.

Olsen donated his Superior photographs to the Douglas County Historical Society, which made them available for publication. The historical society also had in its collection a number of newspaper stories that provided useful information. Our thanks to director Kathy Laakso and volunteer Bob LaBounty.

Russell Olson, the dean of Minnesota streetcar historians, used the materials cited above to produce a large chapter in his authoritative book *Electric Railways of Minnesota.* Maps from that book, drawn by Kent Dorholt, were invaluable and, modified with additional information, are reproduced herein. Continuing his research in the years following the book's 1976 publication, Russ produced an addendum with corrections and new information. He assisted with fact-checking for this book, as he did for *Twin Cities by Trolley.*

The late James Kreuzberger was a Duluth native who spent his last thirty years researching the Twin Ports streetcar system. He wrote an incomplete manuscript for a book of his own, organized with plenty of support data, and a few years ago he generously donated his text to the Minnesota Streetcar Museum, which made it available to the author. Jim researched old newspaper files to understand the politics that surrounded and influenced the construction of the system. He also dug deeply into day-to-day operations, revealing how the streetcar system worked behind the scenes. Following his death in 2010, his widow donated his extensive col-

lection of Duluth–Superior photographs and research notes, plus assorted Duluth Street Railway records, to the Minnesota Streetcar Museum. Many of those photographs appear in this volume.

In addition to those materials cited above, the Minnesota Streetcar Museum also contributed numerous photos and some documents. The author and Russell Olson are members, as were the late Jim Kreuzberger and Wayne C. Olsen, and the author curates the museum's photograph collection, which, with the Kreuzberger additions, includes more than one thousand Duluth–Superior images plus a number of paper artifacts.

John W. Diers participated in researching and organizing the book, and wrote portions of the corporate history and the section on employee strikes. Peter Bonesteel contributed several photographs from his extensive collection. Thanks also to David Schauer for his help identifying photograph locations.

The author thanks Todd Orjala, formerly with the University of Minnesota Press, for initiating this project, and Kristian Tvedten, Erik Anderson, Daniel Ochsner, Brian Donahue, and Rachel Quast for their fine assistance with content, layout, editing, and production.

GLOSSARY OF STREETCAR TERMS

BACKUP CONTROL: With a handful of exceptions, all DSR cars were single ended, with full controls only at the front end. Nonetheless, short backup moves were required to negotiate wyes at the ends of the lines and for switching at the carhouses. To make these moves safely after conductors were eliminated, simple backup controls were installed on the rear platform, consisting only of on and off switches and an air brake lever.

BELL SIGNALS: Gong-type bells mounted on the front and rear platform ceilings were connected by a leather pull cord. The motorman and conductor communicated with one another by way of bell signals, such as two rings to go forward and three to back up.

BLOCK SIGNAL: An automatic electric signal used to prevent collisions on sections of line having only a single track.

BRAKE APPLICATION, APPLY THE AIR: The streetcars had air brakes, which were applied by opening a valve that released compressed air into the brake pipe, forcing the brake shoes to press against the steel wheel treads, thus slowing the car.

CLUB ROOM: the gathering place for trainmen at the carhouses.

CONDUCTOR, CONDUCTRESS: On a two-man car, the conductor was responsible for collecting fares, interacting with passengers, and handling the money. Women hired during World War I were called "conductresses."

CONTROLLER: The motorman used the controller to regulate the amount and polarity of electricity to the car's motors, thereby determining the car's speed and direction.

DEAD MAN: A spring-loaded air brake valve that served as a safety device to stop the car if the motorman was incapacitated. When released, the springs automatically applied the brakes.

EXTRA BOARD: Motormen and conductors not assigned to a regular run. The extra board employees were assigned to fill in for regular crew members who were absent. Originally, if they did not receive an assignment, they were not paid.

EXTRA: An unscheduled streetcar trip. Extras ran for ball games, parades, and other events. See also Tripper.

FAREBOX, FAREBOX READINGS: Passengers dropped their fare in the farebox. A crank on the side caused the coins and tokens to trip mechanical counters. The crew member would copy the numbers, or "take the farebox reading," and enter them on his trip sheet.

FENDER: A steel mesh basket on the car front designed to scoop up a pedestrian who would otherwise have been run over by the car and killed or seriously injured. The device was often mistakenly called a "cowcatcher."

FLANGEWAYS: Streetcar wheels stayed on the track because of flanges, the wider part of the wheel that gripped the inside of the rail. Because the rails were surrounded by pavement, a special groove, or flangeway, provided a place for the flange to travel.

FROG, TROLLEY FROG: The frog guided the wheel flanges through track switches where the rails divided, which required creating a flangeway across another rail. Trolley frogs performed the similar function of guiding the trolley wheel through switches where the trolley wire divided.

GATE CAR: All DSR standard cars were originally built as gate cars. All passengers boarded and alighted through wire gates at the right rear of the car. During the 1930s, many were rebuilt as one-man cars, with air-operated folding doors replacing the gates.

GATE SIDE, POLE SIDE: The gate side was the right side of the car, where the gates were. The pole side was the left side, or street side. Trolley-wire support poles were originally in the center of the street.

HEADWAY: The time interval between streetcars. A five-minute headway meant that a car arrived every five minutes.

LAYOVER, LAYOVER POINT: The time between trips at the end of the line (layover) was taken at the layover point.

LIGHTWEIGHT: A lighter-weight streetcar built in the 1920s to reduce electric power consumption.

LOOP: a circle of track for reversing a streetcar at the end of the line.

MOTORMAN: The crew member responsible for running the streetcar, either alone or with a conductor.

NOTCH 8, THE COMPANY NOTCH, ON THE BRASS, IN THE CORNER: The controller position that provided the maximum speed.

ONE-MAN CARS, TWO-MAN CARS: As built, all the DSR streetcars purchased before 1919 required a two-man crew: a motorman to run the car and a conductor to collect the fares. Later the cars were rebuilt with front entrances so the motorman could collect fares and the conductor was eliminated, hence a one-man car.

ONE-PIECE RUN, TWO-PIECE RUN, THREE-PIECE RUN: Refers to the number of times a trainman had to report to work per day. Two-piece and three-piece runs were split shifts.

OWL CAR: Streetcars that ran all night long, usually once an hour.

PLUG IN: Motormen and conductors reported to work by placing a wood plug next to their name on the plug board.

POWER LOSS: In some spots on the system, electric voltage was reduced and cars ran slower because of the distance to the nearest substation or because of the number of cars on the line simultaneously.

PULL OUT, PULL IN, DEADHEAD: Leaving or entering the streetcar station, or running while not in service between the station and the route.

REGULAR RUN: Work assigned to the same crew every day. Runs were usually assigned by employee seniority.

RETRIEVER: The spring-loaded reel that gathered in the trolley pole rope and pulled down, or "retrieved," the trolley pole if it dewired, to prevent it from tearing down the wire.

SHORTLINE, TURN BACK: An intermediate point on the line where some streetcars ended their trips.

SKIP-STOPPING: When two cars ran together, they would each stop at alternate stops, thereby expediting the trip for both. Skip-stopping was also implemented as an emergency measure to save energy during World War I.

SPREAD TIME: the number of hours from the beginning to the end of a trainman's day. If it was a split shift, the spread time could be as much as fifteen hours.

SPECIAL WORK: Complex track where lines crossed or diverged.

STANDING LOAD: A passenger load exceeding the car's seating capacity.

STARTER: A supervisor located at certain important intersections to keep cars on time and to reschedule as necessary to meet demand or operating conditions.

STATION, STATION CLERK: "Station" was the DSR term for carbarn or garage. The station clerk handled a wide variety of clerical chores, including assigning crews and streetcars.

SWITCH ROD, SWITCH ROD HOLE: A steel pole with a flattened tip could be lowered through the switch rod hole inside the car next to the motorman's left foot to pry track switches into position. Motormen who chewed tobacco would spit the juice through the switch rod hole.

TERMINAL: The end of the line.

TIME POINTS: Major intersections along the line with a scheduled departure time.

TRAINMAN, TRAINWOMEN: A general term for motormen and conductors.

TRANSFER: A paper slip issued by the conductor or motorman permitting a passenger to board a second streetcar without paying an additional fare. Also, the act of changing from one streetcar to another.

TRIPPER: A short run, usually only one or two trips, added during the rush hours. See Extra.

TROLLEY POLE, TROLLEY WHEEL: The trolley pole reached from the car roof to the overhead wire to access electricity. The trolley wheel at the end of the pole rolled along the underside of the wire.

TURN ON THE AIR, PUMP UP THE AIR: Activate the air compressor, which powered the brakes, doors, and whistle.

WORK CAR: Any of various nonrevenue trolleys that plowed snow, hauled materials, or performed other maintenance tasks.

WYE: A triangle of track on which cars could be turned around at the end of the line. Wying a car required two forward and one backward moves to complete the maneuver.

THE DULUTH STREET

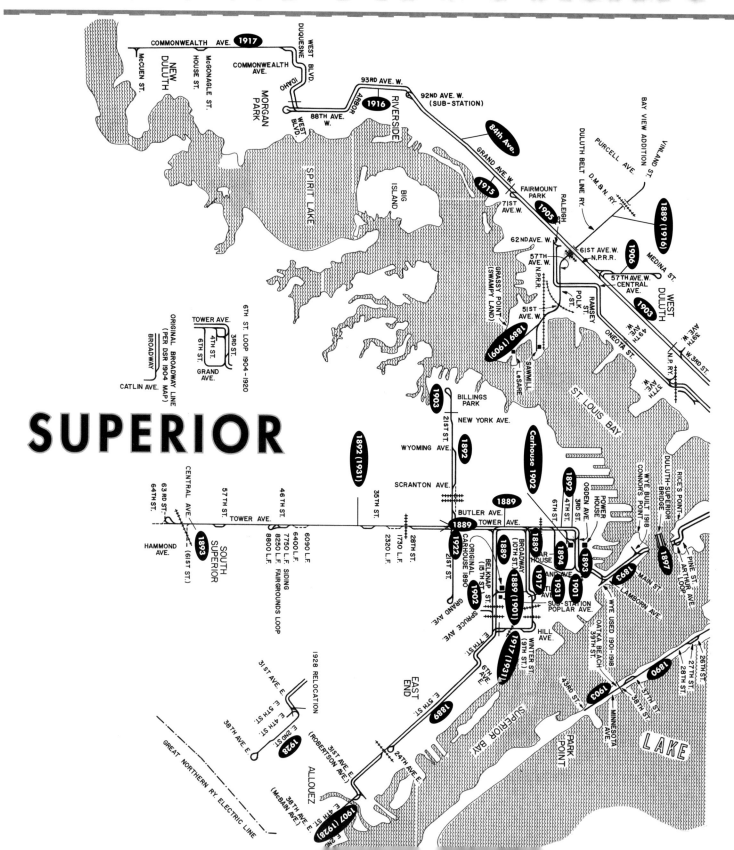

RAILWAY co. SYSTEM

Construction dates are shown for each segment. Abandonments before 1935 appear in parentheses.

DULUTH

SUPERIOR

No. 1

FROM HORSES TO HORSEPOWER
The Dawn of the Streetcar Era

When introducing any history of a street railway, it's appropriate to ask, "Why a railway in a public street?" since trains and automobiles don't mix comfortably today. The answer goes back to the early nineteenth century. Public transportation developed in response to the industrial revolution, which swelled cities to a size greater than walking distance.

This is a typical horsecar, ca. 1888–89. One of 18 owned by DSR, it was lightly built to minimize the mules' effort. Note the snow scraper ahead of the front wheel, which could be lowered to clear the rail. The driver's right hand is on the gooseneck-shaped hand brake.

The first transit vehicles were carriages and coaches called "omnibuses" (origin of the term "bus") that ran regular routes for a fare. At the time most streets were unpaved. They were dusty when dry and turned to mud when it rained. This was certainly the case in Duluth and Superior. Pavement, when it existed, was usually cobblestones, which made for a rough ride on wood wheels. One of the era's breakthrough technologies was the railroad, which appeared in the United States about 1830. It was immediately obvious that iron wheels on iron rails offered less rolling resistance, a smoother ride, and an all-weather road. A horse could pull a heavier load when it was on rails. According to William D. Middleton's authoritative book *Time of the Trolley,* the first urban horsecar line appeared in New York City in 1831. Despite that early start, horse-drawn street railways were slow to develop. It was not until the mid-1850s that they began to appear in large numbers. Thereafter, any city of any size, and many smaller towns, installed horse-drawn streetcars as a matter of course.

When electricity became practical in the late 1880s, it was only logical to electrify the horsecar lines and expand them along with the city. It happened everywhere horsecars were in use, and the Twin Ports were no exception. It was only when the automobile proliferated after World War I that railways began to seem out of place in the streets.

When it reached Point of Rocks, the original line shifted a block closer to the harbor on Michigan Street. This view looks east from about 12th Avenue West. The dark building located between the streetcars is the carbarn at 11th Avenue West. Railroads are in the process of filling in the marshy waterfront. Note the tracks on trestles closest to the water. In a few years that would be solid ground. Ca. 1880s.

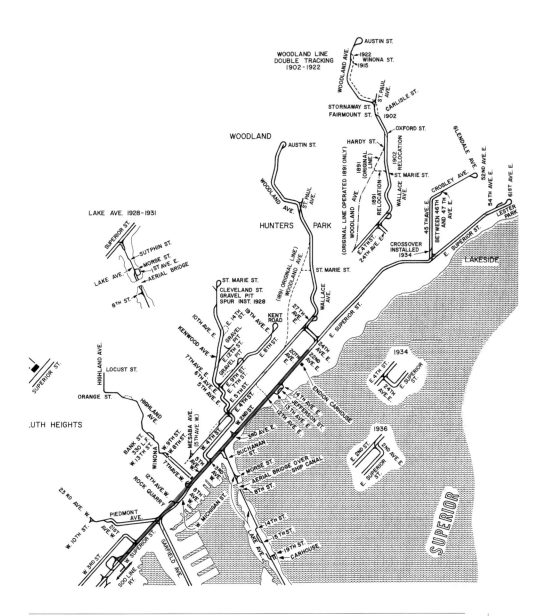

THE ANIMAL-POWERED RAILWAY

DULUTH

The Duluth Street Railway (DSR) was incorporated on October 25, 1881, but several obstacles slowed the construction of the first line. Duluth was a village of 2,500 at that time, so the company had to apply to the state for its charter to operate. Track construction had to wait for Duluth Gas & Water

Company to lay its pipes in Superior Street. Service finally began on July 6, 1883. The line on Superior Street grew in stages, eventually extending four miles from 22nd Avenue East to 28th Avenue West.

To state that DSR had horsecars is somewhat of a misnomer. DSR's stable was mostly mules, which were less costly initially and more economical to maintain as well.

In its July 29, 1956, centennial edition, the *Duluth News Tribune* described life aboard the horsecars:

The single horsecar line on Superior Street was based at this carbarn at 11th Avenue West. Ca. 1880s.

One thing can be said for the mules that pulled Duluth's first street cars in 1883. Neither the Superior Street mud nor the deep winter snow stalled their progress. If the going got bad enough, four mules were hitched up to the little dinky cars and away they went through the drifts and swirling snow.

Weather seemed not to bother the sturdy little animals, but consider the plight of the poor driver. Rain or shine, warm or cold, he stood in a tiny vestibule at the front of the car. When he was frozen almost stiff on a cold winter day, he might occasionally get down and walk alongside the track to get his blood circulating.

The passengers fared somewhat better. In winter a foot of straw was spread on the floor of the enclosed car to keep feet warm. A little stove in the middle of the car was fired up to provide additional heat. The passenger's biggest problem was to be careful not to drop his nickel fare into the straw. If he did, he might just as well forget it. It would be impossible to find.

There were no conductors. The mule car driver had to keep an eye cocked on the register to make sure everyone paid his fare, another on the road ahead, one hand on the hand-brakes and the other on the reins. For all this he got $50 a month.

The late George Roome, who drove the mule cars of the early days, described the street's condition thusly: "In the spring, from 5th Avenue West to 3rd Avenue East, you couldn't see the tracks. I remember once at 2nd Avenue West, in the rain, the car went off the tracks, and I didn't know about it 'til the mules got to the old city hall and Mr. Hoopes, who was the company manager, ran out and yelled, "Hey, George, your car's off the track." The two of us, one on either side, hoisted the car back onto the rail. That's how light those old cars were.

After a long day at the reins, the horsecar driver was obligated to wash his car before going home.

SUPERIOR

The Douglas County Street Railway Company (DCSR) began horsecar service on August 27, 1884. At that time the center of Superior was what is now called the East End, along the Lake Superior waterfront. The line ran from the carhouse and stable at 25th Avenue East and 5th Street to 23rd Avenue East and 2nd Street to Winter Street, a distance of 2.6 miles. It appears to have been unsuccessful. In a short time it was reported that only four daily trips were operated, with hired passengers if necessary, to fulfill the terms of the ordinance. After that it's not clear if service improved or even if it operated at all.

In April 1888, a newspaper reported, "The street car company will at once commence work clearing up and making whatever repairs are necessary to their track." There were eight daily round-trips at this time. How long this service continued is not known. During this period, the location of the downtown shifted to what was then called West Superior, centered on Tower Avenue.

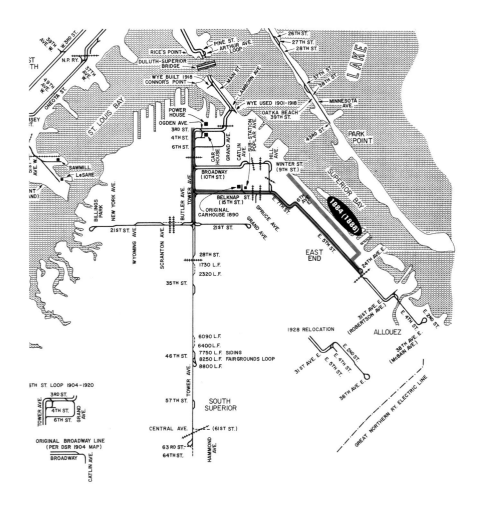

Horse-drawn streetcars ran only briefly and intermittently in Superior. The first line served the East End, at that time the center of town, from 1884 to perhaps 1888. Courtesy of the Douglas County Historical Society.

Horsecars, such as this one on Park Point, were the model for the first electric cars, but soon the cars were built more like railroad coaches. Kathryn A. Martin Library, University of Minnesota Duluth, Archives and Special Collections.

Superior incorporated as a city in March 1889. DCSR was refranchised the same month. On December 23, 1889, operations began on a route starting at 25th Avenue East and 5th Street, then via 5th Street, L Avenue, 7th Street, Belknap Street to Tower Avenue, and on Tower Avenue from 3rd to 21st Streets. The franchise required the completion of a loop line from Belknap Street and Catlin Avenue via Catlin and Broadway to Tower. It's unclear how much of this was operated by horsecars because it was electrified on July 1, 1890, after less than seven months. During the electrification, the *Superior Herald* reported that the company was running only four horsecars and that they ran only every half hour. Although electrification happened quickly, it was an ill-advised decision to continue using the lightly constructed narrow-gauge horsecar tracks. Meanwhile, Duluth had converted to standard gauge. Superior would not complete that process until 1902.

THE DULUTH STREET RAILWAY: A COMPANY HISTORY

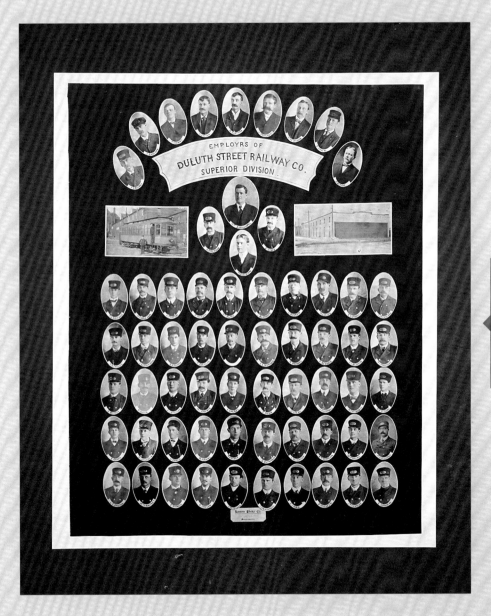

This collage shows the entire Superior Division workforce of the Duluth Street Railway, about 1906. Photograph by Larson Photo Studio.

The Duluth Street Railway Company (DSR) has a rather complicated corporate history. It was incorporated in October 1881 and given a fifty-year charter from the Minnesota legislature. When electrification came along in November 1890, it was operating 4.5 miles of track and owned 18 horsecars and 178 mules. There was a horsecar barn and a stable at 11th Avenue West and Michigan Street on the west end of the downtown. Fifteen-minute service was provided on its single line.

Improvements as part of electrification included widening the track from narrow gauge to standard gauge (4 feet 8.5 inches between the rails), installing heavier

A stock certificate for the Lakeside Railway Company. Collection of Dick Stoner.

rail, street paving, the installation of overhead wire, and the purchase of steam-powered electric-generating equipment. Lines were added and extended, and the incline railway was built up 7th Avenue West. Unfortunately, this period of expansion and electrification exhausted the company's reserves. The effects of the Panic of 1893 proved too heavy a burden, and the company defaulted on its mortgage bonds, entering receivership in 1898.

STREETCAR SUBURBS

Electrification greatly speeded up streetcar service and brought previously inaccessible suburban areas within a half-hour commute of downtown. Three real estate developments, Lakeside, Woodland, and Duluth Heights, tried to cash in on this by building connecting streetcar lines.

LAKESIDE

The Lakeside Railway Company was founded in 1892 by the Lakeside Land Company to help develop the City of Lakeside, located along Superior Street east of 45th Avenue East. Unlike the other land development lines, Lakeside was not physically isolated. The Duluth & Iron Range Railroad had run hourly steam suburban trains to downtown beginning in 1887. Nonetheless, electric streetcars were more frequent, offered a lower fare than trains, and brought passengers closer to their downtown destinations. The line opened on Superior Street from 2nd Avenue East to 61st Avenue East on December 17, 1892. The commuter trains, though faster than the streetcars, lost much of their ridership and quit almost immediately.

Lakeside Railway entered into an operating agreement with DSR. Lakeside would supply the streetcars and DSR would run them all the way into downtown. Like the other development railways, Lakeside proved financially unable to pay DSR's operating contract and also to maintain its track. This led to an 1899 legal dispute between the two companies, and DSR won a judgment for payment of past costs. Lakeside threw in the towel, offering the line to anyone who would pay off the bonds. When DSR emerged from receivership in 1900, it purchased the Lakeside line.

WOODLAND

In 1890 the Motor Line Improvement Company (MLIC) was organized to build a line to Woodland, up Woodland Avenue from a connection with DSR's East 4th Street line. Some of the incorporators were also DSR officials, so it was not a completely independent operation. The company purchased two motor cars and four trailers, built a carhouse at the

end of the line at Woodland Avenue and Austin Street, and commenced operations on April 28, 1891.

It quickly became clear that the motor cars were underpowered and unable to reliably climb the Woodland Avenue hill, so that same year the line was rerouted via East 4th Street to Wallace Avenue to St. Marie Street to Woodland Avenue. Although less direct, the reroute was not as steep and within the streetcars' capabilities.

As it had with the Lakeside Railway, DSR made an agreement to run the Woodland line. The MLIC would provide the rolling stock and cover the operating costs. This arrangement lasted longer than the others. In about 1900, MLIC was purchased by the Woodland Company. The transaction masked the same financial overreach that had afflicted the other developer lines—there wasn't enough revenue from real estate sales to maintain the track. In October 1900 DSR embargoed the line for a week, citing poor track conditions, and did the same again in June 1901. The second embargo brought the dispute to a head, and a couple of days later DSR purchased the Woodland line and immediately began rebuilding it.

HIGHLAND

The Duluth Heights Land Company, succeeded in 1889 by the Highland Improvement Company (HIC), sought to develop real estate atop the ridge northwest of downtown. Given the 600-foot change in elevation, this was easier said than done. The technical solution was the 7th Avenue West Incline that climbed from Superior Street to 8th Street. It was jointly funded by DSR and HIC and opened December 2, 1891. DSR then constructed the first third of the connecting 1.8-mile Highland streetcar line that began at the top of the incline. HIC built the rest of it, and it opened September 27, 1892.

As with the other land development lines, DSR ran it, and HIC reimbursed DSR's operating costs minus fare

Duluth Heights.

The new machinery of the Incline Railway is now completed, and as a consequence we are enabled to offer Duluth Heights residents very much better transportation service and facilities. One fare of **5 Cents** now gives transportation to any part of the city by transfers given to or from any line passing Seventh Avenue West.

Think of it! Lots can be procured, reached by Incline Railway and Electric Cars, only ten minutes ride from the business center of Duluth, and with only a 5 cent fare to every part of the city, at the low price of from $200 to $300, with very easy terms.

Why keep on paying rent?—when you can own your own home, and your payments no larger than you are now paying in rent. We have several **Houses Already Built** for sale, and require only a small cash payment down and the balance in small, easy monthly payments. Come in and see us and secure a home of your own!

Highland Improvement Co.,

208 Herald Building.

Duluth News Tribune, April 30, '94.

This breathless announcement from 1894 promotes the Duluth Heights real estate development, which sat atop the tall ridge two miles northwest of downtown Duluth. Although it was linked to downtown by the Incline and the Highland streetcar line, development was sparse and never met expectations.

revenue. Like the other lines, real estate sales were slower than expected, and HIC was unable to meet its obligations to DSR. The line was sold to DSR in 1894.

PARK POINT

The longest lasting of the independent companies served Park Point. The line was physically isolated from the rest of the Duluth streetcar system until 1930, a year before it was abandoned.

Minnesota Point Street Railway incorporated in 1887 and by December 1888 had laid 1.25 miles of horsecar track. For unknown reasons service did not begin until 1890, when the company acquired four Duluth horsecars made surplus by the conversion to electricity. The line was extended to 39th Street by 1892.

Deep snow and few year-round residents restricted service to summers only for the first few years. Even in the summer traffic was limited. In 1896 stock control shifted from local to Eastern interests. In 1898 the company was sold at auction and renamed Interstate Traction Company. As the name implied, it had designs to reach Superior via Wisconsin Point, but no serious movement in that direction was ever taken. However, the city began steam-powered ferry service across the ship canal in 1899, prompting the company to electrify the line that year and convert it from narrow gauge to standard gauge. To stimulate ridership, a pavilion and picnic ground was constructed at Oatka Beach. It was successful for the first few years. On June 26, 1902, the *Duluth Herald* reported, "The popular dancing party at Oatka Beach auditorium drew another immense crowd last evening. The traction company carried about 350 people to the pavilion and, besides these, there were a large number of campers and about 150 people from West Superior (by boat)." The line was extended to 43rd Street in 1904.

The 1905 opening of the Aerial Bridge improved access to Park Point and streetcar ridership. Interstate Traction ordered new, larger streetcars to meet the demand and converted the line from single to double track. A bigger carhouse was built in 1906. Ridership reached 416,000 in 1910, and the company turned a small profit.

More houses were built on the Point, ridership continued to climb, and the company added two new streetcars. The fleet swelled to 20 cars, including some former St. Paul City Railway cable car trailers.

However, Interstate Traction was unable to meet its bond payments. In 1913 it was reorganized as the Park Point Traction Company. The company saw a small financial loss in 1914. Minnesota Street, which ran the length of the Point, was paved in 1915, ending the streetcar's status as the only reliable form of transportation. Revenue fell off accordingly, and in 1917 the line was purchased by DSR.

SUPERIOR

Superior gained its first street railway in 1884 with the incorporation of the Douglas County Street Railway. It built a 2.6-mile horsecar line that served the East End, at the time the center of Superior. The company was shaky financially, and service was soon reduced to a handful of daily trips to protect the franchise. Service appears to have lapsed by 1888.

The location of downtown shifted to what was then called West Superior, centered on Tower Avenue. In 1889 the company was revived. Electrification had been under study before the company completed its horsecar

About 1891, a single-truck car carrying a "Lakeside Railway Co." destination sign heads west on a barely graded Superior Street near 42nd Avenue East.

lines, and fresh capital allowed the Northwest Thomson-Houston Company to finish the planned electrification in July 1890.

The Superior Rapid Transit Railway acquired the Douglas County Street Railway in August 1892 for 9,987 shares of Superior Rapid Transit stock and $450,000 in bonds secured by a mortgage with the Central Trust Company of New York. A second mortgage was added to finance expansion, and $200,000 in second-mortgage bonds were issued in July 1894. The company, though, ran afoul of the Panic of 1893, defaulted on interest payments on its second-mortgage bonds, and was placed in receivership on January 28, 1896. Thomas Dunn, Twin City Rapid Transit Company's legal counsel, purchased the property at a foreclosure sale on June 16, 1900. Thomas Lowry was subsequently named to the board of directors.

PERCENTAGE RATE OF RETURN

YEAR	DULUTH	ST. PAUL	MINNEAPOLIS
1921	5.07	3.25	5.55
1922	5.61	4.83	7.71
1923	6.00	4.70	7.57
1924	4.73	3.97	6.79
1925	5.10	2.90	6.10
1926	4.32	4.80	7.02
1927	4.50	4.50	6.05
1928	3.81	3.79	5.75

This table shows that despite having only half the Twin Cities' population density, DSR achieved a better financial return than TCRT subsidiary St. Paul City Railway did most years.

Lowry, along with Luther Mendenhall and G. G. Hartley, had earlier incorporated the Duluth–Superior Traction Company of New Jersey in June 1894 with the objective of taking control and consolidating the Duluth and Superior operations.

The relationship between DSR and Twin City Rapid Transit (TCRT) was a strong one but somewhat indirect. DSR seemed to be TCRT's corporate subsidiary, but that

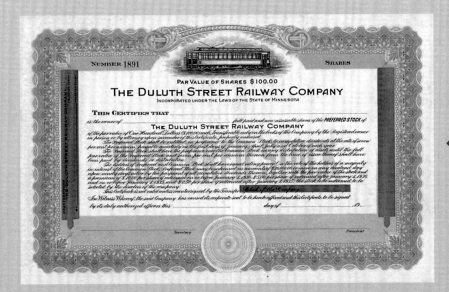

Though perhaps more solid than the Lakeside stock, DSR stock was ultimately not a good investment. Kathryn A. Martin Library, University of Minnesota Duluth, Archives and Special Collections.

was not the case. Instead, they shared some top managers, board members, and shareholders. The most noticeable connection was DSR's reliance on streetcars built in the shops of TCRT.

There followed a series of complicated legal and financial moves that involved the Duluth–Superior Bridge Company, which was then arranging financing for the construction of the Duluth–Superior Bridge. In August 1900 two companies emerged from the maneuverings and consolidations: the Duluth–Superior Traction Company of Connecticut, a holding company, and the Duluth Street Railway Company, which had then emerged from its receivership. The Superior Rapid Transit Railway and the Duluth–Superior Traction Company of New Jersey were merged out of existence.

Three decades of corporate stability followed. However, the company was carrying a mortgaged debt of over $3 million that came due on May 1, 1930, and even though marginally profitable, its earnings weren't sufficient to arrange a refinancing with favorable terms. All of the company's cumulative problems—Duluth's geography and its low population density, its cold and snowy winters, auto competition, and its inability to reduce operating expenses sufficiently, along with the stock market crash—came together, and it was forced into receivership.

For its first 40 years, DSR did minimal marketing because ridership grew on its own. That changed with automobile competition in the 1920s, hence this display in a downtown building.

Service reductions followed, and the first streetcar line was abandoned in 1930 with bus conversions in 1931. Amazingly, the company was able to come up with enough cash to start trolley bus service on a segment of the Lester Park line in 1931.

The Duluth Street Railway was reorganized as the Duluth–Superior Transit Company in January 1933, and it began a program of trolley and gas bus substitutions that culminated with the conversion of most of the system to bus operation in July 1939. Only the 7th Avenue West Incline and its connecting Highland streetcar line remained as a brief footnote to the rail era. More a tourist attraction, the Incline never made a dime in its forty years of operation. It joined the history books on September 4, 1939.

Duluth–Superior Transit continued to operate bus service in Duluth and Superior for the next thirty years. The trolley buses went away in 1957, and the company continued its struggles with the automobile in a regional economy that was moving away from its industrial base. A public agency, the Duluth Transit Authority, was created in 1969. It took over system operation, and in 2013 it continues to run buses in the Twin Ports.

This comparison of the Twin Ports and Twin Cities streetcar systems clearly shows how Duluth–Superior's low population placed its transit system at an economic disadvantage.

STATISTICAL COMPARISON OF DULUTH, SUPERIOR, MINNEAPOLIS AND ST. PAUL, 1928

	DULUTH	SUPERIOR	MINNEAPOLIS	ST.PAUL
AREA IN SQUARE MILES	67.32	42.00	59.50	54.20
MILES OF SINGLE TRACK	84.67	28.69	256.95	179.84
POPULATION	116,800	43,200	455,900	304,221
POPULATION PER MILE OF SINGLE TRACK	1,379	1,505	1,774	1,692
POPULATION PER SQUARE MILE OF AREA	1,735	1,208	7,662	5,613
REVENUE PASSENGERS	20,195,505	4,532,028	107,564,340	61,122,708
REVENUE PASSENGERS PER MILE OF SINGLE TRACK	238,520	157,965	418,620	339,873
REVENUE PASSENGERS PER SQUARE MILE OF AREA	299,992	107,905	1,807,804	1,127,725
PASSENGERS REVENUE	$1,142,412	$322,213	$7,356,343	$4,175,597
PASSENGERS REVENUE PER MILE OF SINGLE TRACK	$17,035	$11,230	$29,407	$23,218
PASSENGERS REVENUE PER SQUARE MILE OF AREA	$21,426	$7,571	$123,636	$77,040

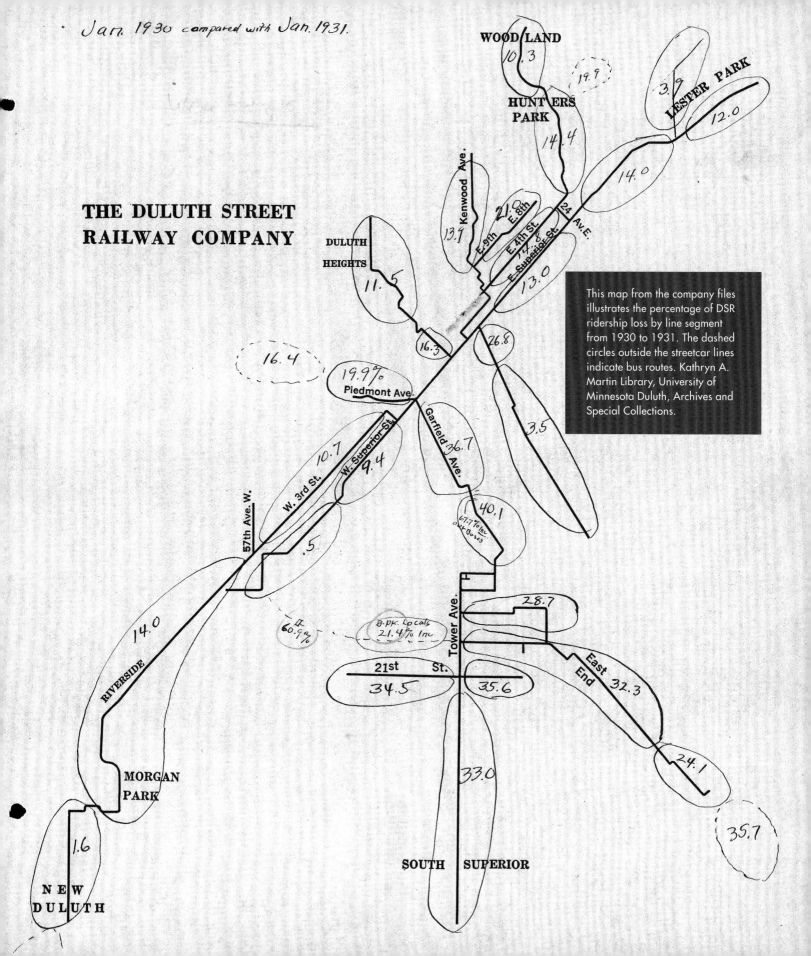

Jan. 1930 compared with Jan. 1931.

THE DULUTH STREET RAILWAY COMPANY

This map from the company files illustrates the percentage of DSR ridership loss by line segment from 1930 to 1931. The dashed circles outside the streetcar lines indicate bus routes. Kathryn A. Martin Library, University of Minnesota Duluth, Archives and Special Collections.

WOOD LAND
10.3
19.9
LESTER PARK
3.9
12.0
HUNTERS PARK
14.4
14.0
Kenwood Ave.
21.0
E. 8th
24 Av. E.
E. 9th
E. 4th St.
14.8
E. Superior St.
DULUTH HEIGHTS
13.9
11.5
13.0
16.3
26.8
16.4
19.9%
Piedmont Ave.
3.5
W. Superior St.
Garfield Ave. 36.7
10.7
W. 3rd St.
9.4
57th Ave. W.
.5
40.1
67.7 To Inc Out Buses
14.0
60.9%
B. Pk. Locals 21.4% Inc
28.7
RIVERSIDE
21st St.
34.5
35.6
Tower Ave.
East End 32.3
24.1
MORGAN PARK
33.0
1.6
35.7
NEW DULUTH
SOUTH SUPERIOR

Here Are the
WINNING DESIGNS

FIRST

Roland Roycraft
1217 East Eleventh St.

SECOND

F. G. Simpson
123 West Owatonna St.

THIRD

Eusebe J. Blais
1739 Dunedin Ave.

FOURTH

M. H. Pearson
613 North 19th Ave. East

FIFTH

James Stickney
625 North 58th Ave. West

IT was no easy task for the judges to select five winning designs from the hundreds of fine ideas submitted in our recent contest. But here are the winners, and below are names of 18 more whose designs earned Honorable Mention.

To Mr. Roycraft, whose design will be used on the new busses, and to all the others who participated, go the thanks of the Transit Company. You have helped make Duluth's new busses smart, colorful and attractive.

HONORABLE MENTION

Doris B. Berg
124 N. Nineteenth Ave. W.

W. F. Bertossi
121 N. Second Ave. E.

Mrs. Glenn Card
1721 E. Third St.

O. Christensen
331 W. Third St.

Roy Holt
605 N. Fifty-seventh Ave. W.

Harry G. Iverson
326 N. 13th Ave. E.

H. W. Johnson
2825 Helm St.

Mary Kathryn Kohlbry
3518 E. Third St.

Jim Kreuzberger
828 Eleventh Ave. E.

John Lewandowski
963 Eighty-eighth Ave. W.

Rebecca Lundmark
930 N. Fourth Ave. E.

O. E. Magnuson
Central Y. M. C. A.

John D. McQuade
4315 Luverne St.

Frank Misiewicz
1419 103rd Ave. W.

E. J. Rafter
991 Eighty-sixth Ave. W.

A. J. Strane
Duluth Junior College

Albert P. Switzer
232 Mesaba Ave.

John A. Yernberg
3806 W. Sixth St.

DULUTH-SUPERIOR TRANSIT CO.

As DSR, now Duluth–Superior Transit, transitioned from street-cars to an all-bus operation in 1939, it wanted a new image. Logo designs were solicited from the public, and the one at the top was actually chosen, at no small savings to the company.

STREETCARS ARRIVE

The Victorian era was a period of huge technological change and a pace of invention that accelerated each year. Horse-drawn streetcars may have been the established norm, but they had numerous drawbacks. They were slow, averaging perhaps five miles per hour. Slow speed meant more cars were required to meet the service frequency, and that increased operating costs and reduced profits. Horses tired. It took at least five of them to keep one car in operation. Teams had to be changed out about once an hour. In Duluth and Superior that meant after every round-trip, as they passed the carbarn. Horses produced enormous quantities of manure that had to be disposed of, and they were subject to disease.

For all these reasons, inventors actively searched for a mechanical power source to replace horses and increase speeds. On the face of it, steam power would have seemed the logical solution. It was an established technology and certainly up to the job. However, locomotives of the time, even small ones, were rolling pollution sources. Their soot settled on everything, their cinders burned through clothes, and their smoke fouled the air. They also tended to alarm horses when they passed. For all these reasons they were usually restricted to lines in suburban and rural areas.

The first cable car line appeared in San Francisco in 1873, the same technology that survives today only in San Francisco. An unpowered streetcar reaches through a slot between the rails and grips a continuous wire cable, which is connected to a stationary power source located in a building. Cable cars traveled about ten miles per hour and could climb any hill. Although extremely expensive to construct and maintain, systems were built in 28 American cities, although no others as small as the Twin Ports.

Cable cars proved to be a bridge technology. For inventors, the holy grail was harnessing what was then called the "electric fluid" to power a railcar. Experimental applications appeared as early as 1879. By the mid-1880s a handful of inventors were approaching commercialization of their patents. The one who prevailed and set the standard for the industry was Frank Sprague, who installed his system in Richmond, Virginia, late in 1887. It was reasonably reliable, much faster than cable cars, and half as expensive to implement. In what was probably the fastest technology adoption in American history, within five years Sprague electric railways replaced over 90 percent of all horsecars, cable cars, and steam-powered streetcars. Duluth and Superior were part of that wave of conversion, and by 1890 their horsecars were gone.

In short order, the streetcar industry had to climb a steep learning curve, modifying car design to the new realities of higher speed while

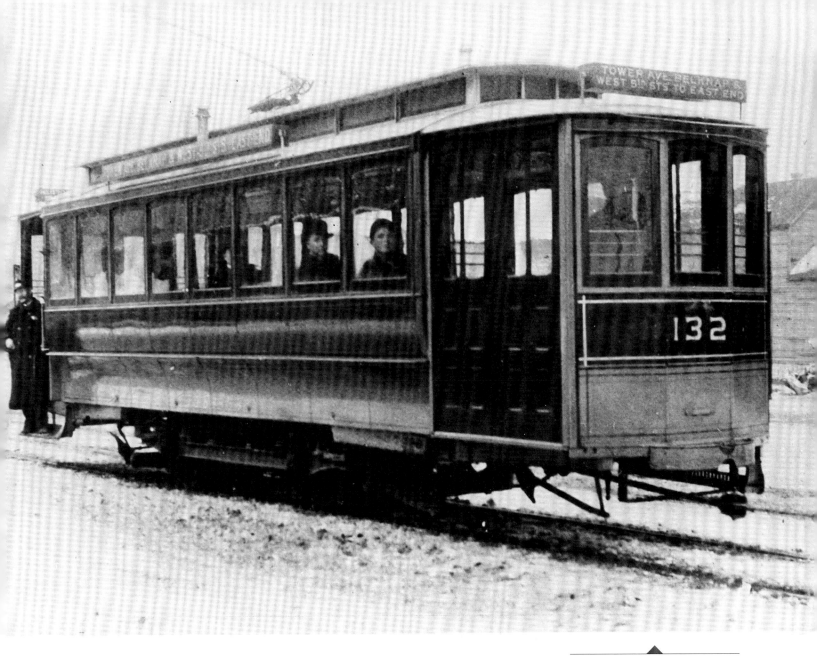

accommodating an explosive growth in ridership. Within ten years, this on-street laboratory would drastically change what a streetcar looked like and how it operated.

Recognizing the limits of animal power, horsecars were built as lightly as possible. Over time, they grew in size somewhat because of the demands of ridership but remained small, spartan vehicles.

The Sprague patents that launched the electric streetcar nationwide were less than three years old, so transit systems and manufacturers were still trying to figure out how to build a good streetcar. The commercial car builders turned out products that were basically enlarged versions of horsecars. They rode on a single four-wheel, two-axle truck, with a motor geared to each axle. The cars were functional, but not comfortable. The

This is typical of the Superior Street Railway cars of the 1890s. When Superior converted to electricity, it retained the flimsy, narrow-gauge horsecar tracks, making them incompatible with Duluth's standard-gauge tracks. This would delay the integration of the two systems by several years. Before the merger with DSR, Superior streetcars were painted green and yellow, with red trucks. Courtesy of the Douglas County Historical Society.

passengers boarded through an open rear platform. Inside the narrow car body, long bench seats faced each other across a center aisle. Longitudinal seating, as it is termed, is uncomfortable when starting and stopping and has never been very popular on transit vehicles.

The electric cars changed the game in several ways, some of which were unexpected. On decent track, they were capable of speeds of 20 miles per hour or more. Aside from the occasional galloping horse, nothing approaching this velocity had ever been seen on a public street before. Concerns were expressed for public safety, and some saw the unprecedented speeds as contrary to the laws of God and nature.

Higher speeds quickly revealed the limits of streetcar and track design. Horsecar track was lightly constructed. Derailments were fairly common but seldom resulted in injury or damage because they occurred at walking speed. Assisted by a couple of passengers, the crew could easily rerail the car and continue on. An electric car on poor track was an injury accident waiting to happen. Single-truck streetcars were—and are—notorious for bucking at higher speeds. They rock forward and backward, and it was not unusual for wheels to lift off the rail. The problem was worse in Superior, which had retained the flimsy horsecar rails after electrification while Duluth had rebuilt its track.

DSR car 47 was a typical single-truck streetcar of the 1890s. With only four wheels and considerable body overhang, it gave a bouncy, lurching ride that passengers disliked. The interior, with its aisle-facing bench seats, subjected passengers to uncomfortable inertia when starting and stopping, and feet in the aisle were likely to be trodden on. The new century would bring larger, double-truck cars that solved those problems.

Streetcar companies quickly discovered that higher speeds created a liability problem no one had foreseen. During the horsecar era, it was accepted practice to stop the car only for women, children, the elderly, and the infirm. Able-bodied men and boys swung on and off the cars as they rolled along. Besides saving time, this practice conserved the horses' limited energy, since starting a loaded car required considerably more effort than keeping it moving.

No one thought to change this practice, and now people were attempting to board and alight at much higher speeds. The result was numerous injuries, including some amputations. Twin City Rapid Transit (TCRT) began installing wire gates on their platforms and requiring motormen to make a full stop for every passenger. DSR, controlled by TCRT interests, followed suit.

A 1902 newspaper story confirmed the wisdom of installing the gates: "The introduction of these safety devices brought about at once a marked reduction in the payments on account of injuries. The payment on account of injuries and damages amounted in 1894 to over $106,000. The next year, when the 'Minneapolis gate' was put in use, the payments were reduced to $80,000, and in 1898 they were as low as $58,000. Last year (1901), when the traffic increased more than 50 percent over 1894, the payments on account of injuries were still less than in 1894."

Horsecar drivers, like all teamsters, had always occupied the open front platform and were exposed to all kinds of weather. Following electrification, the dramatic increase in speed suddenly subjected them to unprecedented wind chills, creating miserable and often dangerous working conditions. One motorman in St. Paul actually froze to death at the controls. The public demanded that something be done. The Minnesota legislature acted, passing a law in 1893 that required all streetcars to be retrofitted with enclosed vestibules to provide protection from the weather. The Panic of 1893 came along at the same time. Streetcar companies fought the bill, arguing that it would drive them out of business. It became law, and they didn't go out of business. By 1895, vestibules were installed in all the cars.

The city also mandated a safety improvement in 1896, a wire net basket, or fender, that projected from the front of the car. Called "kid catchers" in the newspaper, they were designed to hit a pedestrian in the ankle, dumping him or her into the basket and thereby reducing a probable fatality under the wheels to mere bruises and lacerations. Although redesigned some years later, this same basic device, often mistakenly called a "cowcatcher," persisted through the end of service in 1939.

The Woodland Avenue line was constructed by a real estate developer but operated by DSR. This is a typical two-car train of the early 1890s. The vestibule has yet to be enclosed to keep the motorman from freezing. The use of trailers provided needed capacity, but their weight slowed the early underpowered motor cars, which couldn't handle the Woodland Avenue hill. Because of the loose coupling with the motor car, the trailer lurched and banged against it, to the discomfort of the passengers. All were relieved when larger double-truck cars replaced the little trains.

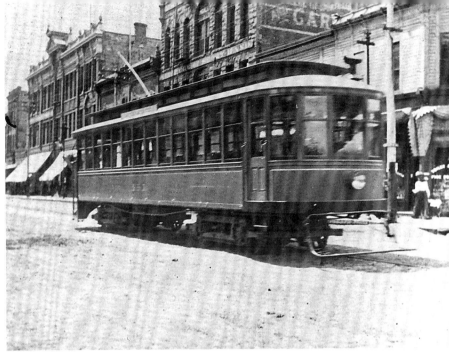

Faced with growing ridership that quickly exceeded the capacity of the small cars, streetcar companies, including DSR, frequently began hauling unpowered trailers. They required a second conductor but achieved a 100 percent increase in capacity for a 50 percent increase in crew cost, since a second motorman was not needed. However, trailers were unloved by both passengers and management. Riders were jolted with every start and stop, described in a newspaper article as "the constant jerking and jamming of two cars loosely coupled." And the underpowered early streetcars were unable to reliably haul trailers up Duluth's hills.

Single-truck (four-wheel) streetcars were a design carryover from horsecars. The double-truck passenger car (with two separate four-wheel sets that swiveled independently, near each end of a much longer car body) had long been standard railroad practice, and soon double-truck cars began to appear on street railways. The ride was much smoother, especially at higher speeds, with no more forward-backward lurching and much less from side to side.

In 1898, TCRT began building large double-truck streetcars of its own design. Having judged commercially built cars to be flimsy and not up to the rigors of Minnesota winters, TCRT went its own way, with a car design that was heavier, wider, and better heated and insulated. Since Twin Ports winters are even longer and more severe, with the added difficulty of steep hills, it wasn't long before TCRT began building streetcars for DSR.

By late 1900 TCRT had built 115 cars and sold 12 of its newest group to DSR to reequip the Interstate line. Thus began a pattern that continued through 1917, when TCRT stopped building its heavy wood standards. With each new group built, TCRT updated its design and added DSR's order. It also sold a number of its own streetcars to DSR.

In 1901, a memo from a DSR official stated that the new double-truck cars "will enable us to do away with the use of trailers. The trailers are a fruitful cause of accidents, and no matter how careful motormen and conductors are, it seems to be impossible to prevent accidents when they are used. The point to be gained by long motors is that when loaded they can make better time and 'take the rails' easier than short motors with a light load can pull a heavy trailer. The trailers, it is said, are a fearful drain on the power house and are expensive to operate, what with an extra conductor and wear and tear of the gearing." Indeed, the larger cars eliminated one of the two conductors, a better vehicle with less crew cost.

Twin City Rapid Transit began manufacturing large double-truck cars of its own design in 1898. DSR adopted these as the standard for its fleet. This is one of the first group delivered in 1902. They went into service on the Interstate line.

Steps.
Car. No 163. 2.26.14
at 13ᵃ Sup. Division
H.H. Brown

A Duluth newspaper in 1900 compared the new TCRT-built double truckers with the old single truckers, saying with the new cars "there is practically none of that constant rocking." Unlike the single truckers, in which all seats faced the center aisle, the new cars had forward-facing seats, which in 1905 the public found much more comfortable:

When the mercury is down to 20 degrees below zero and the wind is blowing at 15–20 mph, residents of Duluth appreciate the fine new double truck cars now taking care of most of the traffic on DSR. Stepping into one of these cars after walking several blocks through such a biting blast is almost as pleasant relief as entering a steam heated apartment. The ride is made in solid comfort, and one cannot help comparing the great superiority of these conveyances over the old cars, with their inefficient heating and their nerve-wracking jolting and teetering along the rails. The traction company is to be commended for making this most desirable change, and it is hoped that it will just as rapidly as possible replace all the old cars with these luxurious coaches. It will certainly pay. For proof, one has but to note the manner in which the small cars, run as extras, are avoided by the people. The new cars are crowded while the old ones are comparatively empty. (Duluth Herald, *February 1, 1905*)

Air brakes appeared in 1902. This was a major safety improvement. Until then, the motorman stopped the car with a single hand brake, actuated by cranking a long gooseneck lever with his right hand. Your author has operated a hand braked streetcar, and its stopping power is much less than an air brake. It requires thinking ahead to avoid overrunning the stopping point. Since the early single-truck streetcars were double ended, the conductor was called on to also apply the rear platform brake when descending Duluth's steepest hills.

Steel underframes replaced wooden underframes in 1905. Beginning in 1908, the newly delivered cars were fitted with 50-horsepower motors, making them noticeably faster than the 40-horsepower motors on the older cars. In the Twin Cities and Duluth–Superior, the older cars with the smaller motors were referred to as "slow cars," and the newer ones with larger motors as "fast cars." The difference was amplified because the newer cars weighed less. Over the years the design was modified to trim

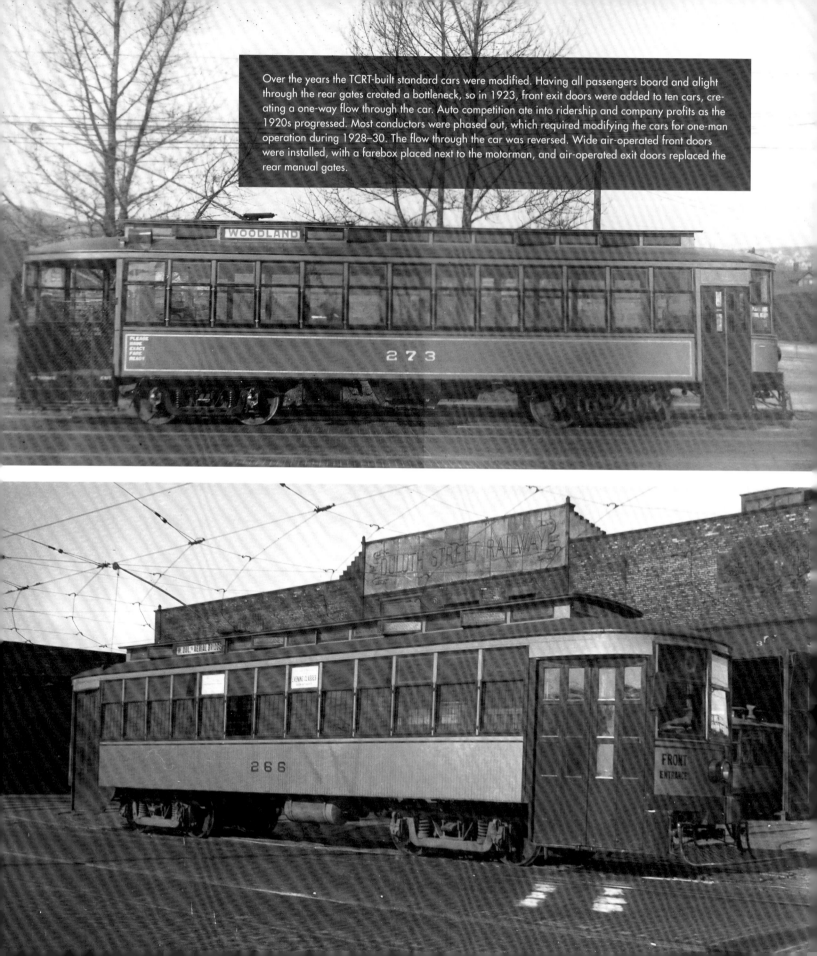

Over the years the TCRT-built standard cars were modified. Having all passengers board and alight through the rear gates created a bottleneck, so in 1923, front exit doors were added to ten cars, creating a one-way flow through the car. Auto competition ate into ridership and company profits as the 1920s progressed. Most conductors were phased out, which required modifying the cars for one-man operation during 1928–30. The flow through the car was reversed. Wide air-operated front doors were installed, with a farebox placed next to the motorman, and air-operated exit doors replaced the rear manual gates.

TRANSITION FROM SINGLE- TO DOUBLE-TRUCK STREETCARS

LINE	FIRST DOUBLE-TRUCK CARS	SINGLE-TRUCK CARS DISCONTINUED
INTERSTATE	1901	1901
LAKESIDE	1901	1905
WEST DULUTH & EAST END	1904	1908
HUNTER'S PARK AND WOODLAND	1904	1908
EAST 4TH STREET	1905	1905
WEST 3RD STREET	1905	1905
WEST 4TH STREET AND PIEDMONT	1912	1912
LAKE AVENUE	1907	1907
EAST 9TH STREET	1912	LINE OPENED 1912
HIGHLAND AVENUE	1913	1913
BILLINGS PARK	1917	

weight: a 1905 car weighed 46,700 pounds, while a 1917 car weighed 41,700 pounds. Lighter cars saved electricity, reduced brake wear, and accelerated faster. As of 1918, DSR rostered 79 fast cars and 56 slow cars. Their speeds reflected their assignments. Because of its steep hills, heavier loads, and longer lines, 69 percent of the cars used in Duluth were fast cars, compared to only 15 percent of those assigned to the flat streets of Superior. As part of rebuilding the core fleet for one-man operation from 1928 to 1930, all the rebuilt cars received the larger motors.

The transition from the small single-truck cars to the TCRT-built double truckers took 17 years, from 1901 to 1917, as shown in the table. However, by February 1912 the *Duluth News Tribune* reported that the double truckers were carrying 95 percent of the passengers.

Streetcars built for Duluth differed from Twin Cities cars in small details. The front fender had a somewhat different design. Headlights were from a different manufacturer. In deference to Duluth's hills, a second set of track-sander pipes were located ahead of the rear wheels to improve adhesion.

From 1900 to about 1930, while conductors were employed, passengers could choose cane-bottomed, forward-facing seats in the front two-thirds of the car or aisle-facing seats in the rear third of the car, which provided more room for passenger circulation to and from the rear gates. 1913, Kathryn A. Martin Library, University of Minnesota Duluth, Archives and Special Collections.

When rebuilt for one-man operation in 1928-1930, a number of the cars received new leather seats shaped for better seating comfort. Passengers entered through the front door, and the front bulkhead that formerly separated the motorman's compartment was removed. The big coal stove remained in place next to the motorman, who finally was given a cushioned seat with a backrest.

STREETCARS INHERITED FROM OTHER COMPANIES

DSR inherited a number of streetcars when it absorbed other neighboring streetcar companies. The Motor Line Improvement Company supplied two single-truck motor cars and four trailers for the Woodland line. Superior Rapid Transit was built to the original horsecar narrow gauge of 3 feet 6 inches, while Duluth was standard gauge, 4 feet 8.5 inches. When DSR took control of the Superior system in 1900, it converted 27 of the Superior single-truck cars to standard gauge. Eleven of the cars remained narrow gauge and continued in service until the last of the Superior lines was made standard gauge in 1902. Thereafter they were stored and appear to have never reentered service.

When DSR acquired Park Point's Interstate Traction Company in 1917, it came with four commercially built double-truck streetcars and one elderly single trucker. The double truckers were retained and continued to run on the Point as needed to haul larger summer crowds and to fight snow in the winter. DSR used single-truck Birneys, which were cheaper to operate, much of the year. When the Park Point line was abandoned in 1931, all its old cars were scrapped.

CONVERTING TO ONE-MAN OPERATION

Conductors were eliminated first between 1912 and 1920 on the most lightly patronized lines, including Highland, West 4th Street, and Park Point. The local lines in Superior followed in 1924. The number of cars required to run these services was small. DSR converted a pair of the old single truckers to handle West 4th Street and modified a pair of early TCRT standard cars for Highland. However, the rest of the old single truckers were worn out, uncomfortable, and unpopular with passengers, so further retrofits were ruled out. Instead, DSR purchased six single-truck lightweight Birney safety cars, then the standard for lightly traveled streetcar lines across North America. They were delivered in 1919. Besides being new, the Birneys reduced power consumption dramatically. They were intended for Superior, but the city refused to allow one-man cars at that time, so the Birneys were deployed in Duluth.

Though economical, they proved to be unpopular with passengers. Like all single truckers, they gave a bouncy, lurching ride. The uncushioned wood-slat seats were uncomfortable. They were poorly insulated, causing them to be noisy and cold in the winter. They were so light they bogged down easily in snow and had a tendency to derail. A 1920 newspaper story related that riders from the Park Point, Kenwood, and East 8th Street lines all protested the Birneys, calling them "neither safe, sanitary, comfortable or suitable for service."

After problematic deployments on the Piedmont, Kenwood, and East 9th Street lines, three of them were assigned to Park Point, where they provided most of the service. The older double-truck cars replaced them during snowstorms and when ridership spiked on summer evenings and weekends.

At the urging of DSR, the City of Superior finally allowed one-man cars in 1924. Three of the standard cars were converted to one-man in 1924 for use on the Billings Park–Broadway line. Conversions of five more cars followed in 1925 through 1926.

DSR was still looking for economies in operations. They purchased a small group of TCRT's new double-truck lightweights. TCRT had been experimenting with lightweights since 1916. In 1925 they licensed the

designs to the Lightweight Noiseless Electric Streetcar Company, which built new cars at Snelling Shops for several cities.

DSR ordered five cars, numbered 301 through 305. They were delivered in 1925. Motors burned out on the steep Duluth hills, so the group was assigned to Superior, where they replaced the heavy wood standard cars on the East End–Allouez and Billings Park–Broadway lines. Although the cars had some brake problems, they rode comfortably and reduced power consumption by half. The converted standards and the five lightweights were sufficient to operate all Superior service as one-man except for the Interstate line to Duluth.

The Superior lines and a couple of the lightest Duluth lines had been converted to one-man operation by the mid-1920s, but the rest of the Duluth system had not. Across North America, many streetcar systems purchased new, lightweight cars designed to be run by a motorman alone. DSR, and TCRT as well, chose to rebuild and reconfigure their heavy wood cars. We can speculate as to why that decision was made. Both systems distrusted that the products of commercial car builders could stand up to Minnesota winters. Both had a tradition of self-sufficient shops that were not inclined to turn elsewhere for help. In DSR's case, poverty probably

In need of one-man cars for its Superior lines, DSR returned to Twin City Rapid Transit and ordered five TCRT-designed lightweights, which were delivered in 1925. Except for excessive brake wear, the cars were successful and remained in service until the end of the Superior lines in 1935.

YEAR	STREETCARS
1885	6
1890	44
1895	108
1900	105
1905	118
1910	144
1915	138
1920	159
1925	150
1930	149
1935	125
1939	69

Duluth Street Railway's passenger car fleet.

played a role: it's doubtful there was sufficient cash on hand to purchase a new fleet.

Whatever the reasons, both systems set about rebuilding their wood standard cars. Most received new trucks and new 50-horsepower motors, upgrading them all to "fast" cars. Passenger flow was reversed. Instead of entering through the rear gates, all passengers now entered through air-operated folding front doors, dropped their fares in a farebox next to the motorman, and exited through folding doors on the rear platform that were actuated by passengers standing on the rear steps.

Many of the cars received new, leather upholstered seats, and the motorman's controls were updated with safety features such as spring-loaded brake valves that would stop the car immediately if anything happened to the motorman.

How to use the Rear Treadle Exit

-1-

Ring the Bell as Usual —

-2-

Walk to the Rear —

-3-

Step on the Treadle Plate —

It opens the door for you as soon as the car stops

Simple, Isn't It?

DO not hesitate to step on the treadle plate while the car is moving. The doors cannot open until the car has stopped.

A pressure of only twelve pounds will operate the treadle.

After the car has stopped, it cannot possibly start again as long as you are standing on the treadle plate or on the steps.

Because of declining ridership and the conversion of the Lester Park line to buses, DSR had a bigger fleet than it needed to run the system. As a result, only 72 of the 128 standard cars were rebuilt during 1928 to 1930. The remaining two-man cars were restricted to rush hour trippers and other extra service and otherwise saw little use during the 1930s. In 1932, almost a third of the fleet was stored as "unserviceable," and by 1935 most of them had been scrapped. The active fleet shrunk from 131 in 1930 to 69 during the last year of service in 1939.

As part of rebuilding its cars for one-man operation, DSR installed treadle controls in the rear step treads, which prevented the rear door from opening unless the car was stopped with the brakes applied and a passenger was standing on the steps. This informational brochure was issued in 1928.

2

A PUBLIC CONVEYANCE

Streetcars and Daily Life

The first day of streetcar service to South Superior on September 14, 1892, may have been the busiest.

What was it like to ride a streetcar in the Twin Ports? Later in the book you'll take trips on three lines of particular interest, but here's a taste to put it in context. Let's say it's a typical summer day in 1925.

Your line runs every 20 minutes, so you consult the folded paper schedule that includes every line in the system, find the time points listed before and after your stop, estimate the minutes between those two points, and time your walk to arrive at the car stop with a couple of minutes to spare. You've done this many times before and likely have the schedule memorized.

The stop is marked by a painted white band located part way up one of the wood poles holding up the overhead wire. The streetcar, warm yellow with an oxide-red roof and touches of green trim, approaches in the distance. It's about a block away when the overhead wire starts to vibrate and sing from the trolley wheel rolling along its underside. The streetcar's steel wheels emit a low rumble. The car almost passes you entirely, but the rear entrance comes to a halt opposite where you're standing. You step off the curb into the middle of the street to board.

Triple-stream wire gates slap open, and you climb the high first step, then two more, onto the spacious rear platform. The sliding pocket doors leading into the passenger compartment are open. One more short step up and you're passing the fare-box mounted on a black pole in the middle of the aisle. There stands the conductor, a figure of authority in his double-breasted, brass-buttoned, navy-blue coat and pillbox hat. Under his watchful gaze you deposit your fare token and request a transfer.

The floor is varnished wood, the seats are clear-varnished and cushioned rattan, a type of wicker. Your seat is next to a large window. To open the window, flip up the windowsill and drop the heavy window down into a pocket in the wall. Flip the sill back down and the stored window disappears. Your elbow sits comfortably on the low sill, which is only nine inches above the seat cushion.

Even before you sit down, the conductor signals the motorman to start up with two quick dings of the overhead bell, muted because it rings inside the fully enclosed motorman's compartment. Immediately the brakes are released with a whoosh of air. The car accelerates smoothly, its speed increasing perceptibly as the motorman notches open the controller. The hum of gear noise from the motors under the car increases in volume and pitch along with the speed, then ceases whenever the car coasts, which is about half the time. The wheels rumble, banging occasionally through a switch, and the car noses gently from side to side, following the undulations of the track. Air pours through the open windows, and the motorman's gong warns cars that venture too close. The streetcar is all wood above floor level, and its body flexes and creaks. Periodically the air compressor under the floor goes thump-thump-thump for a minute or two.

Every couple of blocks the car pauses for more passengers with a hiss

Street Railway Time Table
SUPERIOR LINES
No. 68—Effective April 19, 1925

WEEK DAYS	SUNDAYS AND HOLIDAYS

ALLOUEZ LINE—Leave or Pass 3rd and Ogden for Allouez—
(On connecting East End Cars)

5:00 A. M., 5:10, 5.30 and every 10 minutes until 7:50 A. M., then every 20 minutes until 3:10 P. M., then every 10 minutes until 7:30 P. M., then every 20 minutes until 11:50 P. M., 12:20 A. M.

5:25 A. M., 5:40, 6:00, 6:15, 6:30 and every 20 minutes until 11:50 P. M., 12:20 A. M.

Leave Allouez

5:29 A. M., 5:49 and every 10 minutes until 8:09 A. M., 8:29, 8:49, 9:09, 9:19 and every 20 minutes until 11:59 A. M., 12:09 P. M. and every 20 minutes until 3:29 P. M., then every 10 minutes until 7:59 P. M., then every 20 minutes until 11:39 P. M., 12:09 A. M., 12:39, 12:49

5:59 A. M., 6:19, 6:37, 6:59 and every 20 minutes until 9:39 A. M., 9:49, then every 20 minutes until 6:29 P. M., 6:39, 6:49, 7:09, 7:29, 7:39, 7:49 then every 20 minutes until 12:09 A. M., 12:39, 12:49.

EAST END LINE—Leave or Pass 3rd and Ogden for East End—

5:00 A. M., 5:10 and every 10 minutes until 8:50 A. M., then every 20 minutes until 11:30 A. M., then every 10 minutes until 7:30 P. M., then every 20 minutes until 11:50 P. M., 12:20 A. M.

5:25 A. M., 5:40, 6:00, 6:15, 6:30 and every 20 minutes until 11:10 P. M., 11:30, 11:50, 12:20 A. M.

Leave 31st Ave. and E. 4th St.

5:34 A. M., 5:54 and every 10 minutes until 9:24 A. M., then every 20 minutes until 12:04 P. M., then every 10 minutes until 8:04 P. M., then every 20 minutes until 11:44 P. M., 11:58, 12:14 A. M., 12:45, 12:53.

6:04 A. M., 6:24 and every 20 minutes until 9:44 A. M., then every 20 minutes until 10:44 P. M., 10:49, 11:04, 11:14, 11:24, 11:34, 11:44, 11:58, 12:14 A. M., 12:45, 12:53.

Cars pass Division Avenue 7 minutes after leaving Robertson Avenue

BROADWAY LINE—Pass Broadway and Tower for Hill and Belknap—

5:27 A. M., 5:47, 6:07, 6:19 and every 20 minutes until 11:19 P. M., 4:32, 4:59, 5:15, 5:30, 5:45,-5:59 and and every 20 minutes until 11:19 P. M., 12:03 A. M.

6:39 A. M., 7:09, 7:28, 7:39 and every 20 minutes until 11:19 P. M., 12:03 A. M.

Leave Hill Ave. and Belknap St.

5:40 A. M., and every 20 minutes until 4:00 P. M., 4:15, 4:30, 4:45, 5:00, 5:15, 5:30, 5:45, 6:00 and every 20 minutes until 11:20 P. M., 11:50, 12:20 A. M.

7:00 A. M., 7:20 and every 20 minutes until 11:20 P. M., 11:50, 12:20 A. M.

TWIN PORTS ELECTRIC LINES

A Twin Ports Electric Lines timetable for the Superior Lines, 1925.

of the brakes. Lake Superior is intermittently visible between buildings to your left. As your stop approaches, you push the small round pearl button next to you on the window post, triggering a bell that sounds just like a telephone. You head for the rear platform—it's impolite to keep other passengers waiting. The car stops at the next corner, the gates open, and down the steps you go, unconsciously checking for traffic as you head for the curb. Two dings, the gates slap shut, the brakes whoosh, and the streetcar is gone.

Rapid! Safe!! READ... as you-ride!

Minutes by Street Car to Third Avenue West

30 25 20 15 10 5   5 10 15 20 25 30

By the time you look after gas, oil and tires, close and lock garage doors, drive down town, hunt parking space, back into it, lock up and then walk to your place of business . . . . do you really save much time?

This map from the 1931–32 winter schedule shows travel time from downtown to most points on the Duluth system.

DSR VERSUS THE CITY

Streetcar companies were in business to make a profit. Transit was not subsidized by the government as it is today. The companies were essentially regulated utilities. They were awarded an exclusive franchise from the city in exchange for city regulation of fares, route alignments, and service levels. The franchise was a two-edged sword.

In the world of public transit, almost everything revolves around the schedule of service. It determines where and how often the cars will run. That in turn drives the size of the organization and its operating budget. A successful schedule tries to balance the public's demand for convenient service with the company's desire to maximize profits, a conflict that is inherently impossible to resolve.

The city was always pushing DSR for route extensions and service improvements that the company considered unprofitable. DSR would resist, and this tension created a permanent adversarial relationship between the city and the company. Sometimes the balance of power shifted. For example, in the 1920s, after much lobbying by the street railways, fare regulation was shifted to the state level because no city council would ever approve an increase and some political distance was needed. On the positive side, the franchise kept other streetcar operators out of the market. It also greatly prolonged the life of the streetcar system by smothering the threat of unregulated jitney and bus competition that first appeared in 1915 and resurfaced in the 1920s.

Some residential growth happened where no streetcars ran, so political pressure to build new lines was always present. When housing first climbed the hillside above downtown Duluth, horsecars were physically unable to follow development up the steep hill, and electric cars were still a couple of years away from implementation. In an 1889 address to the City Council, Mayor Sutphin called for transit service to be extended up the hillside above downtown: "I therefore recommend that you take steps looking to the construction at an early day of a track extending as far up as 9th Street on such avenue as shall be designated." A week later the Duluth Tribune called for a cable-powered railway, the only technology that could conquer the slope, up the Central Hillside on Lake Avenue "to the brow of the hill and to a point, say half a dozen streets, farther back." It didn't happen. Electrification finally brought the East 4th Street line in 1890 and the East 9th Street line in 1912. Central Hillside had neighborhoods located higher than 6th Street above downtown by 1900, but their first transit service was a bus route in 1929. To see what climbing the hill was like, your author hiked to the top of Lake Avenue, pausing every block to regroup, and can only marvel at the residents' stamina, since they surely did the same on a daily basis.

The franchise also required the company to pave and maintain the pavement in the track area of the street and to plow snow. This made sense at the time because streetcar snowplows were much larger and more powerful than any plow the city could deploy, but the company received no compensation for these services.

Streetcars were far more capable of hauling heavy loads around the city than the early motor trucks were. Despite this, the franchise forbade the hauling of any freight and thus any profit from providing such a service. This clause was winked at over the years. The streetcars routinely transported mail and newspapers. The company's work streetcars periodically, at the city's request, transported rock and other materials for street work.

Sometimes the company used unconventional tactics to counter initiatives from the city. In April 1890, on the eve of electrification, Thomas Lowry and the DSR directors responded to what they felt were onerous franchise terms by declaring they would stay with horsecars and not electrify after all. Barely two weeks later a compromise in franchise language was apparently reached, because DSR agreed to electrify.

Another dustup occurred when the city, for reasons unknown, suddenly ordered DSR to remove its recently constructed track on 12th Avenue East. DSR removed the track but also eliminated free transfers between streetcars. Free transfers were reinstated at an unknown later date.

The streetcar's monopoly of urban transportation drove the city to require that DSR build ahead of development, which made sense if the development followed, but often that was not the case in Duluth and Superior. To be sure, there were fully developed neighborhoods with reasonable population densities, but the Twin Ports featured long stretches with few people or jobs. There were extended voids between Superior and South Superior, along Oneota Street to West Duluth, between Fairmont Park and New Duluth, and between the top of the Incline and Duluth Heights. The last two major extensions, to Kenwood in 1923 and the Crosley Avenue branch in 1926, remained sparsely populated during the streetcar era.

On a number of occasions, the company was asked to extend service along platted streets before the streets themselves were completed, or in some cases the streets were in place but underground utilities weren't. The track would be laid but then would have to be torn up and relaid.

Duluth's unusual geography further stretched DSR's resources. The city's hourglass shape (a long, narrow hourglass, to be sure) squeezed the lines onto a single street in the middle and spread them out on the peripheries. The results were the Crosley line on the east end and the 57th Avenue West branch. Providing a reasonable level of service on these two lines resulted in too much service on the main trunk. On the other hand, because of the compressed route structure, most lines directly served the city's traffic generators with no transfer required.

FARES

Until about 1920 the nickel fare was an American institution that cities defended and streetcar companies decried as economic starvation. In Duluth, that fight took place over the 1916 extension to the Morgan Park steel plant. DSR demanded a 10-cent fare for trips beyond 71st Avenue West, arguing that an 18-mile ride from Lester Park for 5 cents was beyond all reasonableness. DSR implemented the extra dime fare for a few months, but the city overruled that, and the fare returned to 5 cents.

Riders could save money by purchasing reduced-fare ticket books in advance. With the adoption of fareboxes and pay-as-you-enter fare collection, DSR switched from tickets to metal tokens in Duluth in 1921 and in Superior in 1927. As fares increased to six, seven, and finally eight cents, tokens offered a discount to buffer the fare increases and eliminated the need to pay with multiple coins.

As a public service, often required by the franchise, most streetcar companies allowed uniformed police and firefighters to ride free. In 1895 the *Superior Leader* reported that DSR made a mountain out of a molehill by insisting on a fare from firemen who boarded wearing straw hats instead of the usual uniform caps, unaware that the straw hat was a standard part of the summer uniform. The fire chief was mightily offended, since police could board by only showing a badge, regardless of dress.

State regulation was also a challenge for DSR. In 1893 the State of Minnesota passed a law requiring enclosed vestibules to protect motormen from the cold. DSR was apparently slow to modify its cars. On October 4, 1895, DSR general manager Herbert Warren was arrested for failure to comply with the law.

When fares increased in Duluth from 6 cents to 8 cents in 1926, it suddenly took four coins to pay. For convenience, and to soften the financial impact with a multiride discount, DSR began issuing these dime-sized tokens.

DULUTH		
	CASH FARE	**TICKET/TOKEN FARE**
1883-1922	5 CENTS	
1922-1926	6 CENTS	
1926-1929	8 CENTS	7 CENTS
1929-1941	10 CENTS	7.5 CENTS
1942-1948	11 CENTS	10.7 CENTS
SUPERIOR		
	CASH FARE	**TICKET/TOKEN FARE**
1900-1912	5 CENTS	
1912-1916	5 CENTS	4.2 CENTS
1916-1921	5 CENTS	
1921-1923	6 CENTS	5.8 CENTS
1923-1927	10 CENTS	6 CENTS
1927-1929	8 CENTS	7 CENTS
1929-1941	10 CENTS	7.5 CENTS

Because of separate city franchises, different fares were charged in Duluth and Superior.

Despite these impediments, DSR offered service that was frequent and convenient. The main lines east on Superior Street and 4th Street and west on 3rd Street / Grand Avenue ran every 10 minutes all day and sometimes every 5 minutes. Ten-minute service extended to Superior via the Interstate line and, except in later years, to Superior's East End. Elsewhere, 20-minute off-peak service was the norm, with more frequent service during the rush hours.

DESTINATION SIGNS

Over the years DSR employed different devices to tell its patrons where a particular streetcar was headed. This was more necessary in Duluth than in most cities because every car passed through downtown on Superior

Street. Including the various short turns, from downtown there were 13 eastbound destinations and 17 westbound.

Destination signs evolved over the years as the system expanded. In the early days the cars were assigned to specific lines with the destination painted on the sides of the car. This limited flexibility, so changeable flat, wooden signboards were affixed to the roof—long ones on each side and short ones on the front and rear. Changing them required climbing onto the roof. They were replaced with four-sided wood signs that could be revolved (probably with a pole to avoid climbing on the roof) to display one of four destinations. Painted wood signs were hard to see at night, so small round lights with colored lenses were installed on the car front below the right window. Soon, however, there were more destinations than there were lens colors. Finally, backlit canvas roll signs were mounted on the front and sides of the clerestory roof. To these in 1919 were added separate large backlit numbers and letters in the right front window, each of which referred to a particular destination. Duluth used numbers and Superior used letters. Many were abbreviations of the destination, such as 92 for 92nd Avenue West and Grand Avenue, 61 for 61st Avenue East and Superior Street, A for Allouez, and B for Billings Park.

Chapter 5 describes every line in detail. But beyond the day-to-day normal service, the streetcars played a number of other urban transportation roles.

THE STREETCAR AS SCHOOL BUS

Students were not always bused to school. In the early twentieth century school buses didn't even exist. Elementary school children walked to neighborhood schools. Junior and senior high students walked if they lived close enough. If not, they took the streetcar.

Thanks to Duluth's long and narrow geography, streetcars funneled past its high schools and junior highs. Duluth Central High School on East 2nd Street and Washington Junior High on East 3rd Street were directly served by the East 4th Street, East 8th Street, Kenwood, and West 4th Street lines and were a couple blocks up the hill from every other line in the city. Denfield High School in West Duluth at 46th Avenue West was one block off the main line on Grand Avenue. West Junior High, in the old high school a few blocks away, and Lincoln Junior High, at 25th Avenue West and 4th Street, were also convenient to the Grand Avenue cars. Morgan Park Junior and Senior High was located directly on the streetcar line.

East Junior High was only a two- or three-block walk from the Woodland, East 4th Street, Lester Park, and Crosley lines. In Superior, Central High School, Vocational School, and East High School were all located on the East End line. Most families in town were close to a streetcar line.

Until the late 1920s, the fare for high school students was the same as for adults. In 1929 DSR received approval from the Minnesota Railroad and Warehouse Commission to raise its adult fare to 10 cents or a token (six tokens could be bought for 45 cents, 7.5 cents per ride). The City of Duluth felt that this imposed a hardship on families whose children rode the streetcars to school. DSR was pressured to experiment with a 5-cent fare for trips to and from school. A special ticket was implemented at the start of the school year in September 1929. The fare was only good on weekdays between 7:30 a.m. and 5:30 p.m.

Generations of Duluth high school and junior high students used DSR streetcars and buses to attend school, paying with these books of discounted fare tickets.

SCHOOL	MARCH 20 BOARDINGS	ENROLLMENT	BOARDINGS AS % OF ENROLLMENT
CENTRAL HIGH, WASHINGTON JUNIOR	758	2,702	28
DENFIELD HIGH	562	952	59
EAST JUNIOR	549	1,023	54
MORGAN PARK	122	368	33
WEST JUNIOR	82	824	10
LINCOLN JUNIOR	42	787	5
ALL PUBLIC SECONDARY SCHOOLS	2,115	6,656	32

Typical daily school boardings in Duluth during 1929.

To determine school ridership prior to the reduced fare, counts were taken of students observed boarding or leaving streetcars on March 20 and May 23, 1929. The lower fare increased student ridership by about 50 percent, which more than offset the revenue loss per ride. Although the program was cumbersome to administer because of the need to sell tickets at individual schools, DSR gained revenue. A small number of tickets were also sold to Catholic school students and students at the State Teachers College.

One track extension appears to have been built specifically to better serve East Junior High. The East 4th Street line ended at the wye at 24th Avenue East and 4th Street, half a mile short of the school. The city wanted a track extension to the front door and beyond to Ridgewood Road. DSR resisted, and the compromise was a new turning loop on 4th Street at 27th Avenue East, built in 1929. It brought the cars within a couple of blocks of the school.

UNSCHEDULED SERVICE

DSR ran more service than appeared in the public timetable. Transit's share of the total transportation pie was large enough that any unusual mass movement of people required extra streetcars. This took two forms—extras and charters. Extras, also called trippers, were simply additional cars added to the regular lines. Charters went wherever and whenever the chartering party wanted to go and had the added feature of not being open to the general public.

Extras ran for special events, ball games, and parades. In 1924, 20 extra cars were needed for the circus. Extras ran when the high schools started and let out and transported football teams to away games across town. They ran for certain holidays, such as cemetery visits on Memorial Day and midnight church services at Christmas. During the war years, employment at the Morgan Park steel plant and the McDougall-Duluth Shipyard in Riverside increased dramatically. Every morning more than two dozen extras ran away from the city to bring thousands to work and returned them in the afternoon.

Here's a good example that also captures the politics of Duluth in that era. In June 1923 the Finnish Workers Socialist Alliance informed DSR by letter that three to four thousand people would be attending its annual summer festival in Fairmont Park on July 1, "Therefore we are asking you to put a few extra cars to take people to the park. . . . We need six or seven extra cars to take people back to home from 4:30 to 6 p.m." The regular Sunday service to

Large groups could purchase special tickets for travel on the regularly scheduled cars to and from events. This is a return trip ticket from a Christmas entertainment at the Morgan Park clubhouse in 1935.

DECEMBER 21st, 1935
FROM MORGAN PARK

The Duluth Street Railway Company will honor this ticket as cash fare from the Christmas Entertainment at the Clubhouse in Morgan Park between the hours of noon and five P. M. on the above date.

SAMPLE

Fairmont Park ran every 20 minutes, giving the line a capacity of about 320 passengers in that 90-minute period. The DSR superintendent wrote back, "We are glad to be advised of the proposed gathering . . . and will have the foreman . . . furnish any extra service which may be needed." When these extra services ran, it was not uncommon for the sponsoring organization to purchase special tickets to permit their attendees to ride without paying a regular fare.

> *Yesterday was a record breaker in the business of the DSR Co., the receipts for the day being 108,426 fares, as compared to 60,000 fares collected two years ago, when the company did the largest day's business up to that date. The circus, ball game, theater and other attractions for the day were responsible for the immense street car business, this being the first 4th of July in years when the weather was fine and everybody seemed to have an inclination to go somewhere. During the day the company had every available car and employee capable of running one of them in service. There were 108 cars in service, which is double the usual number in operation in the daytime.* (Duluth Herald, *July 5, 1904*)

In 1919, Duluth observed the Fourth of July with parades downtown and in West Duluth, carnivals at Lester Park and Fairmont Park, a water regatta off Park Point, a community celebration in Duluth Heights, and a church picnic at Lincoln Park. DSR was hard-pressed to handle the crowds. Every car that could turn a wheel was put on the streets. Track Department employees and qualified office personnel were drafted for duty. The superintendent, supervisors, and line foremen were assigned specific areas of the city, assisted by shop men as troubleshooters. Work cars, the wrecker, tower cars, and trucks were ready with crews in the event of equipment failures. Shop men were stationed at railroad crossings to flag and at track intersections to throw switches.

The biggest day in DSR history was February 15, 1927, the day of the Winter Frolic parade, when over 130,000 fares were collected. The Tri-State fair generated considerable traffic on the South Superior line. During the one-week fair in 1934, 43,000 passengers were carried to the fair.

There were other occasions—the Christmas shopping season, Easter Sunday, New Year's Eve—when DSR advertised and provided extra service. In 1926 there were ski tournaments at the Chester Park Bowl on several winter Sunday afternoons when regular Kenwood line service was supplemented with enough additional cars to provide a two-minute headway. Several cars made through runs from Superior.

CHARTERS

Like all streetcar companies, the Duluth Street Railway offered its street-cars for charters, which were free to roam the system as requested by the chartering party. The 1919 brochure "Information Regarding Chartered Cars" described how it worked.

In those early days of electric street railways, trolley parties were quite the fad, as the *Duluth News Tribune* recounted on August 20, 1896: "Miss Helen Haines gave a trolley party last evening to a large number of her friends. It was the first trolley party of the season. The party occupied one of Mr. Warren's open chariots and they rode all over the city tooting horns and making merry."

From 1896 to 1909, DSR maintained a specially appointed luxury streetcar. Rebuilt from a regular streetcar, the St. Louis featured over-stuffed furniture, velvet curtains, carpeting, a bar, electric heat, and a uniformed attendant. DSR management used it to entertain guests and politicians, but it could be chartered by anyone. A contemporary news story introduced the car to the public:

About next Monday the new private car of the DSR Co. will be ready for a trip over the line. It has been built entirely in the shops of the company at the West End barn and not only will it give a handsome car for the use for which it is intended, but it will give evidence of the excellent work which can be done in the shops.

The new car is named St. Louis. One of the old cars has been rebuilt and it is practically new. The vestibules are circular and have curved glass windows and doors. The interior is beautifully finished. The sides and ends are of paneled cherry highly polished. The ceiling is of oak and the floor is of quartered oak highly polished. The floor will be covered by mats and the windows will be hung with draperies. There will be no stationary seats and willow chairs upholstered with silk will be used. There are more than 20 lights inside the car. The center lights are enclosed in beautiful cut glass shades. Along the sides there are lights at each window, their brightness being soft-ened by ground glass globes. In each corner are large round globes with small stars cut into the glass. All the metal work inside the car, including the curtain and strap rods, are of highly polished brass. There will be none of the old-fashioned bell cords, but electric bells are provided with which to call the conductor or motorman. The conductor has an electric bell to call the motorman.

Form 341-A. 500. 3-19.

Information Regarding Chartered Cars

Cars may be chartered only upon personal application at the office of the company and payment in advance of charges.

The rate is $7.50 a trip one way, or $10.00 for a round trip over any local line in Duluth or Superior except on the Morgan Park-New Duluth line. The charge for a trip between Duluth and Superior via the Interstate Bridge is $10.00 one way, $12.50 round trip. From points east of 26th Avenue West to Morgan Park—$10.00 one way, $12.50 round trip. From points east of 26th Avenue West to New Duluth $12.50 one way, $15.00 round trip.

Additional trips may be made over other local lines in connection with above trips at the rate of $2.50 for each one way or round trip over each additional line.

All rates provide for a layover at destination of not to exceed five hours, after which a charge of one ($1.00) dollar will be made for every hour or fraction thereof. Time to be consumed and total amount to be paid must be decided upon at the time of charter.

Cars may be chartered by the hour at rate of $7.50 for first hour and $5.00 for each additional hour or fraction thereof—time to be computed from time of leaving to time of returning to car house.

Cars will not be chartered on Holidays or at other times when the service is taxed by large gatherings.

Chartered cars must leave starting point at agreed time. When chartered car orders are countermanded refundment of payment will be made as follows: If more than six hours before time for leaving car house, the full payment. If within six hours, full payment less $1.00 per car to cover time allowed crew for reporting. If after car has been started, full payment less $2.50 per car.

Information regarding chartered cars will be given cheerfully by telephone but ORDERS FOR CHARTERED CARS WILL BE ACCEPTED ONLY UPON PERSONAL APPLICATION AND ADVANCE PAYMENT AT THE OFFICE OF THE COMPANY. TELEPHONE ORDERS WILL NOT BE RECEIVED.

This rule is necessary in order to avoid errors. When you call at the office you will be furnished with a copy of the written order for cars chartered, with full particulars, together with a receipt for payment. If party desiring to use a chartered car cannot personally come to office to arrange for it we suggest that some one else be delegated to attend to it.

Cars have a seating capacity of 48.

THE DULUTH STREET RAILWAY CO.

DSR's 1919 charter tariff.

Company officials toured the system and hosted guests in luxury in the private car St. Louis, which was equipped with overstuffed furniture, floor rugs, velvet curtains, and a bar. The car was available for public charters and lasted until about 1909.

The car is heated by electricity, six electric radiators being used for that purpose. It requires about as much electricity to supply these as to run the motor. They heat it perfectly and are small and take up but little room.

The exterior of the car is very plain in finish, but is very rich. It is about the same color as the other cars on the line, and has no more ornamentation, except for the name painted on each side. There is, however, around the top a row of electric lights, red, white and blue in color, and at night the car will present a brilliant appearance. This car will be the prettiest thing of its kind west of New York City. It will be used for showing distinguished visitors around the city and will also be at the disposal of any parties not necessarily so distinguished but who have the required price. (Duluth Herald, November 12, 1896)

In 1934, veteran employee W. J. Holmes, writing in the employee newsletter *Transit Topics*, recalled what it was like to crew the St. Louis:

The "St. Louis" played an important role in society as well as in business. Many of the social lights of that gay age—friends of the management and others, directly or indirectly interested in the company, used it for entertainment purposes, such as cruises to the club house at Billings Park and to the Northland Country Club—sight-seeing jaunts around the city and in the winter snowshoeing and skiing parties at Woodland and Lester Park.

A number of streetcar companies ran specially built funeral cars, with side doors for loading the casket and additional seating for the mourners, along with an appropriate black paint job. DSR considered providing that service but never did.

Once buses joined the DSR fleet in the 1920s, charter trip destinations were no longer limited to where the tracks ran. In 1933 DSR partnered with the Northern Pacific Railway to provide local bus sightseeing tours for 50 cents a person.

CUSTOMER COMPLAINTS

Passengers could, of course, complain about the service. DSR logged the complaints and kept multiyear statistics. A report survives that covers the entirety of the 1920s. It shows that disputes involving fares and the use of transfers were the most common, 25 to 50 percent of each year's total. The next most common were complaints about rude motormen and conductors, followed by complaints of narrowly missed streetcars, especially at transfer points.

In order to head off complaints, DSR published a recap of the previous day's late cars and other service interruptions in the newspaper, along with explanations of the causes. DSR made some money hauling prisoners to jail. It was not popular with the riding public:

> *Sentiment among patrons of the East End street car lines is crystallizing against the use of the street cars to transport prisoners from police headquarters to the county jail at the court house, and it is declared that unless the sheriff voluntarily discontinues that method of transportation legal proceedings will be resorted to compel some other system.*
>
> *"It is too disgusting for words," said one prominent resident of the East End who is at the head of the present agitation. "The authorities apparently insist on taking their prisoners to the East End at noon time when many school girls who live in our end of the city are going home to lunch. I have been on the car a number of times when the deputy sheriff appeared with a half-naked, debauched and profane woman of the underworld or with some filthily besotted man whose presence would tend to physically and morally contaminate everybody on the car."* (Superior Evening Telegram, *March 14, 1911*)

One of the most unusual complaints was summarized in a company memo: "The only thing that marred the (concert) performance was right near the close when Tibbett was singing some soft melody, one of our street car whistles on a car standing in front of the Armory started to toot and attracted a great deal of attention. . . . Regardless of what the occasion was for using this whistle, several hundred people listening to this concert no doubt condemned the street cars for this disturbance."

The public did more than complain. Sometimes it sued. One of the more colorful cases was recounted in the *Superior Evening Telegraph*, August 22, 1917:

> *Coming out of her house on last March 3rd, Mrs. Anna Shimerock fell over the carcass of a horse that had been dragged in front of her doorstep by employees of the street car company and broke her nose, according to a complaint filed in the circuit court. Mrs. Shimerock has filed suit for $5000 for the injuries she received and her husband is asking $1000 for the loss of his wife's services while she was recovering. She claims that one of the company's cars ran into the horse and killed it. The car men dragged the dead animal in front of her house to get it out of the way of the cars, she avers. Due to the high*

snow she did not see the obstruction when she came out of the house and fell over it.

Sometimes the tables were turned and customer behavior became the issue:

The DSR Co. is determined to stop the disgraceful practice of spitting on the car floors. An order has been issued by the company requiring the conductors to be constantly on the alert, and when they see a passenger using the floor as a cuspidor, to warn the offender not to do it again. If the passenger persists, stop the car and call a policeman. A maximum fine of $100 or imprisonment for up to 90 days is provided for all offenders. (Duluth Herald, *June 14, 1900*)

Smoking was permitted, but only on the streetcar's rear platform. In fact, brass match strikers were mounted on the window posts. In an age when few women smoked, the rear platform became an all-male hangout. Respectable women passed through it but did not linger.

Some feedback on customer behavior appeared in a Duluth newspaper series titled "How you look to . . . ," in this case how you look to a streetcar motorman or conductor. Motorman A. J. Bloomquist wished that when a streetcar was running late and was immediately followed by another, waiting passengers would know enough to let the first overcrowded car pass and board the second one. Conductor Gustave J. Johnson complained of passengers who stood on the back platform, blocking others trying to board or alight. He suggested this was often the same kind of person who would try to board with an expired transfer or put a slug in the fare box.

CARRYING MAIL, NEWSPAPERS, AND DOGS

From 1890 until sometime around 1915, streetcars held a decided speed and reliability advantage over horse-drawn wagons and early automotive vehicles. It was only logical that they would be employed to transport the U.S. mail within cities. Duluth–Superior was no exception. The streetcars handled closed-pouch mail between post offices.

Company records provide snapshots of the mail service at different points in time. The Duluth main post office was located a block up the hill from Superior Street at 5th Avenue West. A post office wagon brought mailbags down to 3rd Avenue West and Superior where they were loaded on streetcars in the presence of the streetcar starter who was based there. In 1901 it appears that mail was transported between the Duluth main post office and branch offices in Superior, Hunter's Park, Lakeside, West Duluth, and Duluth Heights.

Mail hauls could be substantial. A 1919 memo describes the 6:41 a.m. trip from downtown Duluth to New Duluth. It left downtown with 29 mail pouches weighing 417 pounds destined for the post offices in West Duluth, Riverside, Morgan Park, and New Duluth. At West Duluth it dropped off two pouches and picked up three more weighing 220 pounds.

A 1920 report shows mail service connecting seven Duluth post offices and four in Superior. The one inconvenience of streetcars was that they couldn't drive up to the post office door. The report measured the distance between the tracks and the post office, which ranged from 45 feet to 904 feet. To bridge those gaps, sometimes the streetcar crew carried the sacks into the post office, sometimes a postal worker did it, and sometimes a postal wagon met the car. In downtown Duluth, if the wagon failed to meet the car at Superior Street, the mail would be dropped at the 3rd Avenue West starter booth for later retrieval.

The elimination of streetcar conductors caused the DSR to question whether handling mail was worth the trouble. It was clear, however, that the law at the time required streetcars to carry the mail, so it continued until October 21, 1935.

Twice daily, newspaper bundles were placed on the cars in large numbers. This happened despite language in the city franchise that outlawed the carrying of any packages or freight on the cars. This was not much of a problem in the early morning hours, but the afternoon papers tended to crowd the passengers. In 1928 DSR went to the newspaper publishers and told them that no bundles would be carried on one-man cars. It would take two years to phase out the conductors, but after that period the newspa-

DULUTH STREET RAILWAY CO., DULUTH DIVISION

To Conductor:

Carry................packages of Heralds from

5th Ave. West to...

.......................192..... Signed...................................Supt.

Conductor will see that this form is properly filled out and signed before accepting papers, and will enter time of receiving it below, sign it and turn it in with transfers collected on same trip.

Papers received at................M. ....

Conductor.

Twice a day, DSR streetcars loaded bundles of newspapers downtown and distributed them throughout the city. Slips like this one recorded each delivery.

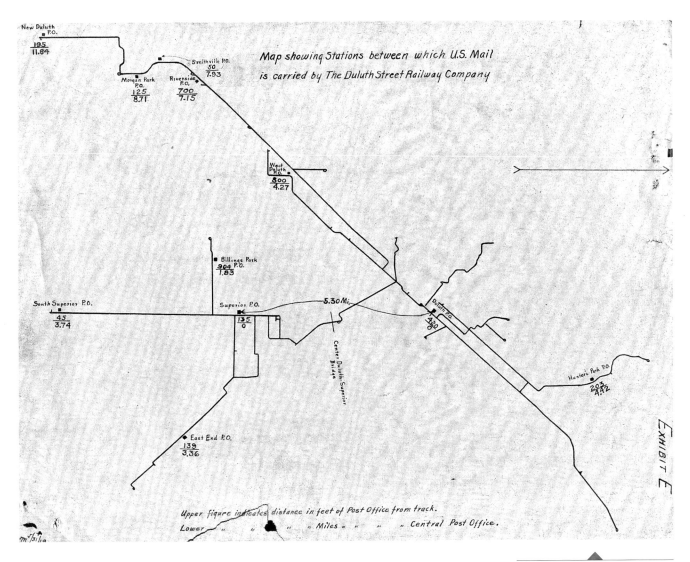

Map showing Stations between which U.S. Mail
is carried by The Duluth Street Railway Company

New Duluth
P.O.
195
11.84

Smithville P.O.
50
7.93

Morgan Park
P.O.
125
8.71

Riverside
P.O.
700
7.15

West
Duluth
P.O.
800
4.27

Billings Park
P.O.
904
1.83

South Superior P.O.
45
3.74

Superior P.O.
135
0

5.30 Mi.

Duluth P.O.
420
0

Hunters Park P.O.
203
4.42

Center Duluth Superior
Bridge

East End P.O.
139
3.36

Upper figure indicates distance in feet of Post Office from track.
Lower   "   "   "   " Miles "   "   " Central Post Office.

EXHIBIT E

m 1/31/19

per publishers would have to buy trucks to deliver the papers, an added expense they did not welcome. In fact, a DSR memo stressed handling the situation diplomatically, so as not to suffer the papers' editorial wrath.

Despite these efforts, almost a year later DSR management and the newspapers discovered that neither was fully aware of whether newspapers were still on the cars. The *Duluth News Tribune* wrote an editorial criticizing DSR for its upcoming discontinuance of newspaper hauling, only to discover that the paper had previously switched everything to trucks. The DSR general manager also was unaware of the switch, thinking newspapers were still being carried on two-man cars.

In the process of discontinuing paper hauling, DSR discovered that one of its shop employees was being paid on the side by the *Duluth News Tribune* to coordinate the placement of papers on the cars.

For some years DSR issued permits for passengers to bring dogs on the streetcars. This was done as a benefit to hunters who would take the cars

This 1919 DSR map shows the mileage from the Duluth Central post office to other post offices, and the distance in feet from the streetcar tracks to the front door.

DULUTH → the all-year
playground of the North   Where Life's Worth Living

DSR's contribution to 1927's
Winter Frolic festival parade
was this highly decorated
streetcar. At that time the
Toonerville Trolley comic strip
with its irascible motorman
The Skipper was at the height
of its popularity, hence the
front-end treatment.

to the edge of town. Permit usage peaked at 274 in 1917 and by 1928 had declined to 129 because "almost everyone who has a dog also has an automobile." So the decision was made to eliminate dogs from all streetcars.

Although the city franchise forbade the hauling of freight on the street railway, the city itself occasionally came to DSR to request that its work cars haul rock for street-paving jobs.

Occasionally the streetcar served the public in unexpected ways. During a 1918 major fire along the Woodland line, it helped residents evacuate, as described in the *Duluth Herald*:

> One Woodland car, with a young woman conductor . . . displayed great nerve in bringing a car load of refugees from the burning district. She not only carried the refugees, but piles of stuff which the people carried with them to save from the flames. "One man brought a large trunk and asked if we would take it on the car," said one conductress. "I told him he could if he was able to get it on. He tried to get it through the gates, but it was too large so we cut a piece off the trolley rope and tied the trunk on the fender. A woman had several geese tied in a sack, and oh my, such a racket. I probably would not have been able to stand the trip, but someone gave me a pair of goggles and someone else supplied me with a mask. For a long distance I had to walk ahead of the car through the thick smoke."

No.
3

TRAINMEN AND STARTERS
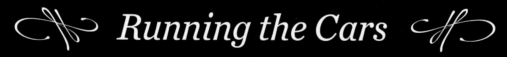 *Running the Cars*

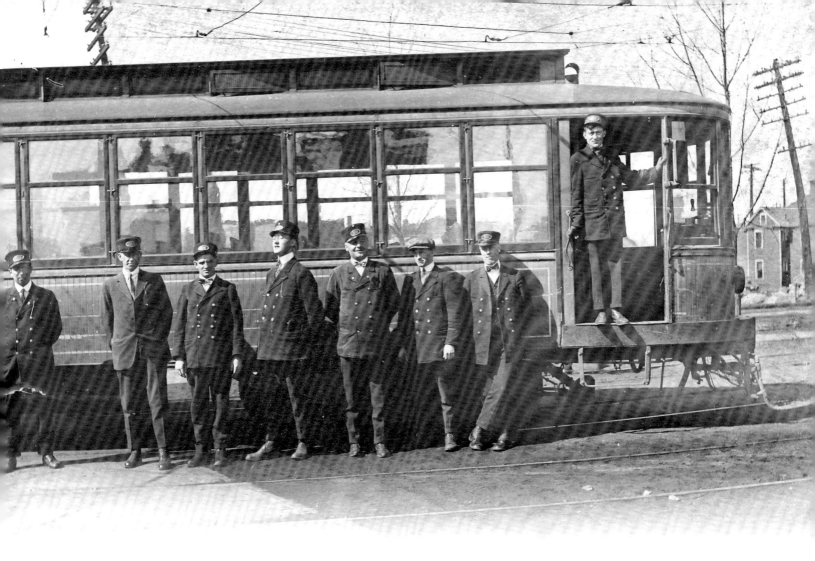

Until about 1930, because they were configured for all passengers to enter through the rear gates, almost every streetcar required a crew of two. The motorman ran the car, and the conductor handled the passengers. Collectively they were referred to as trainmen.

Sometime around 1910, trainmen pose for the photographer outside the Superior carhouse. In the fashion of uniforms of that era, the coats sported brass buttons with the company name or initial. On the fronts of their pillbox hats were oval badges engraved with "MOTORMAN" or "CONDUCTOR" and their employee numbers in raised brass. Courtesy of the Douglas County Historical Society.

THE MOTORMAN

On a two-man car, the motorman was isolated on the front platform behind a closed bulkhead door, and as a rule no one was allowed beyond that door when the car was moving.

What it was like to drive a streetcar? For quite a few years this was done standing up—no seat was provided. Even after a simple stool was installed, the motorman was not permitted to sit when in heavy traffic or approaching any junction or other potential traffic hazard.

The motorman used his hands to operate almost all the controls. At his left was the controller, a waist-high console with two handles on top. The smaller handle was the reverse lever, which determined whether the car went forward or backward. The larger controller handle, which was pulled in a semicircle to the left, was analogous to an accelerator pedal—it set the car's speed. The motorman advanced the handle through eight distinct notches, each a faster rate of acceleration than the last. When fully open, the controller handle was said to be "in the corner," "on the brass," or "in the company notch." Moving the handle to the right from any notch cut the power, and the streetcar coasted.

In the collection of the Minnesota Streetcar Museum are many photographs like this one ca. 1910—streetcar crews posed with their car. Commercial photographers visited the carhouses or appeared at the ends of the lines to solicit this business. The conductor is at left, wearing a coin changer on his belt. His coat has numerous extra pockets to handle transfers and the considerable paperwork that was part of his job. The motorman seldom strayed far from the front platform and was isolated behind a closed door until conductors were largely eliminated beginning in 1928.

Acceleration was not rapid by today's standards. The streetcars weighed over 20 tons and had four motors geared to the axles, developing a total of 200 horsepower. These were referred to as "fast" cars, as opposed to somewhat older cars with only 160 horsepower, which were "slow" cars.

The trickiest part of running a streetcar was stopping it and doing so at the right location. Originally, all the cars had only a hand brake, which the motorman applied with his right hand by turning a long brass gooseneck handle. Deceleration was gradual, and the motorman always had to think ahead.

Air brakes began to appear in 1902 and were a tremendous improvement, providing significantly more stopping power than hand brakes. An air compressor under the car charged an air reservoir to between 60 and 70 pounds pressure, and that pressure pushed iron brake shoes against the wheel treads. Using a handle at his right hand, the motorman released the air pressure, which lifted the brake shoes from the wheel, allowing the car to move forward. Once under way, selected applications of air pressure pressed the shoes against the wheel, slowing and stopping the car. Applying the air evenly to make a smooth stop at the desired place was tricky, required considerable practice, and was done mostly by feel. The steep hills in Duluth complicated matters. There was only so much air in the reservoir, and it took time to recharge the reservoir. On a long downhill run, as on the Woodland line, too many brake applications could drain the air reservoir and cause a runaway.

To warn pedestrians and other vehicles of his approach, the motorman clanged a foot gong or, if a more urgent warning was required, pulled a wood handle hanging in front of him to blow the air whistle. Once the car was stopped, the motorman opened and closed the rear gates with a large crank handle, not unlike a school bus driver today. Additional controls included an air-operated sander for slippery conditions. A single windshield wiper was powered manually. On a rainy day the motorman needed four hands.

Motormen weren't allowed to smoke while the car was underway, but snoose (chewing tobacco) was permitted and was widely used before 1920. However, the disposal of tobacco juice by motormen was problematic for the company. In those days the streetcar's windshield could be dropped into a wall pocket. Motormen would attempt to spit out the front window, literally spitting into the wind, leaving disgusting deposits on the sill and controls. Company memos railed against this and suggested spitting down the small switch rod holes on the floor of the front platform. Some motormen expectorated into the tin boxes under the front passenger seats that held sand for the sanders, which contaminated the sand so that it was useless.

As part of its marketing, in about 1929 DSR commissioned this line drawing of a motorman at his post, left hand on the controller, right hand on the air brake.

THE CONDUCTOR

The conductor was the captain of the ship, responsible for the streetcar's operation and all interactions with passengers. He stood on the rear platform collecting fares, issuing transfers, calling out the approaching streets, handling the money, and filling out the considerable paperwork that accompanied the job. He communicated with the motorman via signal bells, following a code based on the number of rings. Mounted on the ceilings of the front and rear platforms, the bells were connected by a long leather thong. The conductor dismounted to flag the car across railroad crossings. He was the lookout when backing up. At the end of the day, he had to account for the day's fares.

In the late 1920s, hoping to reduce accident costs, DSR divided its motormen and conductors into several safety teams. This well-turned-out 1926 group is safety teams 3 and 11, separated by that little divider on the ground. Team 11 includes Elizabeth Cook, the last remaining World War I conductress. Along with most of the conductors, she would be laid off in 1929.

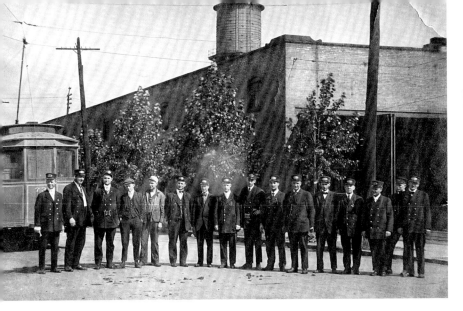

Employees of the smaller Superior Division line up for their portrait in front of the 4th Street and Ogden Avenue carhouse. Although controlled by managers of Twin City Rapid Transit, DSR went its own way with uniforms, choosing double-breasted coats with lapels and oval hat badges. Courtesy of the Douglas County Historical Society.

The motorman and conductor occupied a place in society between blue-collar laborers and office workers. Their jobs were complex, and their navy blue, brass-buttoned uniforms were distinguished, yet a grade-school education was sufficient to be hired. A DSR employment ad called for "men of average intelligence." Still, there was some status attached to the job, the proof being the frequent studio portraits of trainmen in uniform, something not done for factory workers.

The pay was not great, and the hours were long—10 to 12 hours per day, six days a week. Because of the need for more streetcars during the morning and evening rush hours, many of those days were split shifts that could span a 15-hour period from early morning to midevening, especially for lower-seniority employees. Such working conditions resulted in strikes on more than one occasion.

In an age of physical labor in a blue-collar city, motormen and conductors may not have been paid well, but as the public face of DSR they were well-dressed, enjoyed a clean working environment, and from those things derived a certain social status. It is reflected in portraits such as this by professional photographers, which would not have been made of common laborers. Ca. 1910.

From this day card we know that on October 12, 1926, conductor John Hanson and motorman Harry Lawson worked morning run 207. They pulled car 201 out of the Duluth carhouse at 6:33 a.m. and made two round trips to Superior on the Interstate line. They carried 120 passengers, which Hanson dutifully separated into several fare categories. At 10:23 a.m. they turned the car over to another crew at the intersection of Superior Street and Garfield Avenue and deadheaded back to the carhouse on a West Duluth streetcar. This was only the first half of their day. They would probably relieve another crew on the line after lunch and work through the afternoon rush hour.

THE RULE BOOK

In the street railway industry, all aspects of employee behavior were governed by the rule book. DSR's rule book, like many others, opened with these sentences: "To enter or remain in the service is an assurance of willingness to obey the rules. Obedience to the rules is essential to the safety of passengers and employees, and to the protection of property."

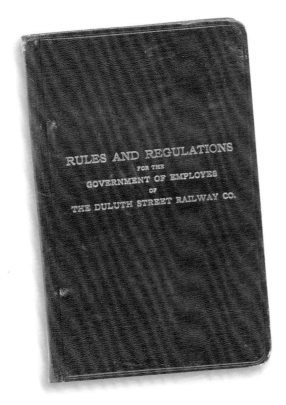

This is copy 31 of the pocket-sized DSR rulebook. It was issued to Elmer J. Johnson when he was hired on March 27, 1920. He carried it for 23 years, and returned it to the company on his retirement in 1943. Inside is a description of the company organization followed by 125 pages of rules covering every conceivable situation and a 23-page index to quickly find the applicable rule.

The rule book was intended to cover every possible situation, but it couldn't. Therefore it was supplemented by a stream of employee bulletins that provided further clarification. This was an era when authoritarian management was the norm, and it was combined with a complete insensitivity to employee comfort and convenience. As if that wasn't enough, employees were expected to balance conflicting rules. The classic example was running fast enough to meet a demanding schedule while conforming to speed limits and other safety rules that tended to slow things down. The result was an endless game of cat and mouse, with employees taking operational shortcuts to ease their workload or increase their comfort and sometimes ignoring rules altogether, and management trying to stamp out such behavior.

CARHOUSES

DSR was divided into separate Duluth and Superior divisions. The Duluth division worked out of the carhouse/shop/office complex that stretched along Superior Street from 26th to 28th Avenues West. From east to west, the complex included:

1. A 13-track carhouse, with dispatching facilities, supervisor office, and club rooms for the motormen and conductors.

2. A long, narrow shop building with four tracks leading into it. Within the building were a paint shop, carpenter shop, machine shop, blacksmith shop, and parts storeroom.

3. A nine-track open storage yard.

4. The general office building. Behind the office building, stretching along 27th Avenue, was a narrow garage and storage shed.

Between 27th and 28th Avenues was a mostly open city block used to store coal, salt, sand, track, and overhead wire materials, as well as a storehouse building. With these facilities, DSR could maintain and rebuild streetcars and administer the day-to-day operations of the entire system.

Because the Highland and Park Point streetcar lines were physically isolated from the rest of the system, each required its own small satellite

This two-story stone carhouse at 11th Avenue West and Michigan Street replaced the original wood horsecar barn in 1885. It was replaced in turn by the much larger 28th Avenue and Superior Street facility in 1893. Kathryn A. Martin Library, University of Minnesota Duluth, Archives and Special Collections.

carhouse. Highland's had room for the line's two cars and was capable of performing the necessary running repairs. Because of its location high on the ridge, moving cars in and out was a major logistical challenge that was undertaken only a couple of times in the line's history. Crews deadheaded between the main carhouse and the Highland line via West Duluth streetcars and the Incline.

Because it had been an independent company from 1890 until the DSR takeover in 1917, Park Point had its own carhouse that performed all repairs. Most of its trainmen actually lived on Park Point. There was a separate carhouse nearby for the fire trolley. It was only in the line's last year, from 1930 to 1931, that operations were consolidated at the main carhouse after tracks were laid over the Aerial Bridge.

Superior streetcars were corporately independent until 1900, when DSR took control. The original Superior wood carhouse was located at Belknap Street and Catlin Avenue. It was replaced in 1902 by a more modern masonry facility at 4th Street and Ogden Avenue. It housed offices and dispatching facilities and could perform light running repairs. Any heavy work was done in Duluth.

This is most, but not all, of the carbarn complex that sprawled along Superior Street from 26th to 28th Avenues West. Out of the photograph at far left is the open-air track and overhead wire yard, then the office building, car storage yard, shop building, and carbarn. Ca. 1910.

The first Superior carbarn for electric cars was this wood complex located at Belknap Street and Catlin Avenue, seen in the 1890s. Courtesy of the Douglas County Historical Society.

Wood carhouses were fire traps, so in 1902 DSR replaced the Belknap and Catlin facility with a brick structure at 4th Street and Ogden Avenue on the north end of downtown. This photograph shows it soon after it opened. Courtesy of the Douglas County Historical Society.

Transit operations are traditionally divided between the carhouse or garage and the street. Trainmen essentially had two sets of bosses. They reported to work at the carhouse, where they would check in, collect the materials and paperwork needed for the day, start up their streetcars, and pull out. During this time they were subject to the control of the carhouse foreman, whose job was to make sure all the work was staffed and all the streetcars left the carhouse in good order. Reporting to the foremen were clerks, usually drawn from the ranks of trainmen, who performed the clerical duties required to assign trainmen to the work. The clerks were functionally the equivalent of noncommissioned officers in the military.

Sometime around 1910, trainmen pose inside the Duluth carhouse. Although it never happened here, electric streetcars inside wood carhouses were a notorious fire hazard. Twin City Rapid Transit replaced its wood buildings with fireproof concrete and steel, but the Duluth carhouse continued to serve even after buses had completely replaced the cars. Note the floor raised on pilings to create pits for undercar maintenance and repairs.

Trainmen reported for work at the foreman's office, nestled between the tracks in the middle of the carbarn. They checked in on the other side of the counter at right to receive their work and car assignments from the station clerk, seated at left. The foreman is in the far office. Kathryn A. Martin Library, University of Minnesota Duluth, Archives and Special Collections.

While management of that era was authoritarian, it was also paternalistic. The model residential communities of Morgan Park and Riverside were extreme examples of this trend. Since the trainmen spent so many hours at the carhouse, the company built club rooms for them with reading libraries, pool tables, and other amenities. It sponsored company baseball teams and a marching band. Because their long hours might require them to work late into the evening and then pull out early the following morning, the carhouse included a dormitory where trainmen could catch a few winks instead of going home.

If they had time before, after, or between runs, the trainmen gathered in the club rooms in the rear of the carhouse. Not unlike a private club, it offered pool tables, a reading area, a kitchen, and a barbershop. Kathryn A. Martin Library, University of Minnesota Duluth, Archives and Special Collections.

In the fashion of many large employers, DSR sponsored recreational and civic activities, including a baseball team and a marching band in 1920. In the latter case, the uniforms were already paid for. Below: Kathryn A. Martin Library, University of Minnesota Duluth, Archives and Special Collections.

STREET OPERATIONS

Once on the street, trainmen were subject to the authority of street supervisors, referred to as inspectors or starters. Starters were stationed permanently in sidewalk booths at 3rd Avenue West and Superior Street in Duluth, and at Belknap Street and Tower Avenue in Superior. Almost all the streetcars passed these points. The starters monitored schedule adherence and ordered service changes as needed. If a streetcar was running too late to make up the time, the starter might short-line it to get it back on schedule. Connected to the carhouse by telephone, he could order additional streetcars if needed to fill in for a late or disabled car or to handle an unexpected rush of traffic. Along with supervisory duties, the starter sold tokens to customers and answered their questions.

In addition to the fixed-post starters, street supervisors moved around the system as needed. They rode the streetcars to check on crew performance. They handled any operational problems that might arise. They also supervised special service to events, dispatching the extra cars as needed.

However, if it was necessary to report a trainman for a rules violation, reprimands and any disciplinary action were handled at the carhouse by the foreman using a demerit system.

On-street supervision was anchored by starters in sidewalk booths at 3rd Avenue West and Superior Street in Duluth and at Tower Avenue and Belknap Street in Superior. In one hour, they could see almost every streetcar in the system and monitor and record their on-time performance. The Superior photograph dates from the 1920s, after an early traffic signal had been placed in the intersection. Duluth photograph (right): Kathryn A. Martin Library, University of Minnesota Duluth, Archives and Special Collections. Superior photograph (below): Courtesy of the Douglas County Historical Society.

ALL IN THE DAY'S WORK OF A CAR STARTER

This firsthand account by E. H. Hassell appeared in a 1934 issue of *Transit Topics,* the company employee newsletter.

"Ding-a-ling-ling-ling," goes the telephone.

"Car starter."

"When do I get a streetcar, please?"

"Where are you please, and where do you wish to go?"

"I'm right here at home and I wish to go to Woodland."

"Where do you wish to board the car?"

"I always take the car at 16th Avenue East and 4th Street."

"The next Woodland car will pass there at 1:10 p.m."

"Thank you so much."

"You're welcome."

As I hang up the telephone to check a few cars, I see a little woman dressed in black waiting at the window.

"Can I buy tokens here?"

"You surely can, Madam. How many do you wish, please?"

"A half dollar's worth."

**"Six tokens and five cents change.
Thank you."**

"You're welcome. I like to get them here so I don't bother the motorman when I get on."

"We're glad to have you get them here."

I hurriedly check more cars as a small boy comes to the window.

"I want to buy some school tickets."

"Got your card?"

"What card?"

"The one they give you at school so you can come here and buy tickets. We can't sell them to you unless you have that card."

"Aw, nurts!"

After running through a car number I turn and look down into the face of a trusting but bewildered old lady. "I left my shopping bag on that last car going up there. It's got an apron in it my niece gave me. How can I get it?"

"That car will be back in 40 minutes. I will try and get it for you. Will you come back to see if I've found it?"

"Oh, my yes. I wouldn't lose that apron for anything."

My next customer is a well-dressed old gentleman who lays down a $5 bill.

"Stack of whites."

"One roll of tokens, $3.60, $1.40 change. Thank you, sir." And with a friendly smile and nod he's gone.

Two blasts of a whistle from a car coming down the hill. That means grab two rolls of tokens, a roll of nickels, lock up the window and door, and run over to meet the car.

"What do you want, George?"

"Roll of tokens. Here's your money. Got some nickels there? Well I'll take them, too. Here's $2 more. Thank you, Ernie."

"You're welcome, George." And I hurry back to check the cars that have passed while I have been out.

A young businessman comes hurrying up to the window and lays down a check.

"Two rolls of tokens, please."

"Yes, sir. That looks like a good check. Thank you, sir."

"Will you give me a receipt, please?"

"Certainly, here it is."

It's 1:49 p.m. Car 203 pulls up, going out to Fairmont Park. A worried operator comes running over.

"Ernie, my rear doors won't work."

"All right, we'll have them fixed." I reach for the station telephone. "Station" (short and snappy). **"Bill, car 203, Fairmont Park, 26th and 3rd Street, 1:59 p.m., rear doors out of order."**

"All right, Ernie. We'll get it."

The next to appear upon my ever-changing stage is an irate old lady who indignantly inquires: "What's the matter with the Woodland cars. I've waited down at 2nd Avenue for over an hour. This service is terrible."

"I'm sorry, Madam. Woodland cars go up over Fourth Street now."

"Oh, dear me. They're always changing things. How do they expect we're going to know? They ought to advertise it in the papers."

"I'm sorry if you have been inconvenienced. They have been running over Fourth Street for months now."

And so it goes from morning to night. Between darting out to catch signs that are slipping, selling tokens and school tickets, looking up lost articles, answering telephones, giving out information, checking cars, and running through car numbers, there is never time to kill. We start work and "Presto!" it's time to check up and go home. Do I get tired? Sure I do, but it's fun.

OFF THE RAILS:
THE DULUTH STREETCAR STRIKES

Labor unrest came early to DSR. During an 1889 streetcar strike in the Twin Cities, there was concern that DSR employees would strike in sympathy with the Twin City Rapid Transit employees, since the two companies had ownership in common. However, the first Duluth strike came in 1893 when the Amalgamated Association of Street and Electric Railway Employees of America led its members out for four days following a wage cut caused by the Panic of 1893.

There was a second strike in 1899. A 1921 company report dryly summarized its causes: "It was necessary to dismiss some of the union employees for good and sufficient cause during the winter of 1898–99, and such dismissal resulted in agitation which necessitated further dismissals and brought about the employment to a large extent of a new force of employees, but the former union employees remained in the city, and on May 2, 1899, they succeeded in inducing the new employees to quit

Trainmen gather in the mid-1890s for a Duluth Federation of Labor event. The first streetcar strike happened in 1893. Kathryn A. Martin Library, University of Minnesota Duluth, Archives and Special Collections.

their work. This brought about the strike of 1899."

Labor took a different view. According to the *Duluth Herald*, there was a "wholesale discharge of motormen and conductors by the DSR Co. The members of the Street Car Employees Union are convinced that it is a war by the company on the union." Indeed, the paper wrote that DSR had never recognized the union, while employees claimed otherwise.

In May 1899 the strike grew violent. Streetcar service was suspended at 10 p.m. on May 7 due to attacks by strikers. Two days later dynamite wrecked a streetcar near the carbarn. A few days later bullets shattered a window of an Interstate car. Shortly thereafter, the strikers gave up. DSR had prevailed.

Herbert Warren was appointed general manager of the Duluth Street Railway in November 1893. He had previously served as chief clerk to Willard J. Hield, then general manager of the St. Paul City Railway. Warren hated unions. He refused to negotiate. He hired spies and strikebreakers, fired pro-union employees, chased organizers off the property, and hired private security firms and off-duty cops to crack heads. In his 45-year tenure as general manager, he suppressed all attempts to organize employees. It wasn't until he retired in 1938 that labor gained a foothold and a contract was signed with the Amalgamated Association of Street, Electric Railway and Motor Coach Employees.

Nineteen years after the 1899 strike, Warren ran afoul of the Duluth Scandinavian Socialists, one of the largest and most active Socialist locals in Minnesota. They held regular meetings and offered lectures featuring nationally prominent figures in the Socialist movement and published an English-language weekly newspaper, *The Truth*. In the summer of 1912 they began holding meetings specifically for street railway motormen and conductors, many of them already members. Wages were low and working conditions harsh for Duluth Street Railway employees, many of whom were recent Scandinavian immigrants. Little had changed since the 1890s. Fifteen-hour days and a system of surveillance and suspensions for rule infractions made streetcar work undesirable, but for newcomers, it was often the only work they could find to support their families.

The 1913 management team and office staff pose in front of the headquarters building at the corner of Superior Street and 27th Avenue West. Large muffs were apparently the trend for keeping female hands warm. Longtime general manager Herbert Warren, who fought the unions during the 1912 strike, is third from the right.

That September a group of aggrieved workers, many of them Socialists, petitioned the company for a wage increase, a reduction in hours, modifications to the disciplinary code, and the right to form committees to present grievances to management. Warren granted a small wage increase but stealthily plotted to break up what seemed to be an effort to organize the workers. That opportunity came on September 2. Axel Peter-son, a Duluth Street Railway conductor and labor activist, was holding a meeting at his home when two informants showed up and forced their way into the meeting. The identities of the nine men in attendance were reported to Warren, who conducted a token investigation and then fired them. Within hours, union organizers delivered an ultimatum to Warren demanding the employees be reinstated, threatening a strike. Warren refused. He had already brought in strikebreakers, and by the evening of September 9 newspapers reported that 100 employees had walked off the job.

On September 10, William E. McEwen, union organizer and editor of the *Labor World,* spoke at a mass meeting. McEwen cautioned against violence and urged the workers to take their cause to the community and organize walking clubs to boycott the streetcars. The following day a formal grievance statement was delivered to the company calling for

The reinstatement of the nine discharged employees.

A ten-hour workday within a spread of 12 hours, rather than the 15 hours then in effect. (Interestingly, on September 12 the trade magazine Electric Railway Journal published an article describing how DSR used split shifts with extremely long spread times to achieve maximum manpower economies.)

Union recognition.

A change in the demerit system. A motorman and conductor explained to the newspapers how the combination of rules conflicted and made it impossible to avoid discipline. One rule stated that cars must wait for connections while another required that cars must always depart the end of the line on time. On one occasion they waited for a connecting car and were late leaving the end of the line. They were given 15 demerits. The next time they failed to wait for the connection but left the end of the line on time and were given 20 demerits. Another round of demerits and they could be fired.

Warren allegedly tore up the grievance petition and chased the petitioners out of his office. The strike was on.

The employees were mostly nonviolent. They detested management but respected their jobs and the company's property. They knew they needed the support of the greater community. However, other groups, notably the Industrial Workers of the World (IWW), used the strike as an opportunity to promote their agenda by provoking riots and acts of vandalism, smashing windows at the carbarn, blockading tracks, even derailing and turning over streetcars. Mobs moved through the city beating strikebreakers and motormen and conductors who crossed picket lines. These demonstrations quickly took on the character of a general strike with other businesses and industries reporting walkouts.

Many businesses took a stand against the strikers simply because they opposed unions. At first the Duluth Merchants Association made an effort to settle the dispute by volunteering to organize arbitration but later showed disapproval of the strikers and sided with the street railway company. Another leading opponent was the Duluth Real Estate Exchange, which publicly announced a boycott against the struggling union.

But public sympathy was with the workers. Citizens refused to ride, even when the company stopped collecting fares. Walking clubs flourished, and entrepreneurial auto owners organized a jitney service. Parades and fund-raisers raised money for strikers and their families. Wives of the strikers sold buttons in support of the streetcar boycott. The Duluth City Council sought a court order to end the strike and initiated proceedings to annul the company's franchise. It offered to organize an arbitration board, but Warren wouldn't budge.

Duluth–Superior was a hotbed of union activity, and the 1912 streetcar strike was particularly bitter. Strikers marched peacefully through downtown Duluth but attacked when the company brought in scabs to replace them. Below: Kathryn A. Martin Library, University of Minnesota Duluth, Archives and Special Collections.

Flashlight of
Damaged Cars during
Street Car Strike
Superior, Wis.

Greenfield Photo

Besides refusing to meet with the strikers, Warren tried to obtain an injunction against the strike leaders restraining them from picketing or otherwise disrupting operations. The judge denied the injunction commenting that strikers have a right to picket.

Warren knew that time was on his side, and he was confident that he could break the strike. The company had appealed the city's actions to the State Supreme Court, but the hearing was set for April 1913 and winter was coming fast. He dug in his heels and held on. It was one thing to walk to work and boycott the streetcars in the fall, quite another in the snow and subzero cold of a Duluth winter.

Despite community solidarity with the workers, by the end of October the strike had collapsed. Other businesses lined up with Warren against the strikers and the governor refused to intervene. Local alderman Joseph Gibson, who had been appointed to lead a strike settlement, quit in despair. Said Gibson, "I do not believe Warren ever intended to have the strike settled." Union leader Max Hall added that he was in total agreement. None of the strikers got their jobs back. Most of them drifted away, finding jobs in the Twin Cities.

SPEED LIMITS

Streetcars were not equipped with speedometers but nonetheless were subject to speed limits in Duluth that were usually slower than the speed limits for automobiles. As a rule, autos were permitted 15 to 20 miles per hour in developed areas, and streetcars were restricted to 12 miles per hour. In more or less open country, such as Commonwealth Avenue near Morgan Park, the auto limit was 35 miles per hour, but streetcars were held to 20.

Needless to say, this placed the streetcar at a competitive disadvantage and drove up operating costs. In 1929 DSR successfully lobbied the city council for more liberal speed limits. This effort raised the limit in "closely built" areas from 12 to 15 miles per hour, and in "closely built, traffic controlled," and "residential" areas from 12 to 20 miles per hour. Outside those areas, the limit was raised from 20 to 45, although the company self-imposed a limit of 35, noting that some of their cars topped out at that speed.

NAVIGATING THE HILLSIDE

One cannot discuss Duluth streetcars without talking about the city's hills, the tallest and steepest streetcar hills in Minnesota. The Piedmont, Kenwood, East 8th Street, Woodland, and Crosley lines all climbed away from the mostly level spine on Superior Street.

Three lines made it to the top of the mighty ridge. The westernmost was the isolated Highland line, in combination with the 7th Avenue West Incline, which together rose 640 vertical feet. The Incline accomplished the first 520 feet from Superior Street. The streetcar, which started from the top of the Incline, wandered upward another 120 feet to the Duluth Heights neighborhood.

The Kenwood and Woodland lines achieved the summit on their own. Starting from the corner of Superior Street and 3rd Avenue West in downtown, they climbed 620 and 750 feet, respectively. No other elevation changes in the state even came close. Duluth's other significant climbers included the East 8th Street line at 405 feet, Crosley at 380 feet, and Piedmont at 310 feet. Add to that Lester Park at 220 feet, West 4th Street at 180 feet, and West 57th Avenue at 140 feet.

It's one thing to climb a long gradual hill but quite another if the hill is steep. Steam railroads were generally limited to about 2 percent (two feet

17th Ave. & 8th St. taken from point 30 paces north of north end of approach. 3:00 P.M. 7/2/23. E.T.M.

Taken in 1923, during construction on the East 8th Street extension, which traveled across the hillside, this photograph captures the steepness of the hill the streetcars had to negotiate to reach downtown. Kathryn A. Martin Library, University of Minnesota Duluth, Archives and Special Collections.

of rise per 100 feet of distance) with extremes of 4 percent found on mountain narrow-gauge lines. Streetcars, which usually had all axles powered, were able to handle much steeper hills. The steepest modern adhesion grade was the 12.5 percent on Pittsburgh's Fineview line, which lasted into the 1960s. Steep grades are particularly problematic when there is ice and snow. For modern light rail, anything over 5 percent is potentially unreliable when icy.

Besides having the highest hills, Duluth had the steepest grades in the state. One indicator of the steepness of the Central Hillside neighborhood is the pitch of the 7th Avenue West Incline, which ranged from 15 to 25 percent.

The conversion of the Lester Park line to trolley bus in 1934 shifted the Woodland and Crosley lines from Superior Street to 2nd Street through

downtown. There was an immediate outcry from passengers who were un-happy about climbing those two blocks to return home. DSR responded by reopening the Superior Street tracks from 3rd Avenue West to 2nd Avenue East, then building two blocks of new track up the hill on 2nd Avenue East to 2nd Street. WPA crews did the pavement work. The new track held the distinction of being the steepest ever on a Minnesota streetcar line, about 10.6 percent. It lasted until the end of service in 1939.

Less severe, but still steep grades included:

8.7%	3rd Avenue West from Superior Street to 2nd Street
8.6%	5th Avenue East from 4th Street to 5th Street
7.6%	Piedmont Avenue from 1st Street to 8th Street (up to 9 percent in places)
7.1%	6th Avenue East from 5th Street to 7th Street
6.6%	5th Avenue East from 2nd Street to 4th Street
6.5%	Kenwood Avenue above 11th Street
6.5%	57th Avenue West from Cody Street to Medina Street
5.7%	7th Avenue East from 7th Street to 11th Street (up to 7.2 percent in places)
4.7%	24th Avenue East from Superior Street to 4th Street (up to 7.1 percent in places)

This is the steepest streetcar hill in Minnesota, 10.65 percent, on 2nd Avenue East from Superior Street to 2nd Street, seen about 1938. To put that in perspective, the front end of the streetcar descending the hill is five feet lower than the back end. Despite the severe grades, DSR never had a runaway.

SENIORITY (AND EXCEPTIONS TO IT)

Motormen and conductors were assigned work based on seniority. Several times a year the schedules were changed, the runs were rearranged, and trainmen selected them based on years of service. There were a few exceptions where the company first required a special certification before the employee could pick the work. This applied to operators on the Incline and the Highland line because those jobs were viewed as having greater than normal responsibilities. Because of its isolation, Park Point residents were given priority over other Duluth residents when picking work on the Park Point line. There was a specially trained pool of snowplow crews. After the Birney safety cars with their different operating characteristics were acquired in 1919, only employees qualified on those cars were allowed to pick Birney runs. Those runs were usually poorly patronized shuttles that stayed away from downtown traffic, the sort of work that went high on the seniority list. However, the company drew the line at letting high-seniority motormen pick them without first being certified to run them. This caused some controversy within the ranks. Further controversy resulted as DSR phased out conductors, starting in 1928. Instead of being deployed all day, two-man cars were restricted to rush hours, and high-seniority conductors found themselves working only split shifts.

CONDUCTRESSES

The sexist but historically accurate terms "one-man" and "two-man" were not exactly so during the 1920s. Twenty-one women were hired as conductors during World War I. The company dubbed them trainwomen (the men were trainmen) or conductresses. The first was hired on May 10, 1918. Having women as crew members was controversial enough that they were not assigned to crews randomly. DSR consulted with the women and paired them with hand-picked motormen. They were generally barred from the Interstate line, with its more complex operating procedures.

A company bulletin goes into quite a bit of detail about the required uniform: "The regulation uniform of conductresses will consist of a uniform cap exactly the same as that prescribed for conductors; a uniform coat similar to that prescribed for conductors except it may be cut to fit the figure; a plain skirt made of the same material as that prescribed for the

Here stand three-fourths of the conductresses hired in 1918 to replace men gone off to war.

coat, the skirt to be made without unnecessary fullness, but with plaits on the side to give freedom of movement, and to be of a length to reach the shoe tops; black hose and plain leather shoes either black or tan with tops not less than 9" from the ground and with broad heels not more than one inch in height."

The women continued on after the war. Eighteen were still employed at the beginning of 1922. In the company files is a list of them, divided into two groups: those married with husbands working and those "who are dependent upon this work for support." Another list divided the women into "married," "single," and "widowed." Five were still employed in 1924.

An August 1928 *Duluth News Tribune* article featured the remaining two, Christine Pearson and Elizabeth Cook:

Veterans of the service, these girl conductors today are wearing the gold "hash marks" of service on the cuffs of their uniform coats. They have stayed with the service and accepted its hardships ten years, and both express their intentions of remaining. The job, they said, offers better opportunities than most situations open to women, both from a standpoint of salaries and promotions; and they said they find the work most interesting.

"We see people in all moods each day," said Miss Cook. We find them in their "morning grouch," their "evening smile" and just in the rough; humanity as it really is and not submerged in the subterfuge of business or society. Yes, we have our troubles, too, occasionally. There are fresh boys and intoxicated lads, and then there are those who are a bit rough, but we handle them all and, honestly, I like the contact with people. They treat us wonderfully at the office and, while we do not claim any advantages because of our sex, the shop men are most pleasant to us. I expect to remain in the service.

DSR employees observe Flag Day on June 14, 1918. Many of the men have respectfully removed their hats, perhaps honoring colleagues now gone off to war. Present are some of the women hired to replace them.

> *Miss Pearson said, "I like the excitement of meeting folks and I like the work. It is different from the usual run of employment and I have no intention of quitting my conductor's job for something less interesting."*
>
> *Under the state employment laws, which require women to work only 54 hours per week, these two cannot hold the regular all-day run to which they are both entitled under their seniority rights. They are working morning and evening runs and they work every day of the week.*

Despite their desire to continue working, both women were gone by May 1929. During 1928 and 1929, DSR converted 54 streetcars to one-man operation. The roster of conductors was reduced, and eleven years' seniority wasn't enough to avoid a layoff.

DANGERS OF THE JOB

Beyond the risks of vehicular collisions, trainmen were assaulted more often than one would imagine. Ornery drunks were always a problem. On July 4, 1893, the *Duluth News Tribune* reported,

> *The trouble arose over two very beery passengers who insisted on taking a keg of beer in a sack out to Lester Park with them. The car was crowded, the keg took up too much room on the platform, and the conductor told the owners they would have to put it off. They demurred and a difficulty ensued. Lt. Donovan happened along about that time and was appealed to by the conductor. The Lt. told the conductor to put the keg off and the conductor started to do so when the owner raised an objection. The conductor, whose car had been delayed about ten minutes, then lost patience, and after shouting to the sober passengers to 'stand clear' fired the keg owners out on the street. They started back with the avowed intention of paralyzing the employee, but Lt. Donovan's hands simultaneously grasped two coat collars and they desisted.*

A small number of passengers simply refused to pay the fare, and that could escalate into an assault. During the days of two-man crews, the rulebook instructed the trainmen to eject unruly passengers and fare evaders, stopping the car first and using no more force than necessary.

The elimination of conductors changed the odds in favor of fare evaders and thieves. Motormen carried change, and the fares cranked through the farebox were readily accessible. As a result, holdups were not uncommon. A particularly memorable one was recounted in a 1934 issue of the employee newsletter *Transit Topics*:

BATTLE OF DULUTH HEIGHTS

The night of July 15, 1921, was a pleasant one. LeRoy Gillette was making his last trip at 12:33 a.m. on the Highland line. He had one passenger—a young man who sat dozing on the front seat just inside the bulkhead window. Two more passengers boarded the car at Lake Avenue, a large man and a small one. The small man went inside and sat down beside the dozing passenger, while the big man stood behind Gillette.

Gillette got out and threw the switch at the turnout, thinking that in just two minutes his day's work would be over and then—home. He returned to the car and had just applied the power when WHAM! He was struck on the head and the blow was repeated. Gillette did not drop, but started to turn. His assailant then fired the gun he had been using as a club. The first shot missed but the second went through LeRoy's right arm.

Meanwhile the smaller ruffian attacked the passenger while the car was running, twisting and turning, swaying from side to side. Gillette swung around, grabbing the thug around the neck with his right arm, turning his head to look into the muzzle of a Colt .38. LeRoy felt his life depended upon gaining possession of the gun. All over the vestibule they struggled. Blood was streaming from Gillette's head and arm. All the vestibule windows were broken, as well as the glass in the doors. Meanwhile the passenger kept the other thug busy while the car continued its wild course. Finally Gillette managed to seize the hold-up man's wrist and suddenly got possession of the gun. Here the Battle of the Heights ended as quickly as it had started, for both the ruffians fled through the car and jumped out the rear window.

The car was just pulling into the station and Gillette stopped it at the right time and place and got off. He was taken to the hospital for treatment but refused to stay there. The hold-up men were never found. LeRoy has the gun as a grim souvenir of that memorable evening.

THE OBSOLETE CONDUCTOR

The 1920s saw the beginning of the long decline in transit ridership as auto ownership and paved roads became universal. The streetcar companies adapted, buying lightweight streetcars to lower power consumption and upgrading their older cars to be more attractive. Their largest cost was labor, and by far the biggest opportunity for cost cutting was to eliminate conductors, reducing the crew size from two to one. However, doing so created problems and complications.

The value of the conductor was most obvious on heavily traveled lines. The crowd would pile aboard and take their seats before paying. The conductor would try to remember who had boarded and collect the fares while the car was underway to the next stop. Not surprisingly, many passengers hid in the crowd, hoping the conductor wouldn't recall them. This was

An industry-wide innovation of the early 1920s was pay-as-you-enter (PAYE) fare collection. Previously, boarding passengers took their seats, and the conductor circulated through the car collecting their fares, which he placed in envelopes in his many coat pockets. Revenues were lost when passengers hid from the conductor in crowded cars and conductors skimmed fares. PAYE required each passenger to pass a farebox and drop in the fare under the conductor's watchful eye before sitting. The farebox recorded the number of fares mechanically. DSR took this a step too far by installing turnstiles in several cars. Passengers complained loudly, and they were soon removed.

particularly difficult if there was a standing load. In those days, there were no fareboxes. The conductor deposited the fares in separate envelopes for each trip, and the envelopes went into one of his many coat pockets. He rang the fares up on an overhead fare register.

Pay As You Enter, abbreviated to PAYE, and sometimes also called Pay As You Pass, required that everyone deposit their fares in a farebox as they entered the car. It was implemented in Superior in 1924 and in Duluth in 1926. The fareboxes contained mechanical coin counters that helped reduce skimming of fares by conductors. DSR even tested turnstyles in a few cars. Besides reducing seating capacity, the public response to the turnstyles was quite negative, and they were quickly removed.

There were a few lightly traveled lines where conductors had always been an extravagance. The lightest of all were the isolated Highland line, which went one-man in 1912, and the West 4th Street line, which shuttled back and forth on a mile of track and averaged three passengers per trip. DSR rebuilt a pair of old single truckers for double-ended operation and converted West 4th Street to one-man in 1919.

Running with only a motorman meant that passengers had to enter through the front instead of the rear—the opposite of how the streetcars were configured. DSR had to install front doors and remove the bulkhead that isolated the motorman from the passenger compartment. Those changes were made in the company's own shops, along with seating improvements and safer operator controls.

Conductors had always provided a lookout when backing into a wye or the carhouse. Now, the motorman had to do it alone from the front end. The company promulgated rules and procedures for backing the cars without a lookout in the rear. Even so, backing up was dangerous. The company replaced five wyes with loops, eliminating the need for backup moves at those locations, and eventually backup controls were installed on the rear platform, allowing the motorman to control the car from the rear.

Calling streets had always been the conductor's responsibility while the motorman was isolated behind a wall. That barrier was removed, and the motorman now called the streets. However, where the conductor could face into the car to project his voice, the motorman was farther from the passengers and facing away from them. A company bulletin explained, "It will be necessary for operators to use their voices strongly in calling streets and avenues so the passengers in the rear part of the car can hear them."

It was standard DSR policy for conductors to dismount at railroad grade crossings and flag the car across. The car would move forward while the conductor flagged and then stepped aboard as it passed. Without a conductor, the company required the motorman to leave the car, walk forward to the grade crossing, determine that no train was coming, return to the car, and proceed across the tracks. It had to take more time, especially on lines like the Interstate and Billings Park–Broadway, which had several grade crossings.

If there was one overriding concern about eliminating conductors, it was that more time would be required for the runs, which in turn would require more streetcars. A September 1928 memo voiced the need for more layover time at the end of the line: "When a one-man operator gets to the end of his route he has to do all of the conductor's clerical work which the conductor on a two-man car usually does while his car is running or nearing the terminal. Some of these duties are: Enter passenger figures, check up his transfers and put them in an envelope, change the side signs in the car, look through the car carefully for lost articles, punch transfers ahead, etc. A motorman operating a streetcar nowadays needs 3 or 4 minutes relaxation after a 30 or 45 minute run through the present street traffic. If his running time is too tight so that he cannot even get his scheduled 5 or 6 minute layover time and then has to work in a frenzy to get his day car work, transfers, sign changes, ventilation, and other duties taken care of, he will soon think that one-man operation is very burdensome."

As the rebuilt cars entered service, the company tried to quantify the delays. In November 1928 a checker compared similar trips with one-man and two-man cars on the Lester Park and Woodland lines and found that passenger boardings and alightings on one-man cars took 60 percent longer per person than on two-man cars, and that one-man cars spent twice as much time standing still to load and unload.

A December 1928 newspaper story reported complaints of one-man cars being slower. In response, DSR scheduled them to alternate with two-man cars on the Lester Park and Woodland lines. An check of that arrangement showed no measurable difference in on-time performance. Completion of the conversion to one-man operation coincided with the onset of the Great Depression. Ridership dropped sufficiently that one-man cars had no problem making the scheduled running time.

THE EMPLOYEES' BUSINESS-GETTING CAMPAIGN

The 1920s ridership decline accelerated dramatically with the onset of the Great Depression. By the end of 1930, the situation was becoming dire. The lightly patronized West 4th Street line was abandoned, and others would follow in the next two years.

Duluth had always been a strong union town, and bitter conflicts between labor and management occurred with some frequency across a variety of industries. There had been a street railway strike as recently as 1912. However, in the mid-1920s, DSR instituted an experiment in participatory management, organizing its employees into safety teams that encouraged a safe work place and holding regular meetings to discuss operational issues. From the records that are available, it appears that employee suggestions to improve safety were taken seriously. If so, this was a major departure from the traditional authoritarian style of transit management and may have laid the foundation for a desperate effort on the part of the employees to retain street railway jobs.

On November 20, 1930, a rather remarkable document was approved at a meeting in the carhouse club room attended by 225 of the company's 350 car men. Thus started the Employees' Business-Getting Campaign:

Whereas, the employees of the Duluth Division of the Duluth Street Railway Company, realizing that street railway patronage in the city of Duluth has decreased steadily over a period of years, resulting in the present receivership, and

Whereas, further loss of patronage may bring about abandonment of operation, or at least drastic curtailment of service, with loss of employment to us and hardship to those who depend on the street cars, and

Whereas, we are convinced that the street cars render an essential service,

necessary to the welfare of the people of Duluth, the maintenance of our schools, the preservation of property values, and the success of retail business, and

Whereas, we desire to assist our company by special effort at this time to provide the best possible service to encourage greater use of the car,

Therefore it is resolved, that all employees of the Duluth Street Railway Company join in a whole-hearted and spirited independent employee movement to regain lost patronage:

That we will be courteous and considerate to passengers under all conditions,

That we will run on time—never ahead of schedule,

That we will make all transfer connections consistent with good service,

That we will distinctly call all streets and avenues, and keep a sharp lookout for passengers,

That we will keep posted as to time of cars on all lines so that we may be able to give accurate service information,

That we will keep our cars clean, properly heated, and well-ventilated,

That the safety of passengers and the public will be our first consideration always.

Be it further resolved, that the Executive Committee is authorized to appoint committees to work out ways and means of making the service as nearly one hundred percent perfect as is humanly possible under the present conditions, and of selling people on its advantage to them in economy and convenience.

The volunteer committee that called the meeting felt that the ridership decline could be reversed. To that end, the resolution basically commits employees to doing their jobs the way they should be done, arguing that poor service was self-destructive.

The Employees' Business-Getting Campaign had a higher goal—to preserve jobs. Higher-seniority car men began to voluntarily take more days off and give up their "extra work" (overtime) so that lower-seniority men could remain on the payroll.

The next step was a publicity campaign to persuade the public to drive less, ride the streetcars more, and refrain from picking up free passengers who would otherwise have ridden the streetcar. The committee immediately took their case to the local newspapers and received both publicity and editorial endorsement.

By the end of 1931, memos from the committee state that the top 80 percent of the trainmen were giving up sufficient hours to keep the 50 men with the lowest seniority employed. *Keep 50 men employed* became a primary slogan of the campaign.

There was an attempt in 1931 to repeal the Duluth jitney ordinance that prohibited buses and private autos from cruising streetcar routes and carrying passengers in exchange for a fare. The employee committee joined DSR in opposing repeal and was successful.

In May 1932, the campaign pioneered a convenience that had not occurred to the company, the posting of streetcar schedules at stops. It passed out copies of timetables to streetcar riders and local officials, along with a letter describing the campaign, with the request that they post them in public places. Few opportunities to spread the word were missed. Seventy-five copies went to the Duluth public schools superintendent, urging students and staff to ride the streetcar.

The campaign also made the assumption that reducing DSR's costs would save jobs. The following letter to fellow trainmen urged saving electricity:

If each of us would save 25 cents worth out of the approximately $3.00 worth of power used each day, the power bill would be $10,000 less per year. Let us study and follow these ten suggestions:

1. Release the air entirely before applying power in starting.

2. Feed up the controller to the eighth point in six seconds under normal conditions.

3. Avoid running on the resistance points.

4. Coast down grade and a reasonable distance before each stop. Don't "fan" the brakes.

5. Save unnecessary braking by keeping a safe distance behind street cars and other vehicles.

6. Use the gong freely.

7. Avoid stopping in curves if possible.

8. Look well ahead. Anticipate stops or slow downs. Coast to them.

9. Turn off lights when not needed.

10. Avoid unnecessary conversation and other distractions which affect the efficiency of operations.

Did it work? Even though ridership continued to decline, memos from the committee speculate that it would have been worse without the campaign. The file contains several letters from businessmen in support of the campaign. N. F. Russell, president of Bridgeman-Russell Dairy Products (Bridgeman's ice cream) wrote,

*A representative of your organization called for
the purpose of trying to get the auto owners to
stop picking up people standing on the corners
waiting for street cars. I, no doubt, living in
Lakeside as I do, have picked up as many as
anybody has. I never looked at the matter in the
same light after talking to your representative,
but will say that I have already discontinued
this practice and in the future will follow London
Road instead of Superior Street.*

The information about this campaign came from a DSR
file. The last page in the file is a February 14, 1933,
memo from the employee association president to the top
company officials. It notes that the campaign is entering
its third year, and thanks to it, there is "a clearer under-
standing of our problems by the traveling public and . . .
a friendlier attitude toward the company and employees
generally." And with that the file ends.

No. 4

KEEPING THE WHEELS TURNING

Behind the Scenes

Track construction on downtown
Superior Street in 1922.

In 1925 DSR employed 485 people. Only 58 percent of them ran streetcars. The rest worked behind the scenes to support street operations. Unseen by the public, they wrote the schedules, laid the tracks, strung the overhead wires, repaired the cars, and handled administration and clerical chores.

SCHEDULE MAKING

Public transit is a precise business, and it is not easy to do it well. The goal is for an employee with a clock to pilot a large vehicle to a preassigned location where it will intercept a customer who also has a clock (set to the same minute) and knows the scheduled departure time. This isn't like the airlines, which require the customer to buffer on-time performance by showing up an hour early. In transit, the window for the vehicle and the rider to meet is measured in a few minutes, sometimes seconds. That same coordinated meet between strangers happened in Duluth–Superior many thousands of times each day, and the forces acting to prevent it were many.

The Schedule Department relied on load checks taken at multiple points across the system to assemble ridership profiles of all the lines. These were used to set the running times and fit the service frequency to the demand.

Scheduled running time is an exercise in averaging. It requires a good knowledge of where and how many people ride, traffic conditions, the streetcar's performance capabilities, and semi-intangibles such as weather. It was common practice to increase running time in the winter due to weather conditions and heavier passenger loads. It was the motorman's job to adjust his speed whenever conditions deviated from the norm.

Once the running time was established, the schedule maker had to tailor the number of trips to meet the demand. In most cases that meant adding quite a bit of service during rush hours, when ridership doubled and even tripled on some lines. A typical schedule consisted of an all-day base headway (frequency) of every 20 minutes on most lines, but every 5 or 10 minutes on the heaviest lines. To these would be added "trippers," short assignments that made only a trip or two during the rush hour.

The hard part was assigning these varied pieces of work to trainmen to make the most economic use of the available manpower, a process known as "run cutting." A century ago trainmen worked 10 to 12 hours a day, six days a week. Work was generally assigned by seniority, and in most cities the senior trainmen got to work "straight runs": they worked their 10 or 11 hours and were done for the day. Everyone else worked "split" or "two-piece" runs.

DSR achieved the most efficient possible runs but only by exploiting its employees. Therein lay one of the grievances that caused the 1912 strike. According to a 1912 article in the *Electric Railway Journal*, which was actually published during the strike, "In order to furnish crews for the rush hour service and at the same time not have a large number of short-hour men, all crews are required to take out trippers in addition to their regular runs." This meant everyone worked split shifts, an average workday of 11 hours, spread over an average of 13.6 hours and sometimes as long as 15.5 hours. For example, trainmen reporting to work at 6 a.m. might work until 8 a.m., go home, return to work at noon, and finally get done for the day at 9 p.m.

To add to the trainmen's woes, all the split shifts involved "making relief," which meant replacing a crew on the line at a location distant from the carhouse. The travel time between the carhouse and the relief point was unpaid, and each relief consumed about 15 minutes. Most runs included two reliefs per day, or about a half hour of unpaid time. A few runs were "three-piece," three different assignments per day separated by unpaid time. Split shifts are still universal at transit systems today, but the spread between the start and end of the day is usually 12 hours at most.

TRACK, OVERHEAD, AND POWER DEPARTMENTS

Although confined within a city, DSR was still a railroad, and not a small one. At its peak in 1930 there were 114 miles of track to maintain, the equivalent of the distance from Duluth to Grand Marais. Much of that track was embedded in pavement that had to be disassembled to make repairs, then replaced. Any railroader will tell you that the most labor-intensive sections of track are sharp curves, which wear quickly, and switches, with their moving parts and frogs (gaps where rails cross one another) that get pounded by the steel wheels. DSR owned 210 sharp curves and 265 switches, many more per mile than the typical railroad. To maintain all this, the Track Department employed 50 people, including curvemen who did nothing but grease the sharp curves to minimize wear and wheel noise. Track work was mostly manual labor.

A 1913 editorial praised the DSR track crews, noting that the franchise required the company to relay its tracks whenever the city improved a street. When it came to grading, "Its [DSR's] crew is put on the work and its big cars

Over the years, track laying was only partially mechanized. This photograph shows the Piedmont Avenue line under construction in 1910. Kathryn A. Martin Library, University of Minnesota Duluth, Archives and Special Collections.

Pieces of rail were welded together to make switches, crossings, and other special work. These were loaded onto crane-equipped work cars for transport to the construction site. Kathryn A. Martin Library, University of Minnesota Duluth, Archives and Special Collections.

The square block between 27th and 28th Avenues was devoted to the track and overhead wire departments. 1916.

In the yard west of the office building, the track department assembled the necessary materials. Crossties were manually offloaded from railroad freight cars. Unloading and stacking rails required a derrick. Below: Kathryn A. Martin Library, University of Minnesota Duluth, Archives and Special Collections.

Most track work, especially prior to 1920, was accomplished with manual labor, requiring large crews such as this.

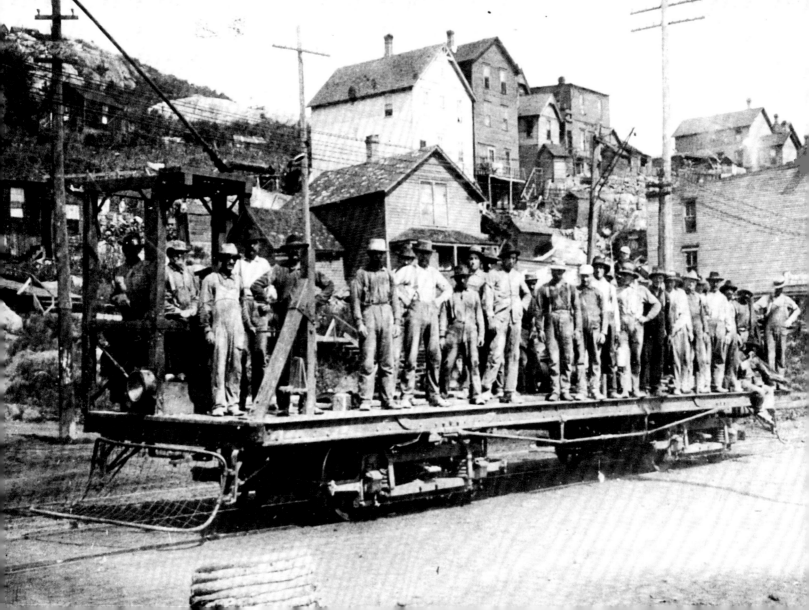

Work car 5 carries a cement mixer as part of a repaving job on Broadway in Superior, ca. 1917.

are used to move the dirt. The result is that this much of the work is done far more expeditiously and is better done than are those parts of the roadway beyond the tracks at either side."

This was an electrified railroad. Over the center of every track ran an overhead wire from which the streetcars drew their power. On the roof of each streetcar was a spring-loaded trolley pole with a wheel on the end that

Laying track required large quantities of gravel, and DSR laid sidings into several quarries. One of them was at 12th Avenue West and Superior Street, accessed by this spur track. 1924.

rode the underside of the wire and brought electricity into the car. The 114 miles of copper overhead wire were supported by almost as many miles of span wire hanging from pairs of wood poles spaced about every hundred feet on either side of the street. Wherever the track curved, additional pull-off wires kept the overhead centered above the track, preventing the trolley poles from losing contact.

The current completed a circuit and returned to the power house via the rails, which were electrically bonded together. The Overhead Department employed special work streetcars and wire trucks with hydraulic platforms that lifted to reach the wire.

Thanks to the Thompson Dam hydroelectric station on the St. Louis River, DSR was able to purchase power without having to own its own power plant. It did, however, have substations to boost the power to reach the far corners of the system. *Transit Topics* was the employee newsletter of the Duluth–Superior Transit Company. In 1934 it included an excellent firsthand description of the electrical system that powered the streetcars (see page 100).

Left: Power is transmitted to the streetcar via the overhead wire; it runs through the car's controls and motors and returns to the powerhouse via the rails, which are electrically bonded. Installing and maintaining overhead wire was a continual job. Initially all repairs were made using a wire car, a work car equipped with a roof platform and the necessary tools and equipment.

Right: Storm damage was a common problem. In this case, sleet has weighed down the overhead wire, snapping a pole. The wire truck has responded, ca. 1920.

As automotive technology advanced, most streetcar companies purchased wire trucks. They were much more flexible because they could get on and off the tracks quickly, which minimized service disruptions. This is the Duluth carhouse yard in 1920.

OPERATION OF THE ELECTRICAL SUBSTATION: THE MACHINERY THAT ALMOST THINKS

By Walfred Swanson, Substation Foreman

No doubt you have passed structures similar to the handsome little building pictured here. "A pleasant place to work," you may have commented, noting the agreeable surroundings and the sunshine flooding the large windows.

It may surprise some of you to learn that except for the man who makes the rounds inspecting them, no one works there.

Yet the functions of this sturdy little establishment are very intricate and of vital importance in the service of the public. To better illustrate the operation of the substation, let us take the power that drives a street car or trolley bus and follow it from its source.

The electrical energy is generated at the Thompson Dam and transmitted at 66,000-volt, 25-cycle alternating current to the Power Company's 15th Avenue West substation in Duluth. At this station it is "stepped down" to 13,200 volts and delivered to our substations where it is stepped down to 430 volts. At this voltage it goes through synchronous converters (rotating machines) where it is changed to a 600-volt direct current to suit the motors of street cars and trolley buses.

In passing, a word of comment about alternating and direct current may be helpful. Alternating current reverses in direction at regular intervals. It can be generated at low voltage or pressure and then "stepped up" by transformers to any desired higher voltage for transmission to distant points. Transmitting power at a high voltage cuts down line losses and effects a saving in copper required.

Direct current flows uniformly in one direction. It cannot be regulated by transformers, and it can be generated only at a limited voltage. Direct current is particularly applicable for street railway use due to the characteristics of the direct-current motor used in this service.

A street car motor is geared directly to the wheels, and the speed of the motor varies with that of the car. The propelling force required is high at slow speeds as in starting and low at free-running speeds. Because it is especially adapted for such work, the direct-current motor is used on street cars.

The control equipment of our automatic substations consists of an assemblage of contactors, relays, master switches, and other devices especially adapted to this service. To explain the functioning of the automatic control from beginning to end would make a long story. I will outline here only the principal steps in normal operation.

The starting up and shutting down of the automatic station is governed by the load demand on the part of the system in which the station is located. As cars or trolley buses enter the section governed by a substation, the voltage on the trolley decreases due to the heavy current demand of the cars or buses. The starting-up indication is given by a master element or voltage relay. The operating coil of this relay is connected to the trolley, and any variation of the trolley voltage causes a corresponding movement of the element in the relay. When the voltage falls to a certain predetermined point, this relay closes a circuit for an automatic time-delay relay, and after a suitable time delay, the other control devices are started in their proper sequence of operation. The time-delay feature prevents the machine from starting up unnecessarily when the voltage drops only momentarily.

The converter starts, builds up to full voltage, and is then connected to the trolley by automatic switches, the whole operation taking about 45 seconds. The station will then remain in constant operation as long as there is sufficient load demand on that section of the system. As the load diminishes to an uneconomical point, a shutting-down indication is given by the operation of an underload relay. If the load remains at or below a certain value for a predetermined time, the converter will shut down, and the high-tension lines are disconnected from the transformer by a 15,000-volt automatic circuit breaker.

Oil circuit breakers are used in high-voltage alternating-current circuits. All contacts are enclosed in tanks filled with oil, and the circuit is closed and opened under oil. A mineral oil of high dielectric (nonconductor) strength is used in the breakers. Our stations are motor operated and fitted with tripping and locking-out devices for emergencies.

In addition to control devices used in the normal operation of the machinery, we have several protective devices to guard the equipment in cases of emergency. Emergencies may arise from heating of bearings, grounded trolley wires, overloads, overspeed and underspeed of the machines, overheating of machine windings, etc. The action of the protective devices in cases of emergency is swift and accurate—much more so than that of any human being. No time is required to think; they act instantly.

Automatic control in our substations has been in service about 15 years. Ours were the first installed in the northwest. Mechanical marvels such as the automatic substation are fair examples of the complex equipment and the ceaseless application of human care and skill which make possible an 18.5-mile trolley ride for very little more than it once cost to ride a single mile behind a mule.

Reprinted from *Transit Topics*, 1934

IN THE SHOP

The 110 employees at the DSR shops on West Superior Street were capable of repairing anything on a streetcar. There was a wood shop, a motor shop, a blacksmith shop, and a foundry. Shopmen worked around the clock, reporting to foremen, who in turn reported to the master mechanic, who reported to the general manager.

Motors required rewinding of the coils. Wheels wore down and had to be replaced. Wood wainscoting on the bodies rotted, the canvas roofs deteriorated, the wicker seat upholstery frayed, and everything needed repainting. Copper contacts inside the controllers burned out. Damage from derailments and collisions meant new windows and rebuilt bodies.

Shopmen (there were no shop women) remove a motor armature from streetcar 82 ca. 1906.

The Duluth Division shop force posed for a rare group photograph in the mid-1920s. Working men wore denim, and almost no head is without a cap. Kathryn A. Martin Library, University of Minnesota Duluth, Archives and Special Collections.

The DSR shop was capable of repairing anything on a streetcar and rebuilt many of the cars extensively during their lifetimes. This is the wood shop. Kathryn A. Martin Library, University of Minnesota Duluth, Archives and Special Collections.

The foundry, blacksmith, and welding shop. Kathryn A. Martin Library, University of Minnesota Duluth, Archives and Special Collections.

The machine shop: note that all the machines were driven by belts off an overhead pulley system powered by large electric motors. Kathryn A. Martin Library, University of Minnesota Duluth, Archives and Special Collections.

Routine daily maintenance included sweeping and washing the cars' interiors, washing the exteriors, greasing the trolley wheel and axle bearings, adjusting the brakes, hanging storm windows before winter and removing them in the spring, keeping the coal heater fires stoked, and filling the sander boxes. When cars broke down on the line, the shop men pulled out the wrecker and retrieved them or fixed the problem on the spot. They did more, rebuilding the cars every few years and making major modifications to a large portion of the fleet during the changeover to one-man operation from 1928 to 1930.

The shops were supplied from this central storeroom. Kathryn A. Martin Library, University of Minnesota Duluth, Archives and Special Collections.

When the trucks under the cars required motor or wheel repair, the car body was lifted by an overhead crane, and the trucks were rolled out from under it.

THE OFFICE

In 1908 DSR moved its general offices from the power house at 11th Avenue West and Superior Street to a new building on Superior Street at 27th Avenue West.

For most of its history, DSR didn't just run streetcars; it built new lines. In the 39 years from 1890 to 1928, new track was built in 27 of them. In addition, worn-out track was replaced, as were significant sections of the overhead wire. Track had to be relaid after street paving projects. All this required an Engineering Department that reported to the chief engineer.

There was a Purchasing Department that bought whatever the company needed, and a Store Department that disbursed those items throughout the company. There were the usual financial functions of accounting, money handling, payroll, and auditing. More than most businesses, streetcar companies were involved in accidents, so the handling of claims was a major concern.

Given the large number of employees and the fact that it operated 24/7, DSR had a lean management staff. A general manager oversaw day, night, and relief carhouse foremen, shop foremen, starters (on-street supervisors), and a handful of trainers and clerical workers.

In 1920, management poses in front of the office building. The only woman holds a clerical position. Left to right: Tranvik, instructor; F. Paul, car starter; J. Boltman, money receiver; Angus McMillan, car starter; J. Mitby, line foreman; C. Huttel, switchman; Pat O'Toole, station foreman; Bernt Stene, line foreman; W. Hafner, station foreman; A. Grytdahl, money receiver; Al Frickman, car starter; R. T. Smallidge, line foreman; Carl Rankin, station foreman; Sangster, station clerk; John Hamilton, starter; Bessy Hintz, money receiver; F. Gallagher, coasting instructor; E. W. Burg, relief foreman; H. H. Brown, superintendent; John Wiski, instructor.

OPERATING CHALLENGES

What could delay a streetcar? Traffic congestion, a problem in bigger cities, wasn't much of a factor in Duluth or Superior, except downtown on Superior Street, where the villain was more often streetcars getting in each other's way.

Every streetcar system had to deal with accidents and delays from varied causes. Streetcars' major drawback was their inability to detour. Anything that blocked the track or severed the overhead wire brought service to a halt. Occasional windstorms blew down trees. If water flooded deeper than about one foot, the motors mounted on the power trucks would short out, requiring expensive repairs. Once, a large boulder fell onto the tracks from Point of Rocks. As the years passed and automobiles became more common, so did auto–streetcar crashes and delays from disabled autos.

Streetcars could derail, disrupting service. A switch might be partially open, or a wheel might break, or the flangeways might fill with ice, causing the car to ride up and leave the tracks.

Railroad grade crossings delayed streetcars, especially in Superior. The Interstate line that crossed the harbor between Duluth and Superior had to deal with swing bridges that opened frequently for lake boats.

"Watch for fallen rock." A particularly large boulder has broken off the Point of Rocks in 1918.

ICE AND SNOW

Severe winter weather and steep hills compounded the challenge of running on time. Duluth averages 86 inches of snow per year, almost twice as much as Minneapolis. The snow season extends from October through April. Factor in the steep hills, and it's a challenging place to keep a street railway running.

Each September, the shop crews prepared for winter. Over 3,500 storm windows were hung, one placed over every streetcar side window. Snow scrapers were installed ahead of the front wheels on each streetcar. Sand and salt were stockpiled and sacked, and sacks were placed on all cars, along with coal scuttles, snow shovels, and hand scrapers. Winter schedules with lengthened travel time were written and implemented. The coal stoves inside the streetcars were inspected, and their fires were lit, often staying lit the entire winter, tended overnight by shop men.

February 22, 1922, was one of the worst storms ever. This car is attempting to enter service after sitting in the carhouse yard overnight. Kathryn A. Martin Library, University of Minnesota Duluth, Archives and Special Collections.

As usual, the 1922 storm was worse on Park Point. This drift at 10th Street defeated the plow and had to be hand-shoveled.

The company's five snowplows were readied for service, and plows were mounted on the streetcars assigned to the isolated Park Point and Highland lines. Each snowplow required a three-man crew. The motorman ran the plow and operated the plow blade mounted on the front of the car. The wingman operated the side or wing plow, which had to move in or out depending on street width and the presence of parked cars. The third crew member handled miscellaneous duties such as stocking the sand and salt bins and hand shoveling as needed.

In 1917, three powerful plows built by Twin City Rapid Transit were the main weapons in the snow-clearing arsenal. Heavier and with larger motors than the streetcars, they were able to clear a street curb to curb in two passes. A three-man crew ran them. The motorman operated the car and the front plow. The wingman moved the wing plow in and out, and a third man assisted as needed.

When all went well, this is how it was supposed to work. A plow clears Woodland Avenue in 1917.

Even the heavy plows could derail, making a bad situation worse. This is Kenwood Avenue at 14th Street, ca. 1925.

In 1915, despite worse snow drifting than the rest of Duluth, Park Point made do with little plow 12, made from a converted 1890s passenger car and nowhere near as powerful or effective as the big Duluth plows.

The Evening Telegram 1-23-29

300 Horsepower
—providing there is elbow room

It takes a mighty big snow drift to even slow up a street railway electric plow.

But even 300 horsepower is useless when the drifts are mixed with automobiles!

Then it's a case of clearing a path by slow hand-shoveling until the abandoned vehicle can be pushed clear.

All this takes time when time can least be spared. Meanwhile, street cars pull up behind and wait. The passengers may be impatient to be on the way, but they have shelter at least, which is not the case with people waiting all along the line.

During one night last winter our crews shoveled out and moved some 45 vehicles from the tracks. Because every one

of these cases caused delay and inconvenience to hundreds of passengers and exposure to many people, we ask your co-operation.

During the next snowstorm please don't keep your automobile or truck out until it is apparent that it will be stalled. If you HAVE to leave it in the street, park as close to the curb as possible; at least try to get clear of the tracks and the wings of our plow.

After the plows have cleared the way, help keep traffic moving by NOT DRIVING DIRECTLY on the rails. Doing so packs the snow and ice so that street cars have difficulty in getting traction.

Thank you!

Twin Ports Electric Lines

Every plow operator who ever cleared a city street has been frustrated by parked cars. In 1929 DSR vented in this newspaper ad, which probably changed nothing.

As auto traffic increased, snow and ice between the rails became ever more compacted. Above a certain height it rubbed against the motor cases on the trucks, slowing the streetcars and even causing the wheels to lift and derail. DSR's solution in 1928 was this ice-cutter car nicknamed Goliath, with rotating blades attached to a third center axle.

A famous tale around the company told of a plow that in 1935 accidentally struck and damaged a parked car in Superior with its wing. When the crew returned to the carhouse to fill out an accident report, they had been preceded by an urgent phone call asking them to forget the whole incident. The car's owner had been visiting a brothel.

Steel wheels on steel rails lose adhesion quickly in icy conditions. Company memos describe the icy surface of the rail as "black." "The first application of sand seems to soften the blackness and then two or three applications flake it." According to another memo, "The sand car was kept working on the different lines nearly all day. On 4th Street where the rail was black in the morning, after two applications and good sun the rail flaked and cleared, but on Superior Street and shaded districts where the sun did not strike, the rail cleared in spots as big as a dollar but did not flake clean." The streetcars were themselves equipped with compressed-air-powered sanders ahead of both front and rear sets of wheels. In the Twin Cities, which had few hills, these same streetcars had only a single set of sanders for the front wheels.

Sleet and freezing rain could be worse than snow. In addition to ice on the rail, the overhead trolley wire might be coated with ice, partially or totally insulating the wire from the streetcar's trolley pole. Unable to get continuous electricity, the cars stalled or ran intermittently while huge sparks flew from the trolley wheel where it contacted the wire. Sleet

DSR's franchises with the city required it to clear the streets on which it operated. The snowplows with their wings could accomplish that in most places, but Tower Avenue was too wide. The costly and labor-intensive solution was to hand-shovel the snow onto a work car and cart it away, as seen in 1916. Bus operators were under no such obligation, and this hastened the streetcars' demise.

Snow was bad but sleet was worse. The tops of the rails became ultra-slippery, ice on the overhead wire starved the motors of electricity, and ice filled the flangeway slots in the street next to the rail, causing the wheels to ride up and derail. Some combination of these ills has stalled motorman Glen Grunseth at the east end of the Lanborn Avenue swing bridge on the Interstate line. Ca. 1932.

cutting blades were attached to the trolley pole; otherwise someone had to ride the car roof and strike the wire repeatedly with a wood pole or a broom to dislodge the ice—assuming the weight of the ice didn't pull the overhead wire down. When that happened on the Allouez line in 1935, DSR abandoned it and permanently substituted buses.

Slippery rails were not confined to winter. Falling leaves each October were crushed on the rails and made them as slick as ice.

An obscure source of delays shows up in two company memos from 1918. "News agents," usually boys selling newspapers, were allowed to peddle them on the cars. DSR policy was that no special stops be made for them; they were supposed to board or alight only with other passengers. This prohibition was ignored by the newsboys, causing conductors to retaliate by passing them up or carrying them past their requested stop. That brought complaints that in turn caused the company to instruct the conductors to refrain from acting and instead file a written report of each incident. This was the least satisfying outcome for the conductors, who viewed themselves as the captains of their ships and already had more paperwork than they cared for.

HALLOWEEN HIJINKS

Streetcars were always the target of pranks, the most common being to run up behind the car, grab the trolley rope, and pull the pole off the overhead wire, thereby cutting off the power ("pulling the trolley"). Greasing the rails was another favorite.

Harmless Pranks Are the Best Fun!

A few years ago pieces of tile piping placed by children on car tracks in a spirit of mischief resulted in derailing and ditching a Woodland Avenue car. The passengers and crew narrowly escaped serious injury.

Halloween is near at hand again and, for the safety of passengers, we appeal to parents to warn their children at this time against breaking the law by placing obstructions on car tracks.

You would not intentionally have your children responsible for serious injury or fatal accident to car riders, but your failure to caution them might have that result.

TWIN PORTS ELECTRIC LINES

DSR employees dreaded Halloween. Pranks ran the gamut from disruptive to destructive. Most common was pulling the trolley pole off the wire and greasing the rails. That escalated to egging trainmen, tipping over waiting shelters, and placing objects on the track that could derail a streetcar. This ad tried to head it off, probably unsuccessfully.

The high point of the year for pranks was Halloween, and the company dreaded it. Boys and young men in groups targeted the cars. A newspaper story on Halloween 1907 contained this classic:

> A street car conductor on the East 4th Street line was given some strenuous exercise Halloween night by some of the mischievous boys near the easterly end of that line. The car had been standing at the end of the track until time for it to leave on its regular trip. The "con" had stepped off for a minute and was standing on the sidewalk. One bright young American saw the opportunity and took advantage of it. He jumped on the car and gave the signal to the motorman to go ahead. The motorman could not see who had rung the bell and supposed that all was well. The boy jumped off and the car started. Thinking that the motorman had started his car to run only a few feet, the "con" lost his chance to get aboard and finally woke up to the realization that his post of duty was fast disappearing down the street. He started on a dead run to catch up and, if the car had not stopped to pick up some passengers, the sprinter might be running yet.

Anticipating the worst, DSR went on the offensive, deploying extra men and vehicles throughout the city to try and stop the pranksters. These measures were largely in vain. A typical day-after report appeared in 1928:

> We had serious trouble with a bunch of hoodlums at the end of the Woodland line about 9:45 last night. C. W. Pearson and Vernon Anderson were looking after trouble on this line and Pearson started to chase a bunch of boys and young men who were pulling trolleys, and they bombarded him with eggs. Pearson's clothing was considerably damaged, and he was struck in the face also. He also tore his trousers.
>
> The waiting shelters at Victoria St. and Hawthorne Road were tipped over and broken so they will have to be brought in. The waiting shelter at 46th Avenue West was also damaged.
>
> About 8 o'clock Supervisor Paul told me that the rails had been greased on 21st Avenue West between Superior and 3rd Street and the sand car had to be ordered out.
>
> An auto tire chain was thrown over the trolley wire between 26th and 26th Avenues West. This fell when a car passed, breaking a couple of windows. There were many bands of small boys pulling trolleys.

Although most of the pranks were a nuisance rather than a danger, a 1924 incident two weeks before Halloween got out of control, according to the

Duluth Herald: "Boys playing at Woodland and Hardy Street threw two sticks, nailed together, over the trolley wire. The sticks caused the trolley pole on a street car to leave the wire. It did so with such force that it broke a span wire which caused other span wires for a distance of two blocks to fall. Lacking means to pump air, the brakes gradually began to slip, and the car started down the hill. Before the car could be brought to a stop the live wire became entangled and tore down a wire pole. Traffic was tied up for more than an hour, people endangered, and a loss of $200 must be stood by DSR."

SAFETY

Accidents that caused personal injury or property damage were always a top concern for streetcar systems. They operated the heaviest, most powerful vehicles on the public street, and any collision was a threat to the company's goal of profitability. Lawsuits could and did put streetcar companies out of business.

On September 12, 1914, car 154, headed for Duluth on the Interstate line, derailed on gravel that had just been deposited on the roadway and almost fell off the ramp to the Interstate Bridge, tying up traffic in both directions.

STREET CAR WRECK ON INTER-STATE BRIDGE, Sept. 12, '14

As the number of autos increased, so did the number of collisions and their cost to the company. Streetcars were by far the biggest and heaviest vehicles on the street, so the auto generally came out second-best, as this one did in 1937.

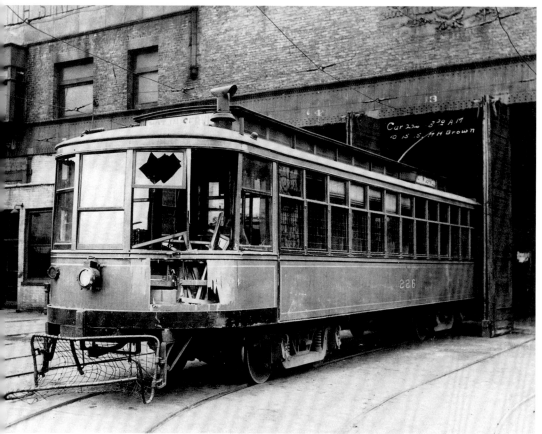

Above the floor, streetcars were made of wood and non-safety window glass. Flying splinters and glass shards were a dangerous combination. 1915.

DSR faced more accident risks than most street railway companies. Streetcars could run away on the steep hills or collide with trains at the numerous railroad crossings. Ice and snow caused derailments. One streetcar on the Aerial Bridge line lost its brakes and toppled into the ship canal. All this was in addition to the usual collisions with autos and pedestrians and passengers falling inside the cars or while boarding or alighting.

Effects of collision at 81st Ave. W. Oct. 14, 1918. E.T.M.

This was the company's worst nightmare, a collision between two streetcars. In this case one rear-ended another at 81st Avenue West and Grand Avenue in 1918.

The company's precautions largely prevented runaways on hills. There is only one recorded case, and it involved a work car rather than a streetcar on 3rd Avenue West. Not that motormen didn't tempt fate. They often used the long downhills to make up time because the streetcar could exceed its normal speed. One company memo tells motormen that speeds downhill should be no faster than uphill. Streetcars had no speedometers, which made enforcement somewhat subjective. In a couple of cases, safety stops were required before starting down a grade, followed by a minimum number of seconds to descend.

The Interstate and Superior local lines had to deal with several railroad grade crossings and thus the potential for collisions with trains. A 1925 company memo recounted five streetcar–train collisions since 1901, as well as eleven near collisions and ten cases where railroads complained of streetcars crossing too closely in front of trains.

January 1927 saw the worst collision in DSR history. The Billings Park line in Superior crossed the Great Northern main line at a grade crossing on West 21st Street. Protections were in place to prevent a crash, but everything went wrong that day. On the 35th anniversary of the crash, the *Superior Evening Telegram* published this article:

Taken 913
7.9.14
H.M. Brown

A streetcar off the tracks can be difficult to retrieve. Here are two examples from 1929 and 1914. Left: at the Billings Park line viaduct over the railroad tracks on 21st Street. In both cases a work car has been dispatched to handle the difficult task.

The tragic scene the night of January 6, 1927, at the 21st Street railroad crossing which resulted from the crash of a Great Northern passenger train and a Billings Park street car, was one of anguish and pain. Six persons were killed instantly and another died later. Sixteen others were seriously injured.

Among the passengers on the ill-fated streetcar who recall the tragedy vividly are postmaster Ralph Nelson, Ray Peterson, Lawrence Barbo, Fred Pearson, Mrs. Vern Wright, the former Lorraine Peterson and others. Nelson suffered serious injuries; Peterson, Barbo and Pearson escaped injury when they were hurled through windows. Pearson, the Evening Telegram *of that day states, "picked himself up nearly 50 feet from the wreck."*

The Evening Telegram of January 6, 1927, gave this account of the catastrophe: "Six persons have died and 17 are injured, three of them probably fatally as the result of the Billings Park streetcar and Great Northern train collision Thursday night which marked the worst disaster of its nature in the history of Superior. Fourteen of the injured are in a serious condition. Included in the fatalities was the locomotive fireman, George Lindberg, who suffered internal injuries and wounds sustained when he leaped from the onrushing engine cab in an effort to escape death. Others were killed instantly, some died on the way to hospitals and others later. The towerman's shanty at the crossing was ripped from the ground by the force of the impact from the streetcar and hurled 15 feet. Towerman Anton Johnson received only body cuts and bruises in a miraculous escape from death. Hot coals from a small stove inside the shanty caught fire to the tinder-like interior and the tower crashed in a mass of flames.

"The register on the streetcar showed a total of 22 paid fares. The cries of anguish and pain from the dying and injured mingled

horribly with the hiss of steam rising from the towerman's shanty as firemen sought to prevent tongues of flame shooting skyward from spreading to the wrecked and splintered street car. Simultaneously, police, pedestrians, and all available help were working frantically to clear the wreckage to get at the injured persons. Desperate men and women fought to gain the interior of the car in an effort to get to the relatives and friends who had boarded the car in Billings Park. Some bodies were carried a distance of 150 yards in the mangled rear of the streetcar which caught on the engine tender."

Frank L. Benedict, then 60, the engineer, told the following version of the accident: "I could see the street car stopped on the right side of the crossing when I was two blocks away. I was traveling about 25 mph and had increased my speed after signaling the crossing. All of a sudden the car moved ahead, stopped directly on the tracks, backed up again and was clear. My train started pounding down on the crossing and when I was about 50 yards away, the car again started across. God, how I tried to stop that engine, I gave her everything I had in brakes, sand even, but the crash I heard sickened me. The next I remembered I was listening to the cries of the dying above the hissing of the steam."

Johnson, the towerman who controlled the gates said: "I tried to stop that car by putting down the gates, but he kept coming. He didn't know what to do I guess. The last I remember I was falling with the shanty."

After an all-day inquest, during which 19 witnesses testified, a Douglas County coroner's jury found that the DSR, the GN and NP, and Wisconsin Railroad Commission were "jointly and equally responsible for the accident." The verdict found no individual responsible, exonerating at the same time the streetcar operator, the locomotive engineer, and the crossing watchman. The verdict said: "The railway companies and commission were responsible through negligence." (Superior Evening Telegram, *January 6, 1962*)

Over a month later, in a letter to a streetcar company official in Connecticut, the DSR general manager described what actually happened. The manually operated crossing gate came down too soon, snagging the rope attached to the trolley pole, which pulled the pole off the overhead wire. Without power, the streetcar stalled with its rear end on the crossing where it was struck by the train.

The crash generated a public clamor to remove the grade crossing. The 21st Street viaduct was extended across all the tracks and opened three years and one day later.

No. 5

TWIN PORTS BY TROLLEY
A Tour of the City

The huge outcropping called Point of Rocks forced Superior Street to detour around it on the way to the West End and the ore docks, 1910.

The streetcar system was really a network of lines that radiated out from the two downtowns. Each line had its own identity and took on the characteristics of the neighborhoods it served. In this chapter we'll travel across the Twin Ports line by line, from east to west in Duluth, then across the bay into Superior.

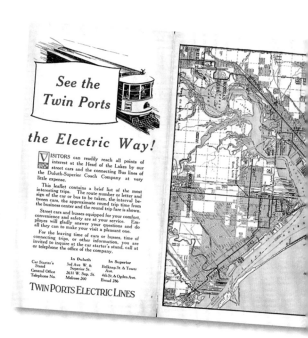

THE DULUTH LINES

DOWNTOWN DULUTH'S SUPERIOR STREET

YEARS OF OPERATION:

Horsecar, 8th Avenue West to 3rd Avenue East, beginning in 1882, extended to 28th Avenue West and 22nd Avenue East by 1889; electrified in 1890.

Due to the city's geography, its downtown retail and commercial core was concentrated along a single mile of Superior Street. The steep hillside begins literally at the north edge of the sidewalk and it inhibited walking. As a result, every streetcar line except the isolated Highland and Park Point lines funneled through Superior Street. Hotels were concentrated around the three railroad stations near 5th Avenue West.

Downtown Superior Street ended abruptly at 8th Avenue West, where it turned to detour around Point of Rocks. A streetcar is visible in the off-street turning loop, where cars to points east of downtown were staged. 1906.

At 7th Avenue West, streetcars on Superior Street passed the Incline's base station and transferred passengers. Note the sidewalks that paralleled it up the hill. Ca. 1935.

By the mid-1930s heavier auto traffic had made it unsafe to walk into the middle of Superior Street to board a streetcar. In Duluth and many other cities, in-street "safety zones" were created, demarcated with lines on the pavement and a yellow X sign, such as this one at 4th Avenue West. Photograph by Robert Mehlenbeck, Krambles-Peterson Archive.

Duluth's three downtown railroad depots clustered together near Superior Street and 6th Avenue West. Accordingly, the largest hotels were built nearby. In the foreground is the Soo Line Depot, which also hosted the Duluth, South Shore & Atlantic. Beyond it is the peaked roof and train shed of the Union Depot, home to the Great Northern, Northern Pacific, Duluth & Iron Range, and Duluth, Missabe & Northern. Not visible beyond the Union Depot is the Chicago & North Western Depot, which also served the Duluth, Winnipeg & Pacific. 1911.

Looking east on Superior Street from 6th Avenue West, this illustrates why the city of Duluth was frustrated with horsecars. They couldn't climb the hill (at left) to serve the rapidly developing neighborhoods above downtown. A cable railway was proposed on Lake Avenue but never built. Several years after this photograph was taken in the late 1880s, electric cars began serving new hillside lines.

The bustling corner of Superior Street at 5th Avenue West, bracketed by the Spalding Hotel and the Lyceum Theater, was probably the most photographed place in downtown Duluth. The small light on the right front of the approaching car changed colors to indicate the destination. Its use was discontinued when the number of destinations soon exceeded the available colors. Ca. 1915. Photograph by Gallagher's Studio.

Superior Street at 2nd Avenue West about 1910, during the transition away from horse-drawn vehicles. Note the sign for the Glass Block department store at far right. Photograph by McKenzie Studio.

At 3rd Avenue West the "hill lines" to East 4th Street, West 4th Street, East 8th Street, and Kenwood climbed away from Superior Street on an 8.7 percent grade. The camera is looking down the hill toward the junction, which was the hub of the Duluth streetcar system. A supervisor, referred to as a "starter," was stationed in the small booth visible on the corner at right. 1914. Kathryn A. Martin Library, University of Minnesota Duluth, Archives and Special Collections.

The conversion of the Lester Park line to trolley bus in 1934 shifted the Woodland line from Superior Street to 2nd Street through downtown. There was an immediate outcry from passengers who were unhappy about climbing those two blocks to return home. DSR responded by reopening the Superior Street tracks from 3rd Avenue West to 2nd Avenue East, then building two blocks of new track up the hill on 2nd Avenue East to 2nd Street. The new track held the distinction of being the steepest ever on a Minnesota streetcar line, 10.65 percent. It lasted until the end of service in 1939. In 1938 a westbound Woodland car is turning from the 2nd Avenue East hill onto Superior Street. This photograph shows the complex mix of streetcar and trolley bus wire at the intersection. Kathryn A. Martin Library, University of Minnesota Duluth, Archives and Special Collections.

Despite the steepness, many of the city's important institutions were located on the first couple of blocks up the hill from Superior Street. These included city hall, the county and federal courthouses, Central High School, St. Mary's and St. Luke's hospitals, the YMCA, the Masonic temple, and a number of churches. These destinations added to the ridership mix.

PASSENGERS	LOAD CHECK LOCATION
1,105	SUPERIOR AND FIFTH AVENUE EAST
1,010	EAST FOURTH STREET AND FIFTH AVENUE EAST
90	INCLINE
1,650	SUPERIOR AND SEVENTEENTH AVENUE WEST
120	LAKE AVENUE/PARK POINT
100	INTERSTATE
4,075	**TOTAL**
PASSENGERS	**ORIGINATING FROM**
2,235	EAST OF DOWNTOWN
1,840	WEST OF DOWNTOWN

Passengers entering downtown Duluth in the morning rush hour.

At Lake Avenue (left foreground), the Aerial Bridge line left Superior Street for its short run to the ship canal, where it connected with the isolated Park Point line. Photograph by Charles P. Gibson, ca. 1915. Minnesota Historical Society.

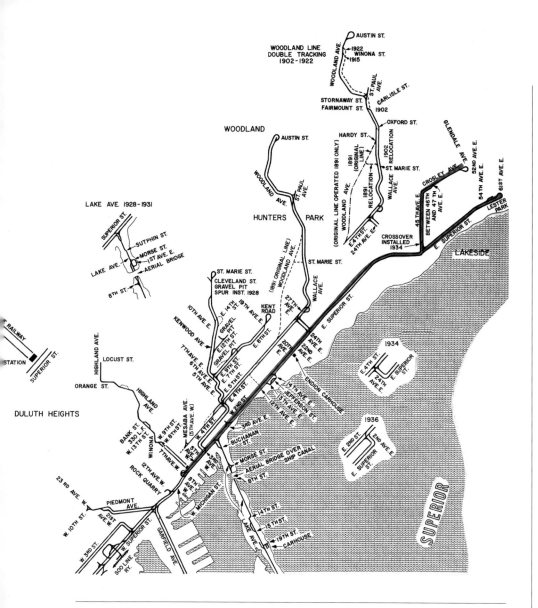

LESTER PARK

YEARS OF OPERATION:
1892 to 1934 (electric trolley bus service continued to 1957)

SERVICE FREQUENCY:
10 minutes peak; 20 minutes off-peak

The Lakeside Land Company developed a new suburb, the City of Lakeside, along Superior Street east of Duluth. It was originally connected to Duluth by commuter trains of the Duluth & Iron Range Railroad, which made 15 daily round-trips. Despite that, the company incorporated the Lakeside Railway Company in 1892 to provide competing and more frequent street-car service. By December 1892, service began over new track extending

At 13th Avenue East the line crossed Chester Creek and passed the G. G. Hartley mansion. 1913.

At 8th Avenue East, London Road
(beyond the barricades) and its
shuttle bus met Superior Street. This
1934 photograph appears to show
the aftermath of a derailment. Note
the curved mark on the pavement.

from the end of DSR's Superior Street line at 22nd Avenue East to 61st Avenue East. Competition from the streetcars soon put the commuter trains out of business.

DSR ran the line using Lakeside's streetcars. After a few years, Lakeside was unable to properly maintain the track, leading to a court dispute with DSR. As happened with all the suburban development trolleys, the solution was for DSR to buy the line, and so it did in 1900.

Superior Street, the center of downtown, is also the spine of the East End, extending seven miles to the Lakeside neighborhood, where development stopped at the Lester River and the rugged North Shore began. Superior Street hugs the lakeshore as far as 10th Avenue East, passing the Fitger Brewery. A shuttle bus serving London Road fed the streetcars at 8th Avenue East. At 13th Avenue an around-the-block loop was built in 1927 to serve the Armory, Curling Club, and Amphitheater and to stage extra streetcars. It replaced a wye at 3rd Avenue East.

Beyond 14th Avenue East, the area is mostly residential, and Superior Street is centered in the neighborhood about half a mile from the lake. The

Superior Street at 19th Avenue East in 1924.

Lester Park and Woodland lines shared the track, each running a 20-minute off-peak frequency so that between 24th Avenue East and downtown they combined to create a 10-minute off-peak frequency. For several years, Crosley cars also shared the track as far as 45th Avenue East, before that line was cut back to a shuttle.

At 24th Avenue East, the Woodland line turned left and climbed away from the lake. Beyond, additional trippers signed "East End" terminated at 24th Avenue, which runs along the crest of a tall hill, while Superior Street drops down to Tischer's Creek and then passes through the Northland Country Club. The business district of Lakeside at 45th Avenue is centered around the site of the former Duluth & Iron Range Lakeside suburban station for commuter trains. Crossing the Lester River, the line terminated at the Lester Park loop.

The outer end of the line, beyond 45th Avenue East, was converted to a trolley bus shuttle in 1931. The entire Lester Park line was converted to trolley bus in 1934.

In 1927 a loop was installed on 13th Avenue East, Jefferson Street, and 14th Avenue East to better serve the auditorium, armory, and Duluth Curling Club. Here track is being laid at 13th and Superior Street.

Looking south at 24th Ave. E.
& Superior St.
3:00 P.M. April 8 1920
F.T.M.

The Woodland line diverged from the Lester Park line and Superior Street at 24th Avenue East. This was also the terminus for cars carrying an East End sign. After the demise of the streetcars, an off-street turn loop was built for the trolley buses. 1920 and ca. 1945. Left: Kathryn A. Martin Library, University of Minnesota Duluth, Archives and Special Collections.

In 1910, two work cars loaded with 50 tons of rail apiece perform a stress test on the Tischer's Creek bridge at Superior Street and 32nd Avenue East.

McKenzie, Photo

Looking west on Superior Street at 43rd Avenue East in 1936. Kathryn A. Martin Library, University of Minnesota Duluth, Archives and Special Collections.

Superior St at Country Club
4.15 P.M. 1-21-16. E.T.M.

Between 36th and 40th Avenues East, the line
followed Superior Street through the Northland
Country Club. 1916. Kathryn A. Martin Library,
University of Minnesota Duluth, Archives and
Special Collections.

The east end of the Lester Park line was converted to a trolley bus shuttle in 1931. Shortly thereafter a company photographer documented the passengers transferring to the through Crosley car to downtown at 45th Avenue East.

A westbound trolley bus through-routed to Piedmont Avenue is at 49th Avenue East and Superior Street in 1935. In the distance is St. Michael School. The Duluth & Iron Range Railroad to Two Harbors is beyond the fence at right. Photograph by L. P. Gallagher.

The tracks crossed the Lester River and immediately spread apart to form the Lester Park loop, seen here in 1930.

Two views of the Lester Park loop, about twenty years apart. A streetcar crew takes its layover in 1910. The line was converted to trolley bus in 1931. The loop is still used by city buses, and the waiting shelter still stands.

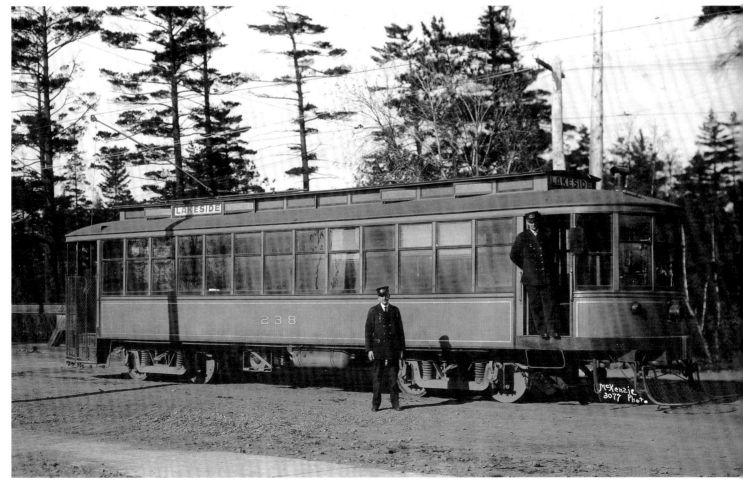

CROSLEY

YEARS OF OPERATION:
1926 to 1939

SERVICE FREQUENCY:
10 minutes peak; 20 minutes off-peak

Beyond 45th Avenue East, the steepness of the hillside recedes, opening up an area for development beginning in the 1920s. The last new construction in the system, the Crosley Avenue line branched off the Lester Park line in 1926 to serve this residential area. Despite the fact that little housing was built along the line, and even though system ridership was declining, DSR created a new through route to downtown. On East Superior Street it duplicated the service already being provided by the Lester Park and Woodland Avenue cars. During 1926–27, in an attempt to reduce car miles, the Crosley line was combined end-to-end with the Interstate line, which already ran through downtown Duluth to 14th Avenue East. The result was an extremely long line interrupted by numerous railroad grade crossings and two cross-harbor swing bridges. Keeping the cars running on time proved impossible. DSR installed telephones at the Interstate and Lamborn Avenue swing bridges so crews could report delays of six or more minutes. In theory this would give

It's opening day for the Crosley line in 1926 and work car 3 is dealing with some last minute details on 45th Avenue East at Gladstone. Kathryn A. Martin Library, University of Minnesota Duluth, Archives and Special Collections.

Photographs of the Crosley line are rare. This one dates from the late 1920s and shows a car descending the long gradual grade on 45th Avenue East at Jay Street. The destination is 21st Street and Grand Avenue in Superior, so this was during the brief period that Crosley was through-routed with the Interstate line. The company was trying to reduce duplicate mileage, but delays due to bridge openings and railroad crossings defeated the effort.

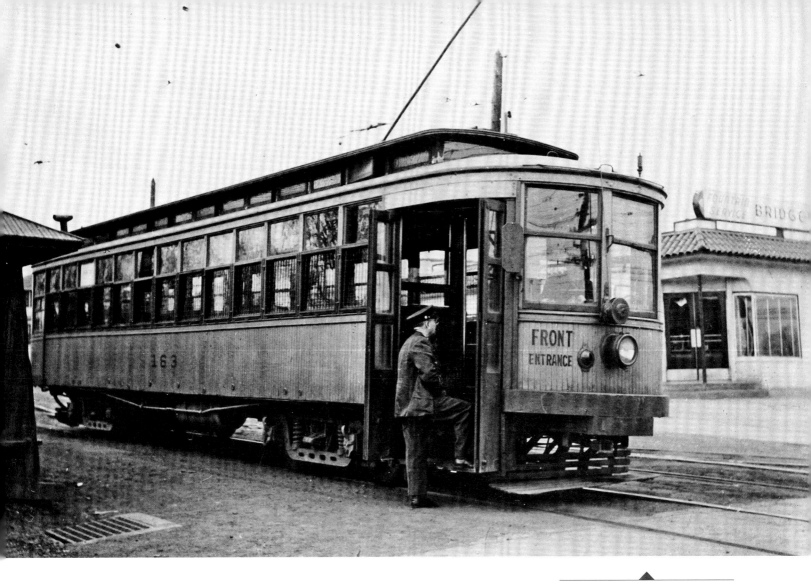

the company dispatcher an opportunity to add a fill-in trip down the line. Apparently it didn't work, and the through-routing of Crosley and Interstate was discontinued.

Separate all-day Crosley service to downtown continued until the Lester Park line was converted to trolley bus in 1934, causing the abandonment of track on Superior Street between downtown and 24th Avenue East. For a short time the East 4th Street line was extended to Crosley via 24th Avenue and Superior Street, but this was apparently unsatisfactory. The answer was to run a double-ended shuttle car on the Crosley branch that fed the Lester Park trolley bus at 45th and Superior. Some through cars to downtown ran rush hours only, but these were discontinued later. The Crosley streetcar shuttle continued because the streets it traversed were not yet paved and suitable for buses. This required keeping 2.4 miles of double track from 45th and Superior to 4th Street and 24th Avenue East in service solely to deadhead the Crosley shuttle to and from the carhouse. This rather awkward situation lasted until the end of all streetcar service in 1939.

Although the entire Lester Park line on East Superior Street was converted to bus in 1934, the streets used by the Crosley branch weren't yet suitable for buses. Crosley was converted to a shuttle using specially modified car 163 that fed the trolley buses at 45th and Superior. This meant retaining the track and overhead wire on Superior Street from 45th to 24th Avenues East, and on 24th Avenue to 4th Street, for the sole purpose of deadheading the shuttle car to and from the carhouse each morning and evening. In this photo, the rather worn looking shuttle car is waiting for its connection at 45th and Superior.

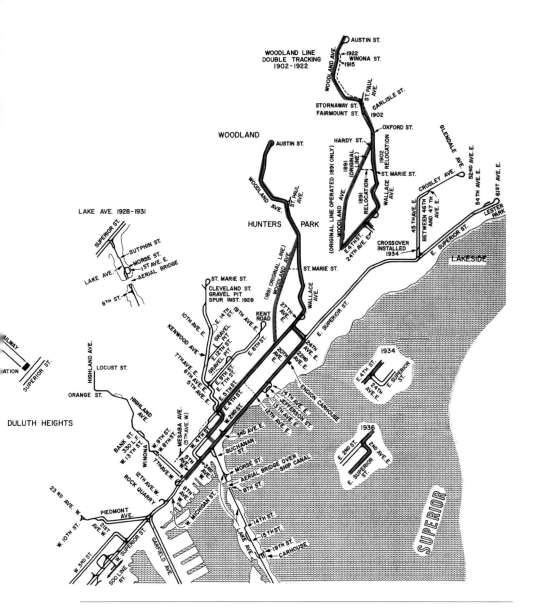

WOODLAND LINE
DOUBLE TRACKING
1902-1922

AUSTIN ST.

1922
WINONA ST.
1915

WOODLAND AVE.

STORNAWAY ST.
FAIRMOUNT ST.

ST. PAUL AVE.

CARLISLE ST.
1902

WOODLAND

OXFORD ST.

WOODLAND AVE.

ST. PAUL AVE.

AUSTIN ST.

HARDY ST.

1891
(ORIGINAL LINE)

1902
RELOCATION

GLENDALE AVE. E.

52ND AVE. E.

61ST AVE. E.

HUNTERS PARK

ST. MARIE ST.

1891 RELOCATION

WALLACE AVE.

CROSLEY ST.

45TH AVE. E.

54TH AVE. E.

LESTER PARK

LAKE AVE. 1928-1931

SUPERIOR ST.

SUTPHIN ST.

MORSE ST.

1ST AVE. E.

AERIAL BRIDGE

LAKE AVE.

8TH ST.

(1891) ORIGINAL LINE WOODLAND AVE.

(ORIGINAL LINE OPERATED 1891 ONLY)

E. 4TH ST.

24TH AVE. E.

ST. MARIE ST.

WALLACE AVE.

BETWEEN 46TH AND 47TH AVE. E.

E. SUPERIOR ST.

CROSSOVER INSTALLED 1934

LAKESIDE

RAILWAY

STATION

SUPERIOR ST.

ST. MARIE ST.
CLEVELAND ST.
GRAVEL PIT
SPUR INST. 1928

HIGHLAND AVE.

LOCUST ST.

ORANGE ST.

HIGHLAND AVE.

DULUTH HEIGHTS

10TH AVE. E.

KENWOOD AVE.

7TH AVE. E.

5TH AVE. E.

E. 14TH ST.

8TH AVE. E.

GRAVEL PIT

E. 12TH ST.

GRAVEL PIT

E. 9TH ST.

E. 6TH ST.

E. 4TH ST.

KENT ROAD

27TH AVE. E.

24TH AVE. E.

20TH AVE. E.

22ND AVE. E.

E. SUPERIOR ST.

1934

E. 4TH ST.

24TH AVE. E.

E. SUPERIOR ST.

1936

E. 2ND ST.

2ND AVE. E.

E. SUPERIOR ST.

SUPERIOR

ENDION CARHOUSE

4TH AVE. E.

JEFFERSON ST.

3RD AVE. E.

13TH AVE. E.

23RD AVE. W.

BANK ST.

330 L.F.

W. 13TH ST.

MESABA AVE. (5TH AVE. W.)

WINONA

W. 9TH ST.

W. 8TH ST.

7TH AVE. W.

12TH AVE. W.

ROCK QUARRY

PIEDMONT AVE.

W. 10TH ST.

21ST AVE. W.

W. 3RD ST.

W. SUPERIOR ST.

SOO LINE RY.

GARFIELD AVE.

W. 4TH ST.

W. 2ND ST.

3RD AVE. E.

BUCHANAN ST.

MORSE ST.

AERIAL BRIDGE OVER SHIP CANAL

8TH ST.

W. MICHIGAN ST.

14TH ST.

15TH ST.

19TH ST.

LAKE AVE.

CARHOUSE

WOODLAND

YEARS OF OPERATION:
1891 to 1939 (trolley bus service continued to 1957)

SERVICE FREQUENCY:
10 minutes peak; 20 minutes off-peak

The Woodland line originated as the independent Motor Line Improvement Company, providing the streetcar service necessary to develop the Hunter's Park and Woodland suburbs high on the hill east of Duluth. Track was laid on Woodland Avenue from a junction with the Duluth Street Railway's East 4th Street line, and service began in April 1891.

The Woodland line climbed away from Superior Street on 24th Avenue East at 1st Street, passing the high-quality housing typical of the East End. Photograph by Charles P. Gibson, ca. 1915. Minnesota Historical Society.

Woodland climbed higher than any other line, 750 feet above Superior Street in downtown. However, the primitive early electric cars hauling trailers couldn't handle the steep grade on lower Woodland, so a less direct route was selected and opened in December 1891. It followed East 4th Street to Wallace Avenue, snaked up Wallace along the face of the hill, and rejoined Woodland at St. Marie Street. The reroute bypassed some significant population, a void that was partially filled when the East 8th Street line was extended almost to Woodland Avenue in 1923. Farther up the hill, the reroute created an indirect jog in the line at St. Marie Street, which was removed by a second reroute in 1902 that extended the track on Wallace Avenue north to an intersection with Woodland.

Beginning in 1892, DSR took over operation of the line using the Motor Line's streetcars. The line had its own carhouse, located at the outer end of the track. It burned in 1894.

The Motor Line was acquired in 1900 by the Woodland Company. By this time the tracks had deteriorated badly, and DSR suspended service twice during that period. The solution was for DSR to buy the line, which happened in 1901. Track was upgraded, and the line was double-tracked.

At two points in time, the Woodland line curves through the north end of Hunter's Park. The older view from about 1900 shows the original center poles holding up the overhead wire. Well before the second view from the 1930s, they were replaced by poles along the curb connected by span wires. Kathryn A. Martin Library, University of Minnesota Duluth, Archives and Special Collections.

Wallace Ave. looking S. from

11. A.M. 12. 1. 13. H. H. Brow

Victoria St.

Wallace Avenue provided a less steep, if more circuitous and less populated, route for the Woodland line because the early streetcars could not handle the stiff grade on lower Woodland Avenue. 1913. Kathryn A. Martin Library, University of Minnesota Duluth, Archives and Special Collections.

At 24th Avenue East and 4th Street, Woodland cars met the end of the East 4th Street line and turned right. At 27th Avenue East, the curbs ended, revealing the raw rock still to be blasted away. In 1929, a loop was constructed behind the camera, and the East 4th Street line was extended to this point from 24th Avenue East to better serve the new East Junior High School.

Despite the line upgrade and relocation, service from downtown ran only as far as Hunter's Park, and Woodland passengers had to transfer to a shuttle car. Connections between the two were not reliable. This was the cause of much complaint until the shuttle was replaced by through service in 1905.

In 1907, new track was built on 24th Avenue East connecting 4th Street and Superior Street, and thereafter the Woodland line used Superior Street into downtown instead of 4th Street. After the Lester Park line was converted to trolley bus in 1934, Woodland cars once again used East 4th Street until abandonment in 1939.

The line on Woodland Avenue terminated at the small business district at Austin Street in the suburb of Woodland, which was annexed by Duluth in 1894. Apart from neighborhood businesses, the line was mostly residential and served a generally well-to-do population. It passed the State Normal School, which became the original campus of University of Minnesota Duluth, as well as East Junior High School. Like so many lines in the Twin Ports, development was scattered and often low density. Even today, Hunter's Park and Woodland feature pockets of housing interspersed with what looks like the north woods.

After 1920, a pair of shuttle buses fed the Woodland line. The Morley Heights bus made a short loop through the hilltop neighborhood above Hunter's Park. In 1923 the Duluth City Council ordered DSR to extend the streetcars along Calvary Road to the city limits. Instead, a Calvary Road shuttle bus met the streetcars at the Woodland loop.

This humorous 1905 postcard is based on the fact that bears periodically wandered among the houses of Hunter's Park and Woodland, even as they do today.

UNEXPECTEDLY DELAYED.

No. 2. Copyright 1905 by S. A. Thompson, Duluth, Minn.

In its early years, the streetcars doubled as the supply line for the neighborhoods on top of the hill, transporting goods as well as people. The practice ended in 1902, as described in this newspaper story:

After tomorrow the Woodland cars can no longer be used for the delivery of merchandise to the residents of that neighborhood. The practice of accepting goods on the cars for delivery to certain corners has been a source of much convenience to the people out there. The housewife who discovers that her commissary department needs replenishment in certain things has been wont to call up her dealer downtown, give him the order, tell him to place it on the next Woodland car, and at the corner it would be met by someone from the household for whom it was intended. The company claims that the practice has been abused, that it has become a common thing for large cases of goods, and even sacks of flour, to be placed on the cars for delivery. It also claims that frequently there has been no one to meet the consignment of goods, and that they were dumped off at their destination, that they were then lost and complaints to the office and all kinds of trouble engendered. Hereafter, a passenger must accompany any package and reasonable size must be maintained. (Duluth Herald, *September 29, 1902*)

The Glen Avon station at right, built in 1892, still stands along Woodland Avenue at Lewis Street. Photograph ca. 1905–10.

Woodland and Hunter's Park residents had two long-standing complaints: that East End residents traveling to the close-in neighborhoods packed the cars, crowding out Woodland riders, or at least preventing them from getting a seat; and that the trip took too long because of all the stops for close-in residents. In 1902, they took matters into their own hands.

> *Rendered desperate by the failure of the street railway company to provide a suitable number of cars to take them home in the evening, the Woodland Park people took the matter into their own hands last night. When the last car after the close of the Metropolitan Theater was about to depart, and half the people were unable to secure passage, they took possession of the car and ordered the motorman not to leave until another car came to accommodate the crowd. He refused to obey and started the car. The crowd fell upon him and threw him off the platform. He called a policeman, but the motorman was kept off the platform and the car stood still until another was sent for and the remainder of the Woodland passengers were able to secure passage on it.* (Duluth Herald, *December 26, 1902*)

In an effort to solve both problems, DSR instituted express streetcars to Woodland and Lester Park during the afternoon rush hour. These cars made no stops between downtown and 24th Avenue East.

The Woodland line ended at a loop in a small commercial district at Austin Street. There, beginning in 1924, it connected with the Calvary Road shuttle bus. 1923 and 1924. Kathryn A. Martin Library, University of Minnesota Duluth, Archives and Special Collections.

After trolley buses replaced the streetcars in 1939, wires gracefully follow the curves of Woodland Avenue at St. Paul Avenue. Ca. 1945. Kathryn A. Martin Library, University of Minnesota Duluth, Archives and Special Collections.

AERIAL BRIDGE

YEARS OF OPERATION:
1892 to 1931 (some rush-hour Aerial Bridge service continued to 1938)

SERVICE FREQUENCY:
10 minutes peak; 20 minutes off-peak

The Aerial Bridge line branched off Superior Street for less than a mile to a loop at the Aerial Bridge, but it was a mile packed with industry and warehouses, a destination for many passengers who transferred from other lines in downtown. It opened in 1892, two years after the summer-only service began on Park Point. The delay was caused by the difficulty constructing the long viaduct over Michigan Street and the railroad tracks. The Aerial Bridge itself was not opened until 1905, so passengers for Park Point initially used a ferry in warm weather and walked across the ship canal on the ice in winter. Prior to 1930, passengers bound for downtown Duluth boarded the Aerial Bridge gondola and transferred to an Aerial Bridge car on the other side of the ship canal.

Looking downhill on Lake Avenue across Superior Street in 1899, the Aerial Bridge line turns the corner and heads for the ship canal, first crossing over Michigan Street. University of Minnesota Duluth Library: Northeast Minnesota Historical Center collection.

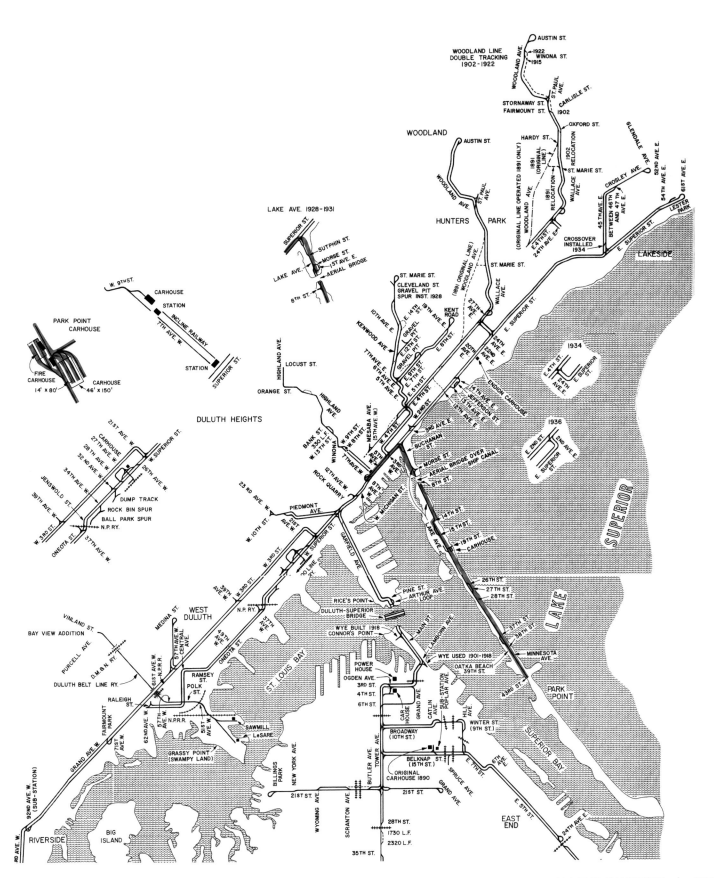

Believers in Murphy's law were vindicated in 1893, as related in the paper:

*Yesterday afternoon streetcar No. 30 running on Lake Avenue jumped the track and went into the ship canal. The car was running about 10–15 mph. The brake failed to work and the car struck the fence at the end of the track, went through it, crashed through the timbers of the pier and plunged into the water. Two passengers were on the rear platform and they and the conductor tumbled off in a heap. The motorman jumped just as the car reached the end of the track. The car landed in the center of the canal where it slowly sank in 20 feet of water. (*Duluth Herald, *September 18, 1893)*

The schedules of the two lines and the Aerial Bridge gondola were coordinated to minimize passenger delay while ensuring a reliable operation. Here is a typical sequence: A northbound Park Point car arrives at the canal at 2:07. The bridge gondola leaves at 2:09, arriving at the north pier at 2:11. The Aerial Bridge streetcar on the Duluth side leaves at 2:14. Similar timings occurred in the return direction. The schedule was disrupted when ships passed through the canal.

The Aerial Bridge line wasn't very long, only about a mile, but it served the concentration of industry, warehouses, and docks known today as Canal Park, and it connected with the isolated Park Point line on the other side of the Aerial Bridge. Photograph by Charles P. Gibson, ca. 1909. Minnesota Historical Society.

Feb. 24 1922
10:45 AM

In 1930 the Aerial Bridge was rebuilt, replacing the traveling gondola with the current lift bridge. Anticipating this, DSR proposed replacing the Park Point line with electric trolley buses, since the track on the Point had reached the end of its useful life. Instead, DSR built tracks in the bridge deck, permitting through service between Park Point and Duluth for the first time. However, the devastating impact of the Great Depression combined with poor track condition led to replacement of Park Point streetcars by gasoline buses only a year later. The Aerial Bridge streetcar line remained in place until 1938 but saw only rush-hour cars after 1931.

The line ended with a wye at Lake Avenue and Morse Street, near the Canal, shown here in 1922. After the elimination of most conductors in 1928, it was replaced with a loop, because backing a streetcar from the front platform was unsafe.

PARK POINT

YEARS OF OPERATION:
Horsecar 1890, electrified 1899, converted to bus 1931.

SERVICE FREQUENCY:
10 minutes peak; 20 minutes off-peak

There are few places in the United States like Park Point and no other like it in Minnesota. Located on the long, narrow sandbar named Minnesota Point, the Park Point neighborhood has a single main road, Minnesota Avenue, which runs the length of it, and the side streets are short half-blocks that end in sand dunes. It is mostly residential with Oatka Beach, a recreational destination, at the far end. There is only one way to reach it without launching a boat, and that is via the Duluth Aerial Bridge. In its early years, Park Point was primarily a summer destination, with seasonal housing, beaches, and a short-lived amusement park. Exposed to the full fury of Lake Superior storms, Park Point's winters are more severe than elsewhere in the city.

For all but the last year of its existence, the Park Point streetcar line was isolated from downtown Duluth by the ship canal. From the beginning of its construction in 1888 until 1917, it was an independent company, the last in the Twin Ports.

From 1890 until electrification in 1899, the Park Point line ran summers only, using the last horse-drawn streetcars in Minnesota. The cars themselves were purchased secondhand from DSR, which had already converted to electricity. Below: Kathryn A. Martin Library, University of Minnesota Duluth, Archives and Special Collections.

Car 2, built by LaClede Car
Company in 1899, was one
of the first electric cars on the
line and was typical of the
small single-truck designs of
the 1890s.

Such was the leisurely nature of life on the Point that streetcar service
was summer-only from the start of service in 1890 until 1906. According to
a 1910 history of Duluth, in 1890 only three families lived there year-round.
For the first two years the cars made only five or six trips a day.

The Minnesota Point Street Railway (MPSR) used horsecars during its
first nine years of summer-only operations. Although MPSR reported on
December 18, 1888, that it had built 1.25 miles of track, there was no operation that year or the following year. The Village granted an extension of the
operating deadline to May 15, 1889. However, the first operation probably
did not occur until the following summer of 1890 when four retired DSR
horsecars were delivered. Single horses were used. Planks were laid on the
ties between the rails for the horses because the tracks were laid in sand;
there were no improved or hard-surface streets. By the summer of 1892,
three miles of track had been extended to Oatka Beach at 39th Street.

The White City amusement park lasted only from 1906 to 1908, long enough to be featured in this postcard. Collection of Peter Bonesteel.

This is the original Park Point carbarn, replaced in 1907 with a new building across the street. Photograph ca. 1900–1907.

This is the end of the line at 43rd Street, well-patronized on a summer day about 1900.

Despite the failure of White City, Park Point and Oatka Beach drew big crowds in the summer. The presence of soldiers implies this is the Fourth of July, around 1905. To accommodate the extra riders, DSR purchased used trailers from Twin City Rapid Transit and towed them behind motor cars.

PINE ST. OR 19ᵀᴴ ST.

The new carbarn at 19th Street, pictured in 1907 and during the 1920s, was built in stages, beginning with the office portion. It was later expanded and lengthened for car storage and repair.

Duluth is snowy, but Park Point gets the worst of it, driven by the winds off the lake. Car 11, one of four purchased new for the Park Point line, confronts the enemy in 1916.

Control of MPSR passed into the hands of Eastern absentee management in May 1896. Serious financial difficulties developed by late the following year. After several corporate changes, the operation emerged on November 16, 1898, as the Interstate Traction Company, with ambitious plans for expansion and improvements.

A short time later, Robert Dunn, the new owner, told the *Duluth News Tribune*, "We do not care to make any expensive improvements until we see what is going to be done about the government ship canal. When that is finished we will . . . put in a wide-gauge system with a solid bottom, and we will use electricity as motive power, doing away with the horse car service entirely."

Electrification and conversion to standard gauge were accomplished by June 30, 1899, bringing to an end the last horsecars in Minnesota. That year the city built the new ship canal and in May 1899 inaugurated steam ferry service across it. As promised, Interstate Traction Company began the conversion to electricity and widened the track from 3 feet 6 inches to 4 feet 8.5 inches, standard gauge, same as the rest of the Duluth streetcars. The conversion was complete in late June, and 15-minute service frequency began. At the same time DSR

The Minnesota legislature passed a law in 1893 requiring the front platforms of streetcars to be enclosed so the motormen wouldn't freeze. Interstate Traction didn't have much money, so it sort of complied by rigging this canvas curtain.

At 12th Street the paved road jogged a block west from Lake Avenue to Minnesota Avenue. The tracks made the shift at 14th Street. Looking beyond the pavement, the loose sand that hampered automobiles can be seen clearly. 1922.

Taken in 1909, this is the only known photograph of a Park Point car towing a freight trailer, the only way to deliver merchandise to residents before the 1915 paving of Minnesota Avenue. In 1914 freight provided 7 percent of the line's revenue.

assigned new cars to the Aerial Bridge line to feed the ferry and Park Point.

In 1900 the company built a hotel and pavilion at Oatka Beach, near the far end of the point. This stimulated heavy summer ridership, and the company purchased old cable car trailers from the St. Paul City Railway to add capacity. They were hauled behind the electric cars.

In 1904, in anticipation of the opening of the Aerial Bridge, the line was extended about one mile farther out the Point. The company also ordered its first two double-truck streetcars, which arrived in 1905, anticipating the start of year-round service in 1906 with the opening of the Aerial Bridge. Before that, passengers crossed the ship canal on a ferry in summer and walked across the frozen channel in winter.

In 1906, the White City amusement park opened at Oatka Beach. To handle the anticipated loads, Interstate Traction double-tracked the line and purchased several used streetcars that formerly ran in Superior, increasing its fleet to a 20-car high. Reality did not match expectations. White City was not successful and folded in 1907. Interstate revived it as Joyland, but that too failed by 1909. The park was demolished except for a dance hall.

That was the high point of ridership. Thereafter, the company struggled with a limited traffic potential, compounded by erosion of the sand right-of-way and terrible winter weather with frequent heavy snowstorms. There were thoughts of extending the track to Superior via Wisconsin Point, but it was never a serious possibility.

When Minnesota Avenue was paved in 1915, the company saved considerable money by converting from double track to single track with passing sidings and shifting from the center to the side of the road, off the pavement. Thereafter, most of the line looked like this 1927 view at 34th Street.

Once the Aerial Bridge was open, it still cost two 5-cent fares to travel to downtown Duluth. In 1908 DSR and Interstate reached an agreement to honor each other's transfers for an extra fare of 2 cents, thus lowering the cost of a one-way trip to 7 cents.

The company was unable to meet its interest payments to bondholders. In 1913, it was reorganized as the Park Point Traction Company. The Aerial Bridge had a 60-ton capacity, permitting autos to access the Point without being loaded on a boat. The city paved Minnesota Avenue in 1915, greatly increasing automobile competition. Rather than incur the expense of replacing both tracks in the paved roadway, the company converted the line to single track with passing sidings and moved its track to the side of the road. Operations remained unprofitable, and in 1917 the line was sold to Duluth Street Railway.

Throughout the industry, old streetcars were recycled as maintenance equipment. Car 5, its revenue days behind it, has been given a roof platform for overhead wire work. The entire carhouse staff seems to be on board.

When the Aerial Bridge was rebuilt from a traveling gondola to a lift span, streetcar tracks were built into the deck, and the Park Point line was no longer isolated. The first streetcar crossed on March 13, 1930. A year later, the Park Point line was abandoned, a victim of the Great Depression. Right: Photograph by A. F. Raymond, ca. 1936, Minnesota Historical Society

Before it was paved, Minnesota Avenue was loose sand. Wagons and autos bogged down, so the streetcar hauled more than passengers. Streetcars pulled freight trailers that carried coal, wood, groceries, and other supplies to residents. The trailers were left along the line where residents were expected to unload them before the streetcar returned in the other direction.

Sand was a problem for the streetcars as well. Where the track passed through a couple of cuts between the dunes, sand would periodically drift across the rails. In 1901 an employee rigged a scraper to the front of a street-car and used it to scoop away the sand that encroached next to the track.

Apparently the streetcar fulfilled another unmet need:

Owing to the impracticality of using a hearse on Park Point, the street railway company has announced that it will run a funeral car whenever the occasion demands. In the past considerable difficulty has been experienced in bringing bodies from this locality to the bridge, but the use of the funeral car will remove this trouble. It will be available at any season of the year. (Duluth News Tribune, *May 3, 1907*)

It appears that DSR discontinued freight delivery when it assumed ownership in 1917. In an April 1918 newspaper story, residents on the outer end of the line beyond 38th Street petitioned the city council to pave the outer portion of Minnesota Avenue because trucks would not deliver "groceries, building materials, laundry, etc." beyond 38th. They also complained of delivery costs three times higher than what the streetcar had charged.

The 1930 rebuilding of the Aerial Bridge converted it from a traveling gondola to a conventional lift bridge. Tracks were laid in the deck and, for the first time, Park Point's streetcars were no longer isolated. DSR seized this opportunity to save money. It closed the Park Point carhouse. With Park Point cars now reaching downtown, a separate Aerial Bridge line was an expensive redundancy. It was reduced to a few rush-hour trips.

Streetcar service lasted only a year after tracks were finally laid across the bridge. Replacement bus service began in 1931. The Aerial Bridge streetcars continued to run during rush hours until 1938.

Duluth Herald 3-12-30

Street Car Traffic Starts Across Bridge

The long-awaited service by street cars, running directly from Park Point to the mainland via a lift span bridge became a reality at 5:28 a. m. today, when the first car of the morning running out of the car barn proceeded directly to Forty-third street, the end of the Park Point line, and returned, picking up Park Pointers early bound for the city proper and work. The Herald "caught" the crossing of a car on the span of the remodeled bridge.

The Duluth News Tribune. 3-12-30

STREET CAR TRAFFIC BEGINS OVER AERIAL LIFT BRIDGE

In 1940 the abandoned carbarn was used as a boat works.

THE PARK POINT FIRE CAR

Fighting fires in Park Point was an exercise in frustration. Until 1905 the point was isolated from Duluth by the ship channel. Even after the Aerial Bridge opened, intermittent closures for ship passages prevented a quick response from downtown Duluth. Built on a sandbar, the unpaved roads were also sand, in which wagons and early autos became mired. The water next to the point was too shallow for fireboats to work close to shore. Only the streetcar line offered easy access to the four-mile-long, one- to two-block-wide peninsula. In 1907, this led to the creation of the only firefighting trolley in North America.

Interstate Traction, then the operator of the Park Point line, sold a single-truck ex-DSR streetcar to the city. It was rebuilt and equipped with ladders, 1,500 feet of hose, a water pump, extinguishers, and all the usual firefighting tools. It was stored in its own carhouse across the street from the Park Point carhouse. The city paid the company $30 per month to store the car, maintain and repair it, and furnish a motorman whenever an alarm was turned in.

A Duluth fireman who lived near the carhouse was appointed chief of the otherwise volunteer Park Point fire department. Alarms were turned in to his home by telephone. Russell Olson describes in *Electric Railways of Minnesota* the response to an alarm: "He would rush to the carhouse, get the motorman (usually the shop foreman), and with headlight on, automatic gong clanging, start down the tracks immediately. Volunteers were picked up along the way, alerted by the clanging of the gong on the car. Motormen of regular cars who met the fire car on the way to a fire were instructed to reverse direction quickly and proceed ahead of the car to the scene of the fire, assist at that point if necessary, or operate shuttle service during the time of interruption."

According to this news account, being on call 24 hours a day took its toll.

Park Point's fire department is tired. He wants some relief. At least that's the way it appeared to city commissioners yesterday when C. E. Worth of Park Point Traction Co. registered an appeal on behalf of W. W. Forsyth—chief and everything else of the Minnesota Point "brigade" for shorter hours. At present Forsyth puts in 24 hours a day in the discharge of his duties—that being all the time he can work in one day. True, he does not have to be at the "station" all the time, but he has to be within reach of the telephone at that place or at his home, both day and night. The annual report of the fire department shows that the Park Point "force" was called upon to make 14 runs during 1917. Mr. Worth points out that branches in New Duluth and Lakeside, with but a few more runs, kept six or seven more men all year. (Duluth News Tribune, January 28, 1918)

Minnesota Avenue, Park Point's main street, was paved in 1915, but the fire car continued in service. According to a 1928 company memo, it responded to 9 alarms in 1925, 3 in 1926, 12 in 1927 and 3 in the first quarter of 1928.

Conversion of the Aerial Bridge to a lift bridge in 1930 caused DSR to close its Park Point carbarn, shifting storage and maintenance work to the main shops on West Superior Street. With no one on the point to run or maintain the fire car, it was replaced by a conventional fire engine, housed in the old carhouse.

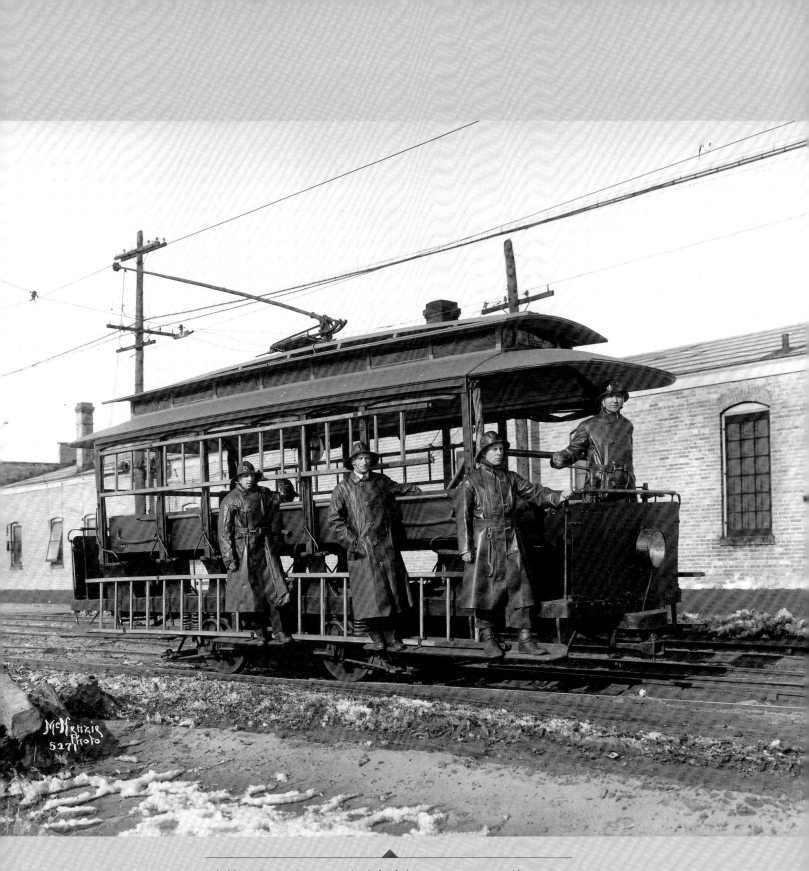

Behold North America's one and only fire-fighting streetcar, spawned by impassable roads on a narrow sandbar. It kept the peninsula safe from 1907 until 1930.

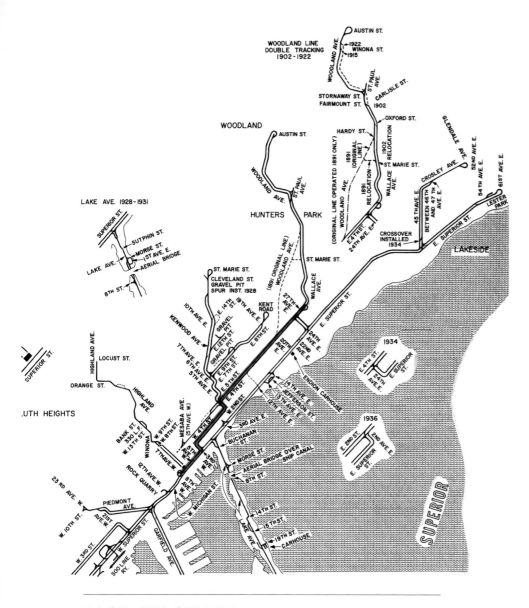

Generations of students rode the streetcars to Central High School, on 2nd Street at Lake Avenue. Ca. 1905.

EAST 4TH STREET

YEARS OF OPERATION:
1890 to 1939

SERVICE FREQUENCY:
5 minutes peak; 10 minutes off-peak

East 4th Street is parallel to and four blocks up the hill from Superior Street. It was the first new electric line built after the conversion of Superior Street horsecars to electricity and filled a long-standing demand for service higher on the hillside. It featured the most frequent service in the system outside of downtown, every five minutes. Unlike most other lines in Duluth–Superior, it had reasonably high population density, with

uninterrupted houses, apartments, schools, and commercial development. It shared track with the East 8th Street and Kenwood lines as far as 5th Avenue East, so all three lines served Duluth Central High School. Near the end of the line at 22nd Avenue East was the Duluth Normal School, later the Duluth State Teachers College and then University of Minnesota Duluth. The East 4th Street line initially ended at 27th Avenue East. When the Woodland line was rerouted via East 4th Street and Wallace Avenue, creating a service duplication, the East 4th Street line was cut back to 24th Avenue East.

In 1928 the Duluth city council tried to force DSR to extend the East 4th Street line to Ridgewood Road, just short of 32nd Avenue East. DSR resisted, and the matter went all the way to the State Supreme Court, which ruled against the city. As a compromise, a turn loop was installed at 27th Avenue East in 1929, putting the line within walking distance of the new Duluth East Junior High School.

The tracks of the East 4th Street line hosted Woodland cars from 1891 to 1907, and again from 1934 to 1939 when the track on Superior Street was removed.

The climb on 3rd Avenue West, 2nd Street, and 5th Avenue East was shared, first by the East 4th Street and West 4th Street lines, and later the East 8th Street and Kenwood lines. The camera is looking east on 4th Street. You can see the downhill grade on 5th Avenue East at right. This photograph was taken before 1912, when an additional block up the 5th Avenue East hill was constructed for the East 8th Street line, crossing the intersection from right to left. The West 4th Street line became a shuttle that met the downtown cars at this intersection. Kathryn A. Martin Library, University of Minnesota Duluth, Archives and Special Collections.

Of all the lines in Duluth, East 4th Street probably passed through the most completely developed neighborhoods. Witness these views taken at 8th Avenue East, 12th Avenue East, and 15th Avenue East.

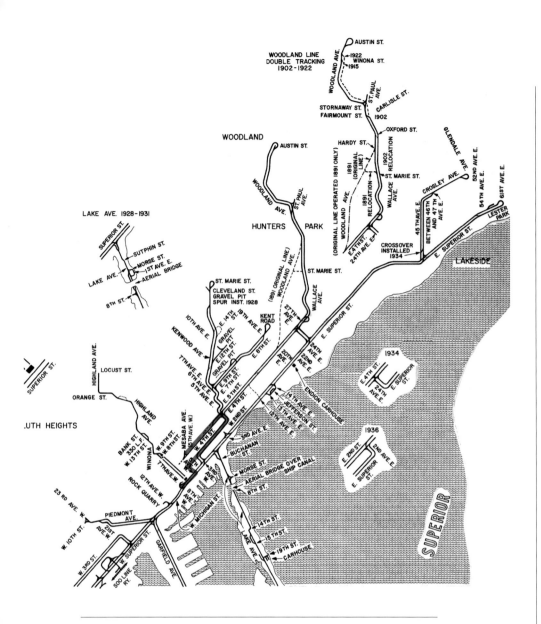

WEST 4TH STREET

YEARS OF OPERATION:
1892 to 1930

SERVICE FREQUENCY:
20 minutes

West 4th Street is only four city blocks above Superior Street. However, the steep hillside made walking a challenge and caused the creation of this dubious line, shaped something like a flattened U lying on its side. From Mesaba Avenue it traveled about a mile east on 4th Street to a junction with the East 4th Street, East 8th Street, and Kenwood lines at 5th Avenue East, whereupon it dropped two blocks down the hill to 2nd Street and reversed direction, passing below where it had just been, before finally dropping again to Superior Street at 3rd Avenue West and terminating at 8th Avenue West. A pedestrian walking up or down the hill could easily beat the street-car, and West 4th Street was the least traveled line in the system. In 1919 it was shortened to a one-mile shuttle along 4th Street between Mesaba Avenue and 5th Avenue East, with passengers transferring to one of the hill line cars to reach Superior Street.

It was assigned the oldest streetcar in the system, the last of the single truckers that had been modified for double-ended operation. Not having to turn the car after each trip saved considerable time. The old car, dubbed the "Dinky" by its riders, became a well-known if unprofitable institution. It averaged only three passengers per trip. This *Duluth Herald* story from 1925 gives a feel for it:

A West 4th Street car in 1907. To reduce cost, it was the first line in the system to run without conductors in 1919. Car 52 was rebuilt as a double-ender with two trolley poles and controls at both ends so it didn't have to be turned after each trip. Along with sister car 57, it was the last of the old single-truckers to carry passengers until the line itself was abandoned in 1930.

The 4th Street line ended at this wye at Mesaba Avenue, seen in 1929. The wye itself was seldom used because the line's regular cars were double-ended. The camera is looking downhill on Mesaba.

Sorrow reigned yesterday on West 4th Street. Denizens of that district wiped many a tear and heaved many a sigh. For the 4th Street dinky, affectionately named "Toonerville" by many, broke a wheel late in the afternoon and had to be withdrawn from the run. A large "yaller" car was pressed into service, and 4th Streeters mourned. No more did the motorman know every customer and stop automatically when the place of residence was reached. For the dinky was gone, and the effect was just like taking the sweet out of "Home sweet home."

The Dinky, car 57, was repaired and continued to serve West 4th Street until 1929. It was the first line in Duluth to be abandoned, in 1930.

The most lightly patronized line in the system was West 4th Street, which narrowed to a single track west of 3rd Avenue East. This view looks west from 1st Avenue West in 1913.

We're back at the intersection of 4th Street and 5th Avenue East. From here, the West 4th Street line ran a mile west to Mesaba Avenue. Beginning in 1919, the line no longer ran down the hill to downtown. It was shortened to a shuttle, feeding the downtown cars at this intersection. This photograph was taken shortly before the line was abandoned in 1930.

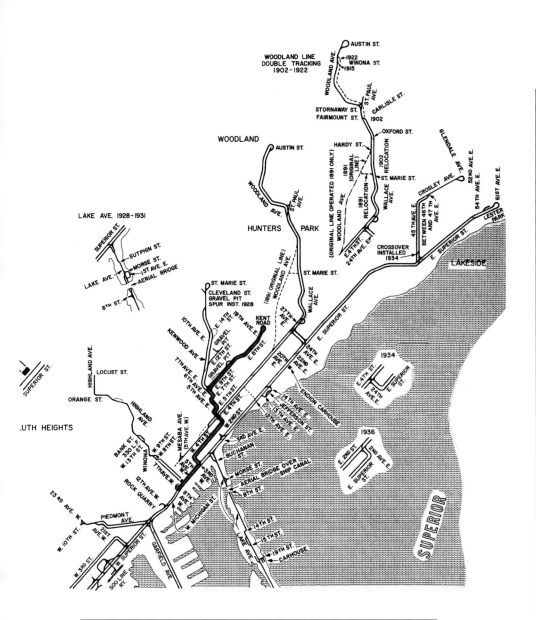

After turning from East 9th Street onto 7th Avenue East, the motorman stops to load a passenger, then releases the brakes and coasts down the steep hill toward downtown in 1937.

EAST 8TH STREET

YEARS OF OPERATION:
1912 to 1939

SERVICE FREQUENCY:
10 minutes peak; 20 minutes off-peak

East 8th Street and the later Kenwood line were the hill lines. They were the steepest, most challenging in Duluth, climbing the Central Hillside 405 and 620 feet, respectively, above downtown. In this area, each city block up the hill places the house roofs of the lower block even with the ground floors of the upper block.

Although the hills were challenging for a streetcar to climb, the downhill run could be frightening. Air brakes only work when there is sufficient air in the system to apply the brakes. A downhill trip was a race between the loss of air for each brake application and the capacity of the compressor to recharge the air tank. To minimize runaways on the downhill trip, the line zigzagged down the hillside. It would descend two or three blocks, then turn right for a block onto a level cross-hill street. This offered a safe place to recharge the air if needed. So daunting was the hill that in 1917 management took the unusual step of handpicking the motormen permitted to run the East 8th Street and Kenwood lines. Normally motormen selected their runs by seniority alone.

Hill line streetcars used the East 4th Street line tracks on 3rd Avenue West, 2nd Street, 5th Avenue East, and 4th Street to climb away from downtown. Grades ranged up to 8.7 percent. The East 8th Street line, originally called the East 9th Street line, diverged from the Kenwood line at 7th Avenue East and 9th Street. In 1923 the line was extended over a new bridge that spanned the Chester Creek ravine and angled onto 8th Street (hence the name change), serving a prosperous neighborhood of single-family homes. The line ended at a turn loop at Kent Road, just short of Woodland Avenue. From 1936 until the end of service in 1939, East 8th Street cars were rerouted via Superior Street and the new track on 2nd Avenue East.

From the line's opening in 1912 until 1923, there was only a single track on East 9th Street, a common strategy for new line extensions. The second track was added as part of extending the line across the Chester Creek bridge and out 8th Street to Kent Road. This is 10th Avenue East in 1916. The streetcar plow has done its job, more than the city could manage with its equipment.

The end of the East 8th Street line looped in the triangle of vacant land at Kent Road. 1923. Kathryn A. Martin Library, University of Minnesota Duluth, Archives and Special Collections.

E. 8th St looking west from Kent Road 2:30 P.M. 12-19-23. FTM

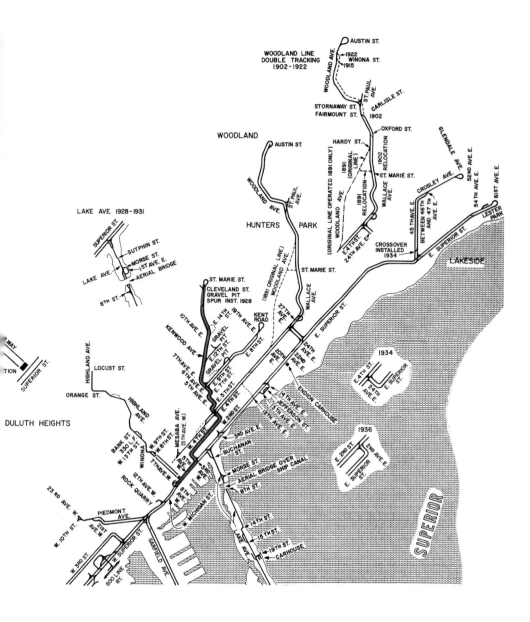

The map contains the following labels:

AUSTIN ST.

WOODLAND LINE
DOUBLE TRACKING
1902-1922

WOODLAND AVE.

1922
WINONA ST.
1915

STORNAWAY ST.
FAIRMOUNT ST.

ST. PAUL AVE.

CARLISLE ST.
1902

OXFORD ST.

HARDY ST.

WOODLAND

AUSTIN ST.

(ORIGINAL LINE OPERATED 1891 ONLY)

1891
(ORIGINAL LINE)

1902
RELOCATION

GLENDALE AVE.

52ND AVE. E.

61ST AVE. E.

WOODLAND AVE.

ST. PAUL AVE.

HUNTERS PARK

ST. MARIE ST.

1891
RELOCATION

WALLACE AVE.

CROSLEY AVE. E.

54TH AVE. E.

LESTER PARK

LAKE AVE. 1928-1931

SUPERIOR ST.

SUTPHIN ST.

MORSE ST.
1ST AVE. E.

LAKE AVE.

AERIAL BRIDGE

8TH ST.

45TH AVE. E.

24TH AVE. E.

BETWEEN 46TH
AND 47TH
AVE. E.

E. SUPERIOR ST.

LAKESIDE

ST. MARIE ST.
CLEVELAND ST.
GRAVEL PIT
SPUR INST. 1928

ST. MARIE ST.

(1891 ORIGINAL LINE)
WOODLAND AVE.

CROSSOVER
INSTALLED
1934

10TH AVE. E.

E. 14TH ST.

19TH AVE. E.

KENT ROAD

27TH AVE.

WALLACE AVE.

E. SUPERIOR ST.

1934

E. 4TH ST.
24TH AVE. E.

E. SUPERIOR ST.

KENWOOD AVE.

GRAVEL PIT

E. 12TH ST.

24TH AVE.
22ND AVE.

HIGHLAND AVE.

LOCUST ST.

7TH AVE. E.

6TH AVE. E.
5TH AVE. E.

E. 9TH ST.

E. 8TH ST.

ENDION CARHOUSE

1936

E. 2ND ST.

2ND AVE. E.

E. SUPERIOR ST.

ORANGE ST.

HIGHLAND AVE.

E. 7TH ST.

E. 6TH ST.
E. 5TH ST.

14TH AVE. E.
JEFFERSON ST.

12TH AVE. E.

DULUTH HEIGHTS

MESABA AVE.
(5TH AVE. W.)

ST. 4TH ST.

E. 4TH ST.

W. 2ND ST.

ENDION ST.

3RD AVE. E.

BANK ST.
330 L.F.

W. 9TH ST.
W. 8TH ST.

WINONA

BUCHANAN ST.

SUPERIOR

7TH AVE. W.

12TH AVE. W.

MORSE ST.

AERIAL BRIDGE OVER
SHIP CANAL

ROCK QUARRY

8TH ST.

23 RD AVE. W.

PIEDMONT AVE.

21ST AVE. W.

14TH ST.

15TH ST.

W. IOTH ST.

W. MICHIGAN ST.

LAKE AVE.

19TH ST.

CARHOUSE

W. 3RD ST.

W. SUPERIOR ST.

GARFIELD AVE.

SOO LINE RY.

WAY
TION
SUPERIOR ST.

After the junction with the East 8th Street line at 9th Street, the Kenwood line climbed another block up the 7th Avenue hill to reach Kenwood Avenue. This photograph looking uphill was taken in 1937, shortly after Kenwood was abandoned.

KENWOOD

YEARS OF OPERATION:
1917 to 1937

SERVICE FREQUENCY:
15–20 minutes peak; 20 minutes off-peak

The Kenwood line was a late addition to the system, opened in stages in 1917 and 1924. DSR had objected that it would never turn a profit and wanted to serve Kenwood with buses, but the city required that it be built. The new line branched off the East 8th Street line. It also served a nonrevenue purpose, with spur tracks to two company-owned gravel pits.

The 1924 extension up Kenwood Avenue to the top of the hill coincided with the conversion of St. Scholastica (at left) from a girl's school to a college.

Although the Woodland line climbed to a greater height above downtown, the Kenwood line was the steepest in the system. The final extension up Kenwood Avenue came in 1924, when the College of St. Scholastica upgraded from a junior college to a four-year curriculum. Because the line served an isolated development on the top of the ridge and because of the difficulty of operating on the steep grades, DSR's prediction of poor ridership proved accurate, and the full Kenwood line lasted only 12 years.

SAMPLE TRIP TO KENWOOD

Turning left from Superior Street onto 3rd Avenue West, the streetcar is immediately on an 8.7 percent grade, meaning the car rises 8.7 feet for every 100 feet of forward motion. The car grinds slowly up the grade for two blocks, turning right onto 2nd Street, which runs across the face of the hill, passing Central High School.

In the course of this trip, the car will attack the hillside four times, each time followed by turning right onto a flat cross-hill street. On the uphill trip, it gives the motors a rest and prevents overheating. On the downhill trip it interrupts the need for continuous braking and gives the air compressor a chance to recharge the reservoir that powers the brakes. After eight blocks on 2nd Street, the car turns uphill again on 5th Avenue East for three blocks, passing St. Mary's Hospital. At 4th Street it transfers a couple of passengers to the waiting West 4th Street shuttle car. Whenever it is necessary to stop for a passenger to alight on an uphill street, instead of making the usual stop just before the intersection, the car slides into the middle of the intersection, which is flatter. To keep from rolling backward when starting, the motorman opens the controller one notch before releasing the brakes.

By the late 1930s, bus design had evolved to place the engine in the rear. An early example of what would become the standard we know today surmounts the hill on East 7th Street, where it replaced streetcars in 1937.

The zigzag up the hill continues, right on 5th Street, left on 6th Avenue and up the hill for two more blocks, right on 7th Street, left and two blocks uphill again on 7th Avenue. At 9th Street, the East 8th Street line turns right, while the Kenwood car continues to climb straight up the hill. Looking out the car's rear windows, a panorama of lake and harbor is spread out below, with Park Point stretching into the distance toward Superior. The car stops every block or two to unload passengers.

The track angles to the right onto Kenwood Avenue. At 12th Street a spur track splits off to serve a gravel pit. Kenwood continues to climb, crossing the Skyline Parkway and leaving most of the development behind. Only a few passengers remain. It enters a deep cut and winds alongside Chester Creek, which it follows for a short distance. Commanding a hilltop to the left is the gothic College of St. Scholastica. Crossing the creek, the line narrows to a single track and climbs one last rise, emerging in the Kenwood neighborhood and terminating at a small business district. The last few passengers depart. The car passes a second gravel pit spur and reaches the turn loop at the end of the line.

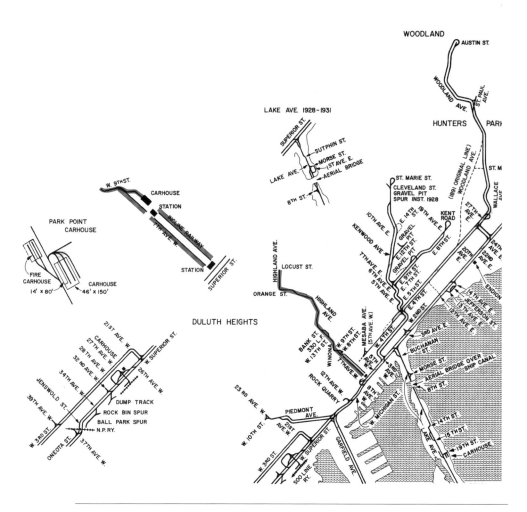

7TH AVENUE INCLINE AND HIGHLAND

INCLINE YEARS OF OPERATION:
1891 to 1939

INCLINE SERVICE FREQUENCY:
15 minutes all day

HIGHLAND YEARS OF OPERATION:
1892 to 1939

HIGHLAND SERVICE FREQUENCY:
15 minutes peak; 30 minutes off-peak

In its first incarnation from 1892 to 1901, the Incline boasted a pair of garage-sized cars capable of hauling wagons or as many as 250 standees. Since they acted as counterweights for each other, the cars always met in the middle of the line at 4th Street.

The Highland Improvement Company was the third of the suburban developers to build a rail link into the city. Duluth's Central Hillside is steepest at Point of Rocks, about 9th Avenue West. Here the uphill–downhill streets are frequently interrupted by sheer drop-offs. The views from the top are spectacular.

In 1889, the Highland Improvement Company (HIC) was incorporated to develop the land atop the hill along Highland Avenue. Thomas Lowry, who held an interest in DSR, was a principal in the company. Without a public transportation link to downtown, development couldn't happen, but the precipitous hillside ruled out a conventional streetcar line. As happened in other similar situations across the country, a

cable-power incline railway was chosen to climb the steepest part of the hill, connecting near the top with an isolated trolley line into the development itself. HIC and DSR shared the construction cost.

The Incline was placed on a steel bridge structure in the platted but unimproved right-of-way of 7th Avenue West from Superior Street to 9th Street. It opened for service on December 2, 1891. Essentially a large, two-track elevator laid on a 15 to 25 percent slope, the Incline climbed 509 feet of elevation in nine blocks. A sidewalk/stairway ran alongside. It ran every 15 minutes.

The original 1892 station at the top of the Incline housed the stationary steam engine and cable mechanism that powered the cars. The pavilion with its various attractions was built next door.

There were three distinct periods in its history. As built in 1891, it was equipped with a pair of garage-sized cars on ten-foot-gauge tracks. They counterbalanced each other—as one went up, the other went down. They were powered by a steam hoisting engine at the top of the hill.

In 1934, motorman R. H. Wellington recalled the original Incline: "The Incline Railway at that time consisted of two very large cars with a capacity of four teams of horses and wagons. They would drive onto the Incline cars loaded with coal, hay, groceries, furniture, and ice. Everything that went up to Duluth Heights went up the Incline. It was nothing unusual for one of the Incline cars to take up 250 passengers at one time."

There was no development at the top, and the connecting Highland streetcar line had not yet opened, so initially sightseeing was the only draw. To create a destination, in 1892 DSR constructed a large recreational pavilion and dance hall and held numerous events such as balloon ascensions to build ridership. Up to 5,000 people rode the Incline on some Sundays.

> There were 10,000 people in and around the Pavilion last evening when Professor Baldwin made a balloon ascension and parachute jump. He had reached a height of nearly 3,000 feet when he made his jump, landing on 11th Avenue West about halfway down the hill. (Duluth Herald, *August 7, 1893*)

On March 29, 1895, the *Duluth News Tribune* reported that DSR had contracted out the entertainment programming to "a circuit of street railway pavilions and summer resorts." Streetcar companies across North America created similar attractions to stimulate ridership. That era ended abruptly in Duluth in 1901 when the powerhouse and pavilion burned. The fire melted the cable, sending one of the cars plummeting down the hillside. It crashed into the Superior Street base station, but no one was injured.

The Incline was out of service until 1902. It reopened with a single, much smaller car capable of carrying only walk-on passengers. It ran on the west track, and a counterweight occupied the east track. The steam hoist was retired. Instead, the single car was self-powered by electric motors, assisted by the counterbalance but still reliant on rail-on-wheel adhesion to climb the hill.

The pavilion was not rebuilt. Four intermediate stations were built along the line. The single car restricted service frequency to every half hour to the top, alternating with half-hourly short trips up to 4th Street, the halfway point. That proved to

After rebuilding in 1910, intermediate stations served hillside residents at 2nd Street, 3rd Street, 4th Street, between 5th and 6th Streets, and between 6th and 7th Streets. This is 4th Street. Photograph by Herman Rinke in 1938.

The disastrous fire of 1901 destroyed the powerhouse and pavilion. It melted the west track cable, causing the car to run away and demolish the Superior Street station. Below: Kathryn A. Martin Library, University of Minnesota Duluth, Archives and Special Collections.

As rebuilt in 1902, the Incline was a reduced enterprise. There was no pavilion or other attraction at the top. A single, much smaller car provided less frequent service. It is seen here at 4th Street meeting the counterweight that rode the east track. For the first time, intermediate stations were opened to serve hillside residents. Power came from electric motors rather than a stationary steam engine. Note the Incline Saloon next to the base station. Library of Congress Prints and Photographs Division, Detroit Publishing Company Photograph Collection.

Viewed in 1912 from atop a harbor front grain elevator, this is the Incline that elderly Duluth residents remember. It ran from 1910 until 1939. From a station on Superior Street it served five intermediate stations before reaching the top, where it fed the isolated Highland streetcar line.

The Incline in the first block above Superior Street and crossing Mesaba Avenue. Largely forgotten is the sidewalk/stairway that followed it up the hill. 1933.

be too infrequent during rush hours, when heavy ridership required most passengers to stand.

In 1911, the Incline was again rebuilt. The single car was replaced by a pair of larger cars built at Twin City Rapid Transit's Snelling Shops in St. Paul. The power system was a conventional funicular, with a large electric hoisting motor at the top that raised and lowered the cars. The cars drew electricity from an overhead wire to power lighting, heating, and an air compressor for the brakes.

Crossing 2nd Street. In the distance the hill line streetcar tracks can be seen passing Central High School. Ca. 1910.

Because the two cars counterbalanced each other, they met every trip at the 4th Street station. The stations were spaced so that both cars were simultaneously stopped at two of them in order to eliminate any unnecessary stops.

From the top of the Incline ca. 1935, Minnesota Point can be seen extending toward Wisconsin.

Two interior views of the Incline cars from 1913 showing the operator's controls, telephone to the engineer, sliding doors, and passenger seats.

LAST CHANCE
DON'T MISS THIS FAMOUS INCLINE RIDE
DULUTH SKYRIDE
VIEW TWIN PORTS FROM 500 FT. ELEVATION STREET CAR FARE

INCLINE SOON TO BE ELIMINATED UNDER DULUTH'S TRANSIT MODERNIZATION PLAN

By 1939 the Incline's days were numbered. Although not profitable, it lasted as long as it did because of the physical difficulty and expense of serving the same neighborhoods with buses. Kathryn A. Martin Library, University of Minnesota Duluth, Archives and Special Collections.

Five intermediate stations located at 2nd Street, 3rd Street, 4th Street, between 5th and 6th Streets, and between 6th and 7th Streets replaced the earlier four stations. The previous stations had been built over the east track, clearing the low-slung counterweight. The new stations were located between the tracks. From 1911 until 1939, the Incline ran every 15 minutes. The cars traveled at six miles per hour, and a one-way trip took eight minutes.

The Electric Railroaders Association newsletter, *Headlights*, in April 1949 gave a detailed account of how the Incline operated:

As it climbed, the view became ever more spectacular. This is at 7th Street, the Skyline Parkway, in 1933.

Each of the two counterbalanced cars had both a trolley pole and a third rail shoe. The trolley pole was mounted close to the devil strip side of the car and contacted a traditional trolley wire to draw off current for the car's lights and air compressors. Because of the intermediate stations a conductor was employed on each car with a number of duties. He opened and closed the doors, collected fares, issued and received transfers, and finally notified the incline operator after each stop when his car was ready to move. The communication between the conductors and the operator was not by buzzer or bell as one might expect, but by ordinary wall-type telephone on each car and via the aforementioned third rail and sliding shoe.

The procedure in the operator's cabin was also something to see. He sat just inside a number of windows giving him an unobstructed view down the hill. His left hand operated a conventional streetcar controller, while his right hand operated a Simplex safety–type air brake valve handle. Both devices controlled the cable machinery. The operator appeared just like an ordinary motorman except for an unusual arrangement. He wore a set of earphones and a chest transmitter. After each stop he would wait for "East Car Clear" and "West Car Clear" from the two conductors and then promptly make the standard streetcar motorman's motions until the large dial next to him indicated that the cars had reached the platform levels of their next respective stations. The station levels were located at symmetrical distances from the midpoint at 4th Street so that both of the counterbalanced cars would be at the exact platform levels at each of the stops.

This clearly shows how the Incline met the Highland line. The small building at the top of the Incline contained a waiting room and the engineer's office. On a typical day, half the passengers walked the short distance to board the Highland car. The other half either alighted at an intermediate station or returned to the Incline after a sightseeing interlude. Ca. 1937.

There were two streetcars assigned to the Highland line, and they were stored and serviced in this small carhouse. One ran all day, providing 30-minute service that met every second Incline car. The other was brought out for the morning and afternoon rush hours, when the service increased to every 15 minutes and Highland cars met the Incline on every trip. Ca. 1937.

A major tourist attraction, many rode to the top of the Incline just for the view. However, the company's report of hourly riders shows a clear pattern of commuters riding down in the morning and returning at night. About half of the Incline's passengers transferred to or from the isolated Highland streetcar line. It's unclear how many boarded at the intermediate Incline stations and how many were simply tourists ascending for the view.

The isolated Highland streetcar line began at the top of the Incline. From there it climbed to the top of the ridge, meandering through the undeveloped hillside area along the current alignment of Orange Avenue. Once on top of the ridge, it served a modest residential area before ending in the business district on Highland Avenue (now Basswood Avenue), just north of today's Highway 53. A portion of the line began service on September 28, 1892, but it didn't reach its full 1.8-mile length until 1894. The Highland development never met expectations, and the company was financially unable to operate the line. It was deeded to DSR in 1893.

Two streetcars modified for double-ended operation were assigned to the line. One ran all day, providing a 30-minute

The Highland car in the late 1890s with the pavilion in the background. The roof of the carhouse is visible to the right of the streetcar.

Having wound its way up the hill along Orange Avenue, in 1931 development was still sparse at the edge of Duluth Heights, looking both ways at Arlington Avenue.

frequency that connected with every second Incline car. During rush hours, the second car entered service to create a 15-minute frequency that connected with every Incline car.

The Highland line's two streetcars were initially hauled to the top of the hill by horse teams. In the course of the line's life, the cars were changed only once, when newer, larger ones replaced the original pair. It required 18 horses to pull them up. The cars were stored inside a two-stall carhouse at the Incline station. Motormen commuted daily from the main carhouse at 28th Avenue West and Superior Street.

In later years, DSR found a way to run the second car during rush hours without adding a second motorman. One-way Incline running time was 8 minutes, followed by 7 minutes of layover before the next one-way trip. On the Highland line one-way running time was 10 minutes, followed by 5 minutes of layover before the next one-way trip. When two cars were running on the single-track Highland line, they met at a siding only five blocks and three minutes up the hill from the Incline station. It was the only passing siding on the line.

The schedule makers realized that there was enough layover time for the Incline conductor to walk his passengers to the Highland car and run the car uphill to the passing siding. There he would switch to the downhill car, run it back to the Incline station, walk the passengers to the Incline car, and pilot it down to Superior Street. Meanwhile the Highland motorman was shuttling back and forth between the siding and the north end of the Highland line.

Despite their dismal financial performance, the Incline and the Highland line were the last of the streetcars to be abandoned because the topography made it so challenging to replace them with buses. A company study found that substituting buses would actually increase the annual cost somewhat because it would be necessary to create two new bus routes, and the one replacing the Highland line would have to be extended all the way to downtown.

A Highland car at the end of the line in Duluth Heights. Kathryn A. Martin Library, University of Minnesota Duluth, Archives and Special Collections.

The Highland line was built to serve the Duluth Heights real estate development. In 1935 the neighborhood remained an island of population along and near Highland Avenue. The camera is looking north on Highland (since renamed Basswood Avenue) at Palm Street, a block south of today's Highway 53 leading to the Central Entrance.

There was little development directly above the Incline station. That was true when this photograph was taken in 1926, and it's still true.

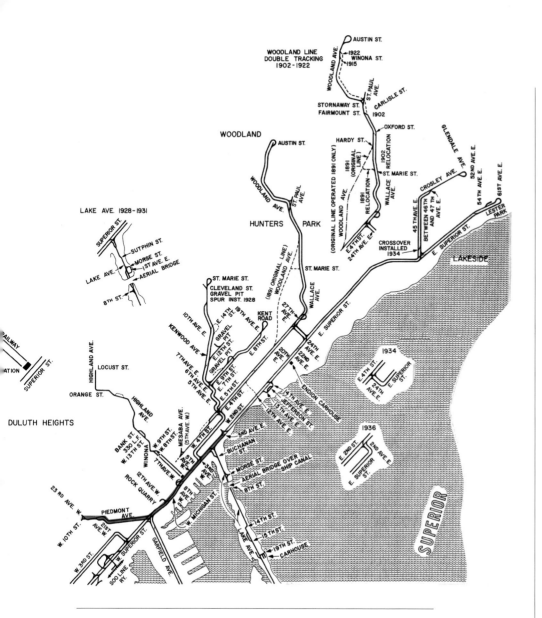

PIEDMONT

YEARS OF OPERATION:
1896 to 1934 (trolley bus service continued to 1949)

SERVICE FREQUENCY:
15 to 20 minutes peak; 20 minutes off-peak

The Piedmont line was a one-mile branch off West Superior Street. Diverging just west of Point of Rocks, it twisted and turned up the steep hillside on an average 7 percent grade to serve a residential neighborhood. As originally built in 1896, Piedmont from Superior Street to 3rd Street was part of the West Duluth main line. However, this required the mainline cars to climb up and over the steep west shoulder of Point of Rocks.

The City requested an extension farther up Piedmont to 13th Street. DSR responded that grades as steep as 12 percent would preclude electric cars and require a cable car line. The extension was finally built in 1910 but only as far as 10th Street, which avoided the worst grades.

In 1912, the West Duluth main line was relocated to a less challenging alternate route with higher ridership via Superior Street and 21st Avenue West. Although short, the Piedmont line provided a needed service to the steep hillside neighborhood. Beginning in 1928, the Piedmont line was duplicated from downtown by a new bus line that extended beyond the streetcar tracks to serve Enger Park and Hermantown. It ran every 40 minutes.

In 1934 trolley buses replaced the streetcars. They were in turn replaced by Hermantown line gas buses in 1949. The construction of new Highway 53 to the Blatnick Bridge removed most of the homes on the west side of Piedmont, greatly changing the neighborhood.

The Piedmont line climbed away from Superior Street just west of Garfield Avenue, where the Interstate line to Rice's Point and Superior (foreground) also diverged and the main line to West Duluth continued straight ahead. When opened in 1896, the line to West Duluth via Grand Avenue followed Piedmont, but in 1912 it was rerouted to a less hilly alignment via Superior Street and 21st Avenue West. This view dates from 1923.

Piedmont Avenue was a challenging place to run streetcars. This view shows track construction at 5th Street in 1910. Kathryn A. Martin Library, University of Minnesota Duluth, Archives and Special Collections.

23 Av. W. 10th St. looking N. 3:30 P.M. 1. 20. 15. H.H. Brown

This is the wye at the end of the Piedmont line, at 10th Street and 23rd Avenue West next to Ensign School in 1915. Kathryn A. Martin Library, University of Minnesota Duluth, Archives and Special Collections.

Looking both ways at 9th Street in 1931. The grades ranged up to 9 percent. Cars descending on the single track at 9th Street ran against oncoming traffic as they rounded a blind corner.

This is the unglamorous West End business district along Superior Street from about 18th to 25th Avenues West in the late 1930s. The car in the distance is using one of the four trolley bus wires. Note the separate streetcar wire at left.

WEST DULUTH VIA ONEOTA

YEARS OF OPERATION:
1891 to 1939

SERVICE FREQUENCY:
15 to 20 minutes peak; 20 minutes off-peak

The West Duluth line served the mostly industrial corridor along the harbor and St. Louis River that extended to Grassy Point. Between downtown and the West End business district at 21st Avenue West, it shared track with the Grand Avenue main line. The main streetcar barns, shops, and corporate offices were located on Superior Street between 26th and 28th Avenues. The Clyde Iron Works Company was located between 29th and 32nd Avenues. Nearby employers included Duluth Brewing and Malting Company.

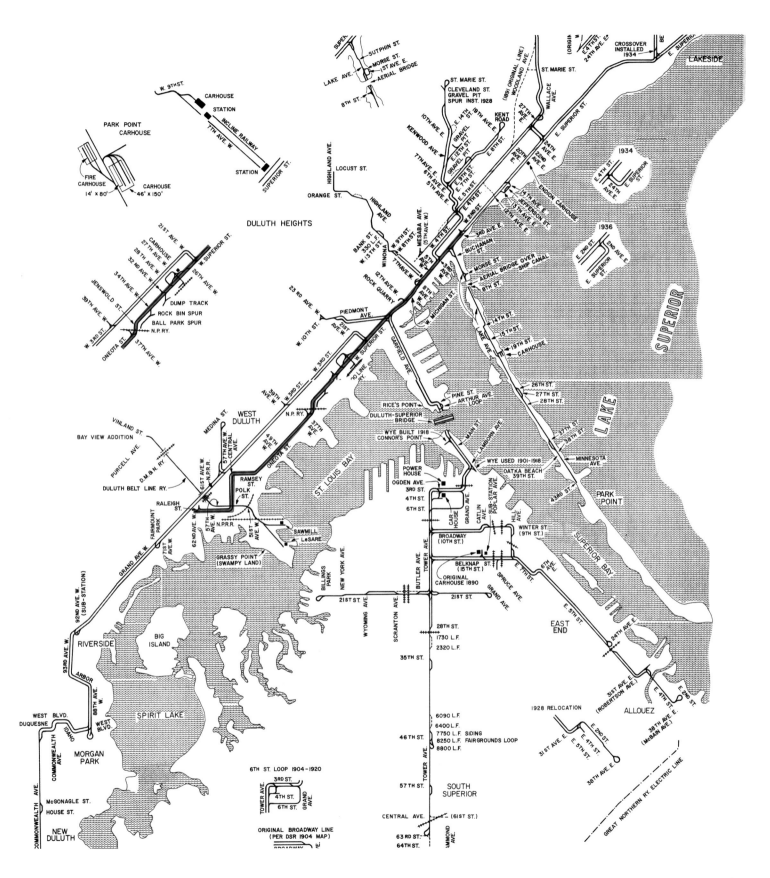

The huge outcropping called Point of Rocks forced Superior Street to detour around it on the way to the West End and the ore docks. Kathryn A. Martin Library, University of Minnesota Duluth, Archives and Special Collections.

Beyond the carhouse and company office, the loop to the track materials yard diverges at 28th Avenue West. The Duluth, Missabe & Northern ore docks are in the distance at 34th Avenue. 1930.

In 1907 a spur track was built at 34th Avenue to stage cars next to the local ballpark.

The Duluth Baseball Club has made arrangements with the DSR Co. for a spur track opposite the baseball park for the convenience of the people attending the games. The track will be long enough to accommodate six to eight double-truck cars and will have a walk alongside. This will do away with the pushing and crowding for places in the cars that has been so distasteful to ladies attending the games. There is a track three blocks west of the park where the cars are sidetracked until the close of the game, but this necessitates a wait of some time before the cars can be gotten to the park. (Duluth News Tribune, June 5, 1907)

Immediately to the west of 34th Avenue, the line passed under the Duluth, Missabe & Northern ore docks, then ducked under the Northern Pacific tracks in the middle of Jenswold Street, which angled right to become Oneota Street. West of the underpass were several coal and lumber docks, National Iron Company, Duluth Refrigerator Company, and Union Match Company. The line reached Central Avenue in 1891, the first service to West Duluth.

Entering an industrial no-man's-land, the streetcars passed under the ore docks, the outskirts of original Duluth, leading to the old villages of Oneota and West Duluth. 1916.

Just west of the ore docks, the West Duluth line ducked under the Northern Pacific's Duluth Transfer subsidiary. The streetcar track is actually in the unimproved right-of-way of Jenswold Street. The underpass is new, having replaced a bridge over the tracks in 1902, and the men on the work car are shoveling ballast onto the recently laid track. Collection of Loren Martin.

Baseball fans rode the streetcars to Athletic Park, on the north side of Oneota Street in the shadow of the ore docks. DSR built a spur track to stage the ballpark extras. In 1923 it hosted early National Football League games. In 1941, it was demolished and Wade Stadium was constructed next door. The street running across the middle of the photograph is Grand Avenue, the second streetcar line to West Duluth. Kathryn A. Martin Library, University of Minnesota Duluth, Archives and Special Collections.

The one-mile stretch on Oneota Avenue west of the ore docks appears almost devoid of development and ridership, and it was, except for employees who worked at several docks a block away. Little changed between 1913 and 1932, when these two photos were taken.

Near 48th Avenue West, Oneota Street passed over a track headed for the Duluth, Winnipeg & Pacific's lumber dock. This is about 1912, when the DW&P track was under construction.

It turned south on Central Avenue through the business district to Raleigh Street. Although this area was commercial and residential, it was a convenient walk east to the numerous coal and lumber docks on Grassy Point, as well as the Alger Smith sawmill and Duluth Brass Works. For twelve years, it was the only streetcar service to West Duluth, until the Grand Avenue line arrived in 1903. However, it had to compete with the commuter trains of the Northern Pacific, which had a station at Central Avenue. The streetcar line turned west on Raleigh Street, which took it away from the waterfront but into a working-class residential area and near the Zenith Furnaces to its final terminal at 62nd Avenue West. It stopped a block short of Grand Avenue to avoid crossing the Northern Pacific Railroad, but it still offered an opportunity to transfer to the Grand Avenue line to reach points farther west.

Because of the concentration of West End and West Duluth industries, rush-hour ridership was heavy in both directions. This was in spite of the stretch along Oneota Street, two blocks away from the waterfront, that appeared to be almost bereft of development.

From 1902 until 1909 the West Duluth line connected with the Duluth Belt Line Railway at Central Avenue. However, most Belt Line passengers transferred to streetcars at Grand Avenue, and fewer than half the Belt Line trips extended to Central Avenue.

Swinging away from the harbor on Ramsey Street, the line entered the West Duluth business district. These photos look both north in 1930 and south in 1912 at the Ramsey Street and Central Avenue intersection. At this point the two West Duluth lines were only a block apart. Railroad stations of the Northern Pacific and Duluth, Winnipeg & Pacific also served West Duluth at Central and Grand Avenues.

Although taken in 1960, little has changed on Ramsey Street, looking both ways at 57th Avenue West, since the streetcar quit in 1939. Kathryn A. Martin Library, University of Minnesota Duluth, Archives and Special Collections.

A Grand Avenue car leaves the West Duluth line at 21st Avenue West and Superior Street. The bus is deadheading back to the garage. Note the heavy trolley bus overhead wires mixed in with streetcar wires. Ca. 1938.

WEST DULUTH VIA 3RD STREET AND GRAND

YEARS OF OPERATION:
1896 to 1939 (trolley bus service continued to 1957)

SERVICE FREQUENCY:
5 to 10 minutes peak; 10 minutes off-peak

The Main Line, as it was called, from downtown to Gary–New Duluth, was long enough and the inner and outer portions of it different enough that we treat it as two separate lines. Grand Avenue and West 3rd Street are actually the same street. The name changes at 39th Avenue West. The line was extended to the blue-collar immigrant neighborhoods of West Duluth in stages from 1896 to 1906. Originally it used the Piedmont line from Superior Street to 3rd Street, which required a steep climb over the west shoulder

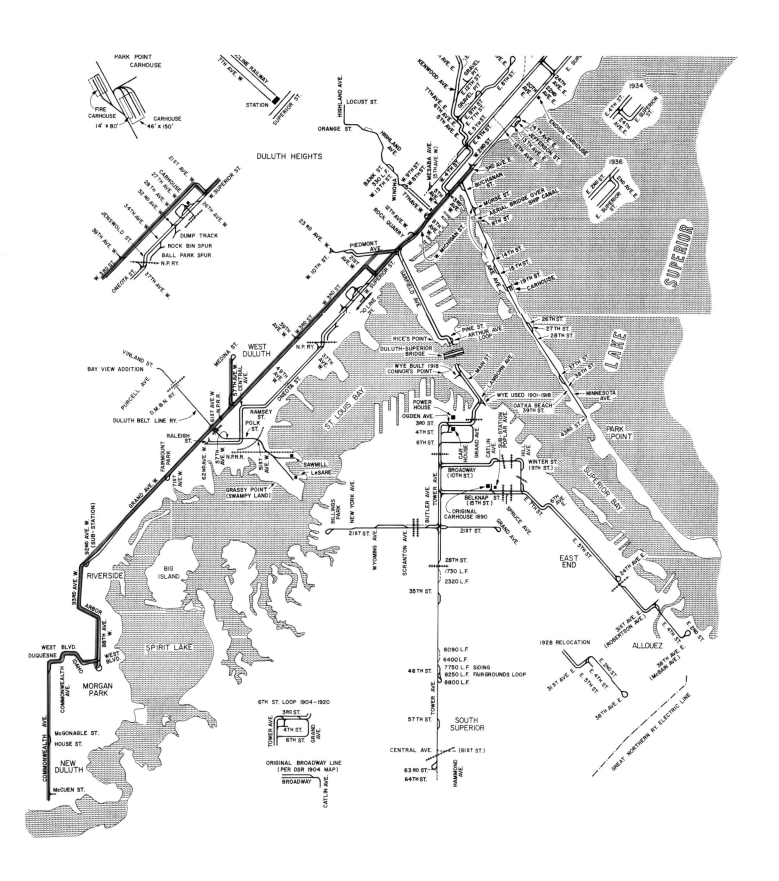

For some reason, 3rd Street changes its name to Grand Avenue at 39th Avenue West. This 1916 view at 24th Avenue West shows how the land flattens west of the Central Hillside and Point of Rocks.

3rd St. looking west at 49th Ave.W.
10:30 AM. 4-4-23.
E.T.M.

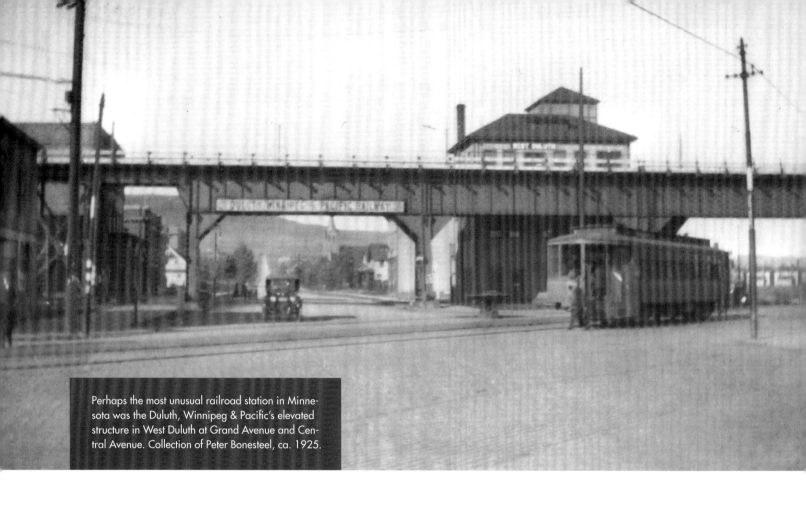

Perhaps the most unusual railroad station in Minnesota was the Duluth, Winnipeg & Pacific's elevated structure in West Duluth at Grand Avenue and Central Avenue. Collection of Peter Bonesteel, ca. 1925.

of Point of Rocks. This routing also caused it to bypass the West End business district on Superior west of Piedmont. In 1912 the line was rerouted via Superior to 21st Avenue West, simultaneously reducing the grades and adding traffic.

The new line paralleled the original West Duluth line that opened in 1891 and ran closer to the harbor on Oneota Street. Eventually there was continuous development along Grand, but for the first couple of decades the stretch from the ore docks at 34th Avenue to 50th Avenue West was largely vacant, although traveling circuses used a site at 35th Avenue West. People's Brewery was a block off the line at 42nd Avenue. Adding to the traffic was Denfield High School, located a block from the line at 44th Avenue.

The West Duluth business district was centered on Grand between Central Avenue and 57th Avenue West. Because the hillside receded somewhat in West Duluth, a one-mile branch was added in 1906 on 57th Avenue West. It climbed away from Grand Avenue for one mile, ending just short of the Duluth, Missabe & Northern tracks that led to the ore docks. There were

Grand Avenue at 39th Avenue West in 1931. The ore dock leads cross in the distance.

We don't know the occasion for this procession, viewed from the DW&P station, turning from Central Avenue onto Grand Avenue ca. 1925.

plans to extend this branch to Proctor, but it never happened. Instead, buses began serving Proctor in 1937.

From 1905 to 1916, the line connected at 61st Avenue West with the Duluth Belt Line Railway. A cable-powered incline, it climbed the hillside to the sparsely developed neighborhood of Bay View Heights. The large Western Rug Company factory was at 63rd Avenue and Grand.

The Grand Avenue portion of the Main Line was heavily traveled. The mix of employment along the entire line, a low-income population, and the geography that squeezed so much traffic onto a single line combined to produce ridership that any streetcar system would envy.

Trolley buses replaced the streetcars on Grand Avenue in 1939. From 1905 to 1915, the Main Line ended at 71st Avenue West, dubbed the Fairmont Park loop for the large park along Kingsbury Creek, site of the Duluth Zoo.

Two blocks west of Central Avenue, in 1906 the streetcar sent a one-mile branch north on 57th Avenue West. The first view dates from 1924. The other, from 1939, shows additional development. The branch was projected to be extended to Proctor, but the extension was made with buses, one of which is approaching from around the corner.

Looking West at 71st Ave. loop
10:00 A.M. Sept. 6, 1918.
E.T.M.

The Grand Avenue line reached 71st Avenue West in 1905, and cars destined there carried the sign "Fairmont Park." As these photos, which look in both directions, show, there wasn't much development there, even 15 years later. Kathryn A. Martin Library, University of Minnesota Duluth, Archives and Special Collections.

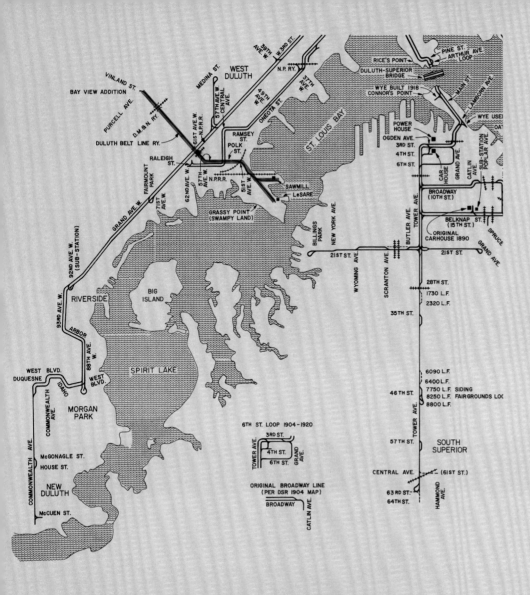

DULUTH-SUPERIOR BRIDGE

WYE BUILT 1918
CONNOR'S POINT

POWER HOUSE

OGDEN AVE.
3RD ST.
4TH ST.
6TH ST.

CAR HOUSE

BROADWAY (10TH ST.)

BELKNAP ST. (15TH ST.)

ORIGINAL CARHOUSE 1890

21ST ST.

28TH ST.
1730 L.F.
2320 L.F.

35TH ST.

6090 L.F.
6400 L.F.
7750 L.F. SIDING
8250 L.F. FAIRGROUNDS LOC
8800 L.F.

46TH ST.

57TH ST.   SOUTH SUPERIOR

CENTRAL AVE. ——— (61ST ST.)

63RD ST.
64TH ST.

6TH ST. LOOP 1904-1920

3RD ST.
4TH ST.
6TH ST.

ORIGINAL BROADWAY LINE (PER DSR 1904 MAP)
BROADWAY

This is the Bay View Heights station at the top of the Incline. Note the freight trailer, which was towed behind the passenger car as needed.

DULUTH BELT LINE

YEARS OF OPERATION:
1889 to 1917

SERVICE FREQUENCY:
Hourly

During the 1880s and 1890s, a series of real estate promoters, hoping to capitalize on the spectacular views, established developments high on the ridge above Duluth. Woodland, Hunter's Park, Morley Heights, and Duluth Heights were examples that achieved some success. Less so was Bay View Heights, located beyond West Duluth and east of the railroad

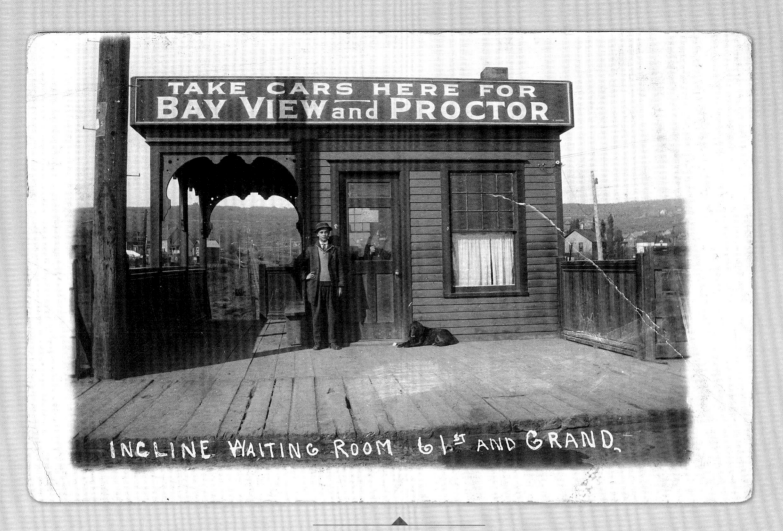

TAKE CARS HERE FOR
BAY VIEW and PROCTOR

INCLINE WAITING ROOM 61st AND GRAND.

The Proctor destination on the depot sign was a bit optimistic. The Belt Line stopped short by about a mile. Kathryn A. Martin Library, University of Minnesota, Duluth, Archives and Special Collections.

town of Proctor. The Myers Brothers incorporated the Bay View Land Company in 1889 and platted 1,250 acres in residential lots.

The area was isolated, so the company incorporated the Duluth Incline Railway in 1888. When the line opened in 1889 the Duluth News declared it "the longest of its class in the world." It was reorganized in 1890 as the Duluth Belt Line Railway. The northern half from Grand Avenue rose 600 feet above the harbor on a grade that topped out at 16 percent and roughly followed the ravine of Keene Creek. The southern half of the line curved through the flats of West Duluth to sawmills on the bay at Grassy Point. The total length was 1.4 miles.

Initially passenger service covered the entire line, with a one-way running time of 20 minutes. Eight of the 13 daily trains terminated at Grand Avenue, with the rest continuing to Grassy Point. Intermediate stations were located at Pleasant View, halfway up the hill, and at Grand Avenue, Central Avenue, and 4th Avenue East in flat West Duluth. Initially the only way to reach downtown Duluth was via a transfer to the Northern Pacific suburban trains at Grand Avenue. The 1891 timetable shows twice-daily connections in each direction. With no streetcar connection to downtown, the company organized the Duluth Electric Street Railway and proposed to build a line to downtown and through to Endion on the East End. Nothing came of the scheme.

With the 1891 streetcar extension to West Duluth via Oneota Street, passengers were able to transfer for downtown at Central Avenue. In 1903, the Grand Avenue car line was extended to 60th Avenue, a block from the cable station, creating a more convenient connection. In 1905, when the Grand Avenue line was extended west to 71st Avenue, the connection at 61st Avenue became even more convenient.

Bay View Heights was appropriately named. The upper portion of the right-of-way still hosts a power line, making it easy to locate. Highway I-35 was built on the lower section.

The Belt line passed under Grand Avenue. This two-level station connected it to the streetcars above.

The stationary steam engine that powered the cable was located inside the Bay View Heights station.

The Belt Line passed under Grand Avenue, and a two-level transfer station was built, connecting the incline and streetcar with a stairway. The incline cars ran hourly and were timed to connect with the streetcars. One-way running time was 10 minutes. Two of the hourly trips each day hauled a freight car to transport supplies. The Belt Line used secondhand streetcars from DSR.

For nearly two months ending in April 1904, the line was closed. Keene Creek, which it paralleled, became blocked with ice, flooding the track, and the overflow froze, making the line impassable.

Initially, much of the line's income came from hauling freight. Timber from Bay View Heights was delivered to the sawmills, and finished lumber was hauled back up the hill. This business dwindled, and in 1909 the line was abandoned between Grassy Point and Grand Avenue.

Extensive improvements were begun yesterday by the Belt Line Railway Company that include the installing of a new cable, remodeling the power plant at Bay View Heights, placing in the power plant some new machinery, remodeling cars, and completing repairs on the roadbed which were started last fall but not completed. The hill station will be repainted and furnished. The cars are also to receive a new coat of paint, and the interiors will be redecorated. (Duluth News Tribune, April 5, 1910)

As automobiles proliferated, business declined. It's unclear whether the line operated beyond 1916, but it was sold and scrapped the following year. The old right-of-way is occupied by a power line and by I-35, so it's easy to spot where it was.

DESTROY ALL FORMER CARDS.
NO. 3.
Takes Effect May 1, 1891, at 12.05 A. M.

DULUTH BELT LINE RAILWAY.

SOUTH BOUND, Down.
From Bay View Heights to Duluth, Iron Bay or Marinette Works.
Connects at West End Station with St. P. & D. Trains to Duluth at 11:55 a. m. and 4:47 p. m.

LEAVE AS FOLLOWS:	No. 1 Daily. Ex. Sun.	No. 3 Daily. Ex. Sun.	No. 5 Daily. Mixed.	No. 7 Daily.	No. 9 Daily.	No. 11 Daily.	No. 13 Daily.	No. 15 Daily.	No. 17 Daily.	No. 19 Daily.	No. 21 Daily. Mixed.	No. 23 Daily.	No. 25 Daily.
	a.m.	a.m.	a.m.	a.m.	a.m.	a.m.	p.m.	p.m.	p.m.	p.m.	p. m.	p.m.	p. m.
Bay View Heights...	6:40	7:30	8:30	9:30	10:55	11:30	1:30	2:30	3:30	4:30	5:30	7:30	8:30
Pleasant View......	6:44	7:34	8:34	9:34	10:59	11:34	1:34	2:34	3:34	4:34	5:34	7:34	8:34
Incline............	6:50	7:40	8:40	9:40	11:05	11:40	1:40	2:40	3:40	4:40	5:40	7:40	8:40
Central Ave........	6:55	......	......	9:45	......	11:45	1:45				5:45		
Fourth Ave. East....	6:57	......	......	9:47	......	11:47	1:47				5:47	......	
Iron Bay or, ...) Marinette W'ks Ar. ∫	7:00	......	......	9:50	......	11:50	1:50				6:00		
	a.m.	a.m.	a.m.	a.m.	a.m.	a.m.	p.m.	p.m.	p.m.	p.m.	p.m.	p.m.	p.m.

Trains No. 5 and 21 run as Passengers on Sunday.

NORTH BOUND, Up.
TO BAY VIEW HEIGHTS.
Connects at Incline [take St. P. & D. trains to West End Station] with trains leaving Duluth Union Depot at 10:10 a.m. and 2:35 p.m.

LEAVES AS FOLLOWS.	No. 2 Daily Ex. Sun	No. 4 Daily Mixed Ex.Sun.	No. 6 Daily	No. 8 Daily	No. 10 Daily	No. 12 Daily	No. 14 Daily	No. 16 Daily	No. 18 Daily	No. 20 Daily Mixed	No. 22 Daily	No. 24 Daily	No. 26 Daily
	a.m.	a.m.	a.m.	a.m.	a.m.	m.	p. m.	p. m.	p.m.	p.m.	p.m.	p.m.	p.m.
Iron Bay or.......) Marinette Works.. ∫	7:05	......	......	10:25	......	12:00 p. m.	2:00	......			6:05	......	
Fourth Ave. East....	7:08	......	......	10:28	......	12:03	2:03	......			6:08	......	
Central Ave........	7:10	......	......	10:30	......	12:05	2:05				6:13		
Incline............	7:15	8:10	9:10	10:35	11:10	12:10	2:10	3:10	4:10	5:10	6:15	8:10	9:30
Pleasant View......	7:21	8:16	9:16	10:41	11:16	12:16	2:16	3:16	4:16	5:16	6:21	8:16	9:36
Bay View H'ts...Ar.	7:25	8:20	9:20	10:45	11:20	12:20	2:20	3:20	4:20	5:20	6:25	8:20	9:40
	a.m.	a.m.	a.m.	a.m.	a.m.	p.m.	p.m.	p.m.	p.m.	p.m.	p.m.	p.m.	p.m.

Trains No. 4 and 20 run as Passengers on Sunday.

N. B.—All Belt Line trains according to this time card have the right to the road. Other roads before using the time of Belt Line trains must get written permission from Belt Line conductors.

H. H. MYERS, Gen. Manager.

MORGAN PARK AND GARY–NEW DULUTH

MORGAN PARK YEARS OF OPERATION:
1916 to 1939

MORGAN PARK SERVICE FREQUENCY:
10 minutes peak; 20 minutes off-peak

GARY–NEW DULUTH YEARS OF OPERATION:
1917 to 1937

GARY–NEW DULUTH SERVICE FREQUENCY:
10 minutes peak; 20 minutes off-peak

Grand Avenue was also Highway 23. This Minnesota Highway Department photograph was taken from the roof of the substation at 92nd Avenue West, looking toward downtown. It shows how the tracks were relocated from the side of the road to the center in later years. Taken in 1938, this photograph probably anticipated the removal of the tracks the following year. Minnesota Historical Society.

The substation at 92nd Avenue West was constructed to provide additional power for all the extra cars on the line to the shipyard and Morgan Park. A turn loop was built here for the shipyard extras.

Until 1915, the Grand Avenue main line to West Duluth ended at 71st Avenue West, the outer reaches of development. Its further extension was due to the World War I construction of the McDougall-Duluth Shipyard at Riverside, specifically Spring Street (about 88th Avenue West) and U.S. Steel's steel plant and its planned town of Morgan Park. In fact, the streetcar was late to the party. The steel plant opened in 1915 and soon employed 1,000 workers. Travel between Duluth and Morgan Park was initially available only via the commuter trains of the Northern Pacific. The trains provided only a limited number of trips at shift times and could only be accessed at depots scattered along the line between downtown and West Duluth. Fares were considerably higher than for the streetcars. DSR resisted the Morgan Park extension because of the city's insistence on a 5-cent fare. DSR asked for a 10-cent fare to make the long trip economically viable, but it did not prevail.

Although Morgan Park was built to house steel plant workers, it was restricted to northern Europeans. Italians, Slavs, and African Americans had to live elsewhere, so most of the employees commuted from West Duluth and Gary–New Duluth.

The demand for transportation combined with pressure to patriotically support the war effort caused the streetcar company to extend service in 1916 through miles of open country to Morgan Park. The line experienced extremely heavy loadings in both directions, carrying commuters to downtown and to Morgan Park.

The next year, 1917, saw a further 2.8-mile extension from Morgan Park to Gary and New Duluth. Along Commonwealth Avenue, it served the

Universal Portland Cement plant, built in conjunction with the steel mill. When the cement plant opened in 1919, a streetcar freight spur was built beneath the West End ore docks, and DSR work cars hauled crushed rock from there to the cement plant.

Gary–New Duluth was home to many steel plant workers, resulting in an unusual pattern of riders who only used the outer portion of the line. At the end of the line in New Duluth, passengers could transfer to a shuttle bus that continued west to Fond du Lac.

Besides U.S. Steel, the McDougall-Duluth Shipyard at Riverside opened in 1917 and, funded by federal contracts, was a major traffic generator. Driven by defense production, ridership peaked during World War I and continued through 1919.

All this open country, seen in 1918, explains why DSR was slow to extend service to Morgan Park and New Duluth. However, the employment at the McDougall-Duluth Shipyard just beyond the far curve quickly ramped up to 4,000, plus many more at the Morgan Park steel plant, resulting in rush-hour service every few minutes here. For several years only half the street was paved, so everyone drove in that lane. Cars that pulled off it to pass oncoming traffic sometimes used the tracks, and motormen were advised to watch out for head-on collisions.

THE WAR EFFORT

When America entered World War I, DSR saw its highest ridership ever, despite a national influenza epidemic that caused the company to limit the number of passengers per streetcar to 85.

Ridership surged along with manufacturing for the war effort. Nowhere was this more evident than the crowds bound for the Morgan Park steel plant and the McDougall-Duluth Shipyard near Grand Avenue and 88th Avenue West. The steel plant opened in 1915 and was reached by streetcar service in 1916. The shipyard opened in 1917 and soon employed over 4,500. Each rush hour required 18 or 19 extra cars.

Ridership became so heavy that in late 1918 DSR purchased a new rotary converter to increase the power at its 92nd Avenue West substation. That year the Northern Pacific added special trains between downtown and Morgan Park. Among the preserved DSR records is a series of load checks taken at Grand Avenue and 57th Avenue West during the morning rush hour (6:00 to 8:15 a.m.). It shows 2,509 passengers on 37 streetcars in 135 minutes. That's a car every 3.6 minutes. The average load was 66 passengers in each car, with 50 seats per car.

An examination of the check shows that the first nine cars were headed for either Morgan Park or New Duluth, probably feeding the 7 a.m. day shift at the steel plant. The rest of the morning, Morgan Park or New Duluth cars ran about every 10 minutes, with more cars terminating at the 92nd Avenue West loop, a few blocks beyond the shipyard. The loop was constructed in 1917 specifically for the shipyard trippers. Most of these cars had a "T" before the run number, meaning they were extra cars, "trippers". Four of the trippers originated at 57th Avenue West. This was the center of the West Duluth neighborhood and proof that quite a few employees lived in West Duluth. An additional ten trips started at 26th Avenue West.

At shift change, the crowds waiting to board at the Morgan Park loop sometimes became unruly and hard to manage. From a company memo to line foremen: "Conductors are complaining that about 5:57 p.m. the workmen at the Morgan Park loop rush the cars and board

Spring Street in Riverside, seen here in 1920, was the stop for the McDougall-Duluth Shipyard, which generated huge loads during World War I.

through the front way when they stop to turn the switch before the car is around the loop."

A blocked track in West Duluth caused a riot one day:

> As a culmination of what had been denounced as unusually poor street car service due, according to street railway officials, to extraordinary circumstances, a crowd of 200 workmen of the Minnesota Steel Company plant almost demolished one of the cars at Morgan Park shortly before 7:00 last night. The car was the first in more than an hour to reach the suburb, having been held up at 61st Ave. West by the miring across the tracks of a truck loaded with potatoes. The mob that smashed the car did not leave a whole glass. Bell ropes were cut and the motorman is said to have been threatened and saved himself by handily wielding the car controller. After getting on the car, the crowd is said to have refused to pay fares. (Duluth Herald, December 4, 1918)

Another bulletin instructed motormen to pull all the way around the loop, leaving enough space to accommodate three cars without blocking the Gary–New Duluth through cars. To speed boarding and alighting, passengers were allowed to leave and enter through the motorman's compartment, which was normally off limits to passengers.

The shipyard traffic, driven by federal contracts, was short-lived. By 1921 it had shut down, leaving behind only a modest neighborhood of company housing.

SAMPLE TRIP TO NEW DULUTH

Having cleared Point of Rocks, the car bangs over the complex switches at Garfield and Piedmont Avenues, where the Interstate line turns left and the Piedmont line diverges to the right. The track drops down a gentle grade into the West End commercial district. At 21st Avenue, the West Duluth line continues straight ahead, while the Gary–New Duluth car turns right and climbs three blocks to 3rd Street. Turning left, the car enters some of the more productive trackage in the system outside downtown Duluth. This is a blue-collar neighborhood with houses, apartments, churches, and factories. The car stops almost every block, discharging passengers and frequently picking up people. At 34th Avenue it passes under the Duluth, Missabe & Northern ore docks, and the street name changes to Grand Avenue. At 44th Avenue is Denfield High School, a major traffic generator. At Central Avenue it passes the unusual elevated West Duluth station of the Duluth, Winnipeg & Pacific Railroad. This is the West Duluth commercial district, and a streetcar branch makes a sharp right turn onto 57th Avenue.

Half of the cars that travel beyond 57th turn at the Fairmont Park loop at 71st Avenue, where the Duluth Zoo adds to weekend ridership. This is the end of continuous development. The tracks shift to the side of Grand Avenue, which is also Highway 23. The motorman puts the controller in the highest notch, and the car accelerates to its maximum speed, probably about 35 to 40 miles per hour (there is no speedometer). No longer running in pavement, the noise from the wheels lessens from a hollow rumble to more of a metallic hiss, punctuated by the clickety-clack across the rail joints.

It's the afternoon rush hour. The car left downtown with a standing load. Most of those riders were dropped off in West Duluth, but the car has almost filled again with workers headed for the Morgan Park steel plant. The car rocks and sways along the highway without stopping for several minutes. Several passengers alight at Riverside, the old company town built by the now defunct shipyard. A few blocks later the car passes the electrical substation and turn loop at 92nd Avenue West. Curving south on 93rd Avenue, it ducks under a concrete arch railroad bridge and enters Morgan Park.

Now running in the grassy median of S-curving 88th Avenue, it enters the company town of houses and apartments, all constructed of concrete blocks. The larger houses of management are to the left, the workers' duplexes, row houses, and apartments to the right. The first major stop is at the streetcar waiting station at Beverly Street, next to a large concrete-block church. As 88th Avenue straightens out, the car stops at every corner to discharge commuters from downtown.

The street ends at the steel plant gate, where the car almost empties out. There is a turn loop straight ahead for extra cars to wait for the rush when the shifts change. A few workers board for the short trip home to Gary and New Duluth. The car abruptly turns right and follows another curving street west out of Morgan Park. This is the back of the neighborhood, where the streets were laid out but the houses never built. Soon the side-of-road track is back among the weeds and brush, ducking under the railroad again and headed back to Highway 23.

Reaching the highway that runs along the base of Spirit Mountain, the track turns left alongside it. Since it left downtown, the car has run on double track, one for each direction. Now it narrows to a single track because there is usually only a single car on this far-flung end of the line. More passengers alight at the Universal Portland Cement plant that was built by U.S. Steel as part of the steel plant complex and fronts on Commonwealth Avenue.

After passing under the Duluth, Missabe & Northern railroad bridge, which connects the Iron Range to the steel plant and Superior, the single track shifts to the center of Commonwealth Avenue, the main drag of Gary–New Duluth. After climbing a short rise, the remaining passengers alight a few at a time on this last mile. Finally, the car reaches the wye at McCuen Street, 12 miles from downtown and 18 miles from Lester Park where the trip started. The Fond du Lac bus is waiting for a small number of connecting passengers.

Morgan Park offered every amenity, including this streetcar waiting station at the corner of 88th Street and Beverly Street. Ca. 1925. Kathryn A. Martin Library, University of Minnesota Duluth, Archives and Special Collections.

No. Boul. looking south between Spirit Lake Transfer Ry. & 5th Street.
3:20 P.M. 12-1-22
F.T.M.

Of all the gray concrete-block buildings in Morgan Park, the most sophisticated, and therefore the most unlikely looking, was the United Protestant Church. Streetcars ran in the grass median through the planned community. 1922.

Streetcars traveled along 88th Street, Morgan Park's main street, past the different styles of employee housing ranging from single family to duplexes to apartment blocks. All were constructed from the same unpainted concrete blocks, visible at right, which were manufactured at the nearby cement plant. Ca. 1925. Kathryn A. Martin Library, University of Minnesota Duluth, Archives and Special Collections.

Rounding the curve on 88th Street, the steel plant at the far end of the street came into view. Ca. 1925. Minnesota Historical Society.

A turn loop was located at the plant gate and extra streetcars started there for the change in shifts. The rest continued on to Gary and New Duluth. Ca. 1935.

Looking west on Commonwealth Ave. from point west of 96th Ave. W. 2:00 P.M. 8/05/22. E.T.M.

Commonwealth Ave. looking north at pole 1921. 5:15 PM. Oct. 1927

Commonwealth Avenue makes a left-hand turn at the base of the hillside, joining Highway 23. The cement plant entrance is at right, seen in 1918. Turn 90 degrees to the right, and the proximity to the steel mill in 1927 becomes clear.

Looking north near

The line ended in New Duluth, 12 miles from downtown, pictured in 1922 and ca. 1935. Passengers could transfer to a shuttle bus to reach Fond du Lac, which was even farther. Kathryn A. Martin Library, University of Minnesota Duluth, Archives and Special Collections.

THE SUPERIOR LINES

INTERSTATE

YEARS OF OPERATION:
1897 to 1935

SERVICE FREQUENCY:
10 minutes all day; 20 minutes all day in later years

The Interstate line that connected Duluth and Superior was definitely a candidate for the most interesting streetcar operation anywhere. It was the longest of Minnesota's four interstate streetcars (the others were Fargo–Moorhead, Grand Forks–East Grand Forks, and Wahpeton–Breckenridge). What set it apart was the complex and sometimes problematic crossing of the harbor.

In the early days, crossing the harbor was neither easy nor convenient. At first there was only ferry service. In the winter the harbor froze, so the ferries were replaced with sleds. The Northern Pacific Railroad built the first bridge across the harbor between Duluth and Superior in 1885. In 1887, short-line passenger train service was inaugurated every 30 minutes from early in the morning until midnight. There was no road bridge, so anyone traveling across the harbor had to buy a train ticket or take one of several competing ferries.

After Duluth's and Superior's fledgling horsecar lines electrified in 1890, connecting them across the harbor became the goal. There were major obstacles: Duluth's streetcars ran on standard gauge tracks, while Superior had retained the narrow gauge inherited from its horse cars, and there was no bridge that could accommodate streetcars.

On the Duluth side of the bay, a line opened

Before the opening of the Interstate Bridge in 1897, a ferry shuttled between the ends of the streetcar lines on Rice's Point and Connor's Point. Kathryn A. Martin Library, University of Minnesota Duluth, Archives and Special Collections.

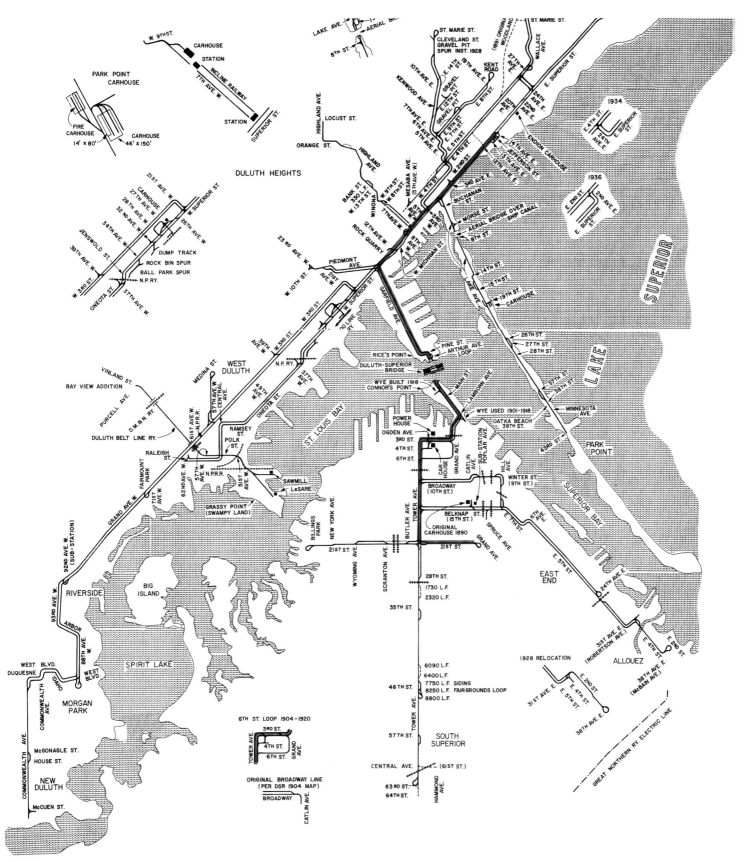

For three winters, from 1894 to 1897, a trestle was built across the ice from Connor's Point to Rice's Point. The smaller, lighter narrow-gauge Superior cars ran over it, and passengers transferred to the larger, standard-gauge Duluth cars on the Minnesota side. The sketch is from the *Duluth News Tribune* in December 1894, showing the Duluth end of the ice bridge. Kathryn A. Martin Library, University of Minnesota Duluth, Archives and Special Collections.

Inter-City Street Car Bridge.

in 1892 on Garfield Avenue, running the length of Rice's Point. That same year Superior Rapid Transit Railway Company reached the tip of Connor's Point via 3rd Street, Lamborn Avenue, and Main Street. In 1893, DSR began running the ferry boat *Estelle* between Rice's Point and the south end of the Tower Bay slip near 3rd and Tower Avenue. The boat made an intermediate stop at Connor Point and connected with Superior streetcars at both locations. Meanwhile Superior Rapid Transit had its own arrangement with a ferry operator to run from Connor Point all the way to downtown Duluth.

When the harbor froze over in December 1893, halting ferry service, DSR operated an electric ferry sled. This ingenious device was an enclosed streetcar-like body on a scow hull mounted on runners. An electric motor on the shore turned a drum around which was wrapped a cable that pulled the sled back and forth across the ice.

The following winter a different method of crossing the ice was employed. After the harbor froze, Superior Rapid Transit built a temporary wood trestle across the ice. It carried the lighter-weight Superior cars, which met the Duluth cars at the south end of Rice's Point. The trestle served during the winters of 1894–95, 1895–96, and 1896–97, being rebuilt each winter. According to a newspaper account, "The bridge is 1200 feet long built upon piling and pontooned at the vessel channel which could not be obstructed by pile or other permanent obstacles."

> *Yesterday afternoon for the first time one of the cars on the Superior line came to this side of the bay with its load of passengers and landed them at the wharf where last summer the [ferry] Lindrup used to discharge its passengers. People who last winter crossed the Rice's Point channel in the car pulled by a cable will not be slow to appreciate the greater convenience and dispatch provided this winter. Last year there were two changes of cars and passengers who were not initiated were inclined to look askance on the queer craft which was to carry them across the ice, and to wonder what would happen if it were to break through into the water. Now there will be only one change of cars.* (Duluth News Tribune, *December 1894*)

The Great Northern Railway finally opened its interstate bridge on September 1, 1897, connecting Rice's Point with Connor's Point. The bridge was a swing span that allowed lake boats to access the inner portion of the harbor. Trains occupied the center section. Separate wood-planked roadways with streetcar tracks in each direction were hung on the outsides of the main trusses. Once the line was open across the bridge, about 600 feet of track to the former ferry terminal at the tip of Rice's Point was abandoned.

The Interstate Bridge opened in 1897, but passengers had to change cars at the Superior end of the bridge until the Superior tracks were widened to standard gauge in 1902. Collection of Peter Bonesteel.

Streetcar service across the bridge did not immediately mean through service between the cities. The Duluth and Superior systems still used different track gauges, so passengers had to change cars at the Superior end of the bridge. Superior Rapid Transit regauged its track from the bridge to Tower Avenue and 21st Street on September 30, 1898. However, through service to Duluth, jointly operated by both companies, did not begin until March 28, 1899. It took until July 8, 1902, to finish converting the rest of the Superior streetcar lines to standard gauge.

The Interstate line began on the east end of downtown Duluth and passed through downtown on Superior Street, track it shared with every other line in Duluth except for the isolated Park Point and Highland lines. It left Superior Street at Garfield Avenue and served the rail terminals, grain elevators, coal docks, and industries of Rice's Point, then crossed the harbor on the Interstate Bridge.

On the Superior side the cars traveled several blocks on Connor Point before crossing another swing span that carried Lamborn Avenue over the Howard's Pocket ship channel. Traveling west on 3rd Street through an industrial area, the line reached Tower Avenue, the commercial spine of Superior. Except for some residential development at the south end of the line in Superior, the Interstate was unusual for serving almost nothing but commercial and industrial neighborhoods.

At various times, the Interstate line was through-routed in Superior with the East End line, the South Superior line, and the East 21st Street line. In Duluth it was sometimes extended east, through-routed with the Crosley line. Through routing with the Crosley and Superior East End lines was terminated because of delays on the Interstate at the numerous railroad crossings and the two swing bridges. DSR informed newspapers daily of streetcar delays. According to a DSR report, on June 26, 1919, which was typical of the shipping season, bridge openings caused nine delays of 6 to 36 minutes.

The Interstate line had built-in reliability problems because it crossed two swing bridges and six railroads. During the shipping season, the Duluth–Superior bridge across the harbor opened about 30 to 40 times on a typical day, totaling about four hours of closure. DSR kept track of delays. During January 1930, with the lake frozen over, the Interstate line averaged only two daily delays of more than five minutes each. In May, the worst month that year, an average day saw 10 streetcars delayed more than five minutes.

Since there was no way to predict these delays, DSR set up contingency plans. Turnarounds were built at each end of the bridge permitting cars to reverse direction. Telephones were installed so motormen and conductors could inform the streetcar dispatcher of the delay and fill-in service could be arranged. A company memo from 1925 authorized crews to short-line themselves without consulting a supervisor at particular points on the line depending on the length of the delay.

Railroad crossings were less of a problem, as most were industry spur tracks. Even so, the conductor had to dismount at each one and flag the car across, which slowed the schedule and increased operating cost.

All across the country, buses appeared in the 1920s to compete with the streetcars. In Duluth, as in the Twin Cities, the streetcar company's strategy was to buy up the buses and run them alongside the streetcars. The Superior White Company started a service that basically duplicated the Interstate Line. In 1925 the line was purchased by Northland Transportation, which wanted White's line from Duluth to Ashland, Wisconsin. A week later, Northland sold the Duluth to Superior service to the streetcar company, which ran it as the Duluth–Superior Coach Company. At some unknown date in the 1920s, another competitor, the Gopher-Badger Bus Company, also began running between Duluth and Superior. DSR's subsid-

In addition to delaying the streetcars with its frequent openings for ships, the Interstate Bridge suffered from collisions. The worst occurred in 1924, when it was knocked off its piers into the channel. Temporary passenger railroad trains ran between the Twin Ports via the nearby Minnesota and Wisconsin draws, and ferries connected the streetcars on the two shores. The Interstate Bridge was returned to service in only four weeks.

In about 1924, buses began running in direct competition with the Interstate streetcar line. DSR bought out the operator but kept running the duplicate service. Although they charged a higher fare, buses offered a faster trip between Duluth and Superior, due to fewer stops and higher speed limits. Here one lays over on Michigan Street in Duluth in 1934.

iary Superior Bus Company purchased Gopher-Badger in December 1931 and discontinued the competing service. A month later, Superior City Bus Company changed its name to Duluth–Superior City Bus Company.

On November 21, 1924, the steamer *Merton S. Farr* hit the Interstate Bridge, knocking the fixed span into the bay. Ferry service began November 23. The railroads implemented hourly passenger train service as an alternative. The bridge was repaired, and streetcar operations resumed December 19.

The Interstate was a transit company's dream, a route with bidirectional ridership at all times of the day, a separate fare for each city, and, at least until about 1930, no extra cars added for the rush hour.

Ridership counts taken in 1926 show peaks of rush-hour ridership in both directions, but it is clear that more Superior residents commuted to Duluth than the other way around. Bidirectional ridership in both rush hours was quite different from most of the streetcar lines in the Twin Ports. Economically, the Interstate benefited from charging a double fare, although this was partially offset by the expense of bridge tolls.

In 1926 the line segments that made up the Interstate line carried these daily ridership totals:

6,919	*Garfield Avenue*
5,497	*Connor's Point to Tower Avenue and 21st Street*
2,186	*South Superior (Tower Avenue from 21st Street to 63rd Street)*
712	*East 21st Street line*

Daily ridership crossing the Interstate Bridge was about 4,100. There were over 5,700 people on the cars when they passed Garfield Avenue and Michigan Street, a block from the West Duluth main line. This reflected the fact that Garfield Avenue, with all its employers, was a destination in itself.

As it did everywhere, the proliferation of the automobile ate into ridership all through the 1920s. Bus competition didn't help. A 1926 load check shows the competing Interstate bus carrying more than 800 daily riders over the harbor bridge, compared to about 4,100 on the streetcars. In 1926 the average streetcar crossed the bridge with 21 passengers aboard.

The Depression hit the Twin Ports hard, dependent as they were on the steel and lumber industries. According to one text, Duluth experienced 40 percent unemployment, the highest among American cities of 100,000 or more. Ridership crossing the Interstate Bridge dropped 40 percent from 1930 to 1931. Furthermore, 1931 ridership was 60 percent below ridership in 1926. It's easy to see why the streetcars were imperiled.

Until 1929, the City of Duluth set lower speed limits for streetcars than for automobiles. On Superior Street through downtown, autos were permitted 15 to 20 miles per hour, while streetcars were restricted to 12 miles per hour. On Garfield Avenue it was 20 miles per hour for cars, 12 miles per hour for streetcars. This put streetcars at a disadvantage when competing with both autos and buses. It also increased operating costs, because more streetcars were required to run the slower schedule. Streetcar travel time from 3rd Avenue West in Duluth to Tower Avenue and Belknap Street in Superior was 36 minutes in 1919. The competing Interstate bus, which made no local stops between the harbor bridge and downtown Duluth, covered the same distance in 24 minutes. In 1929, the separate streetcar speed limit was eliminated, and Interstate streetcars reduced their travel time to about 28 minutes. By that late date, however, the public's impression that streetcars were much slower was established, and auto drivers were unlikely to be convinced otherwise.

Interstate line speed limits within Duluth.

	AUTOMOBILE	STREET CAR PRE–1929	STREET CAR 1929
SUPERIOR STREET, 3RD AVENUE EAST–LAKE AVENUE	15	12	15
SUPERIOR STREET, LAKE AVENUE–3RD AVENUE WEST	20	12	20
SUPERIOR STREET, 3RD AVENUE WEST–GARFIELD	15	12	15
GARFIELD AVENUE	20	12	20

SAMPLE TRIP FROM DULUTH TO SUPERIOR

Pulling out of the wye at 3rd Avenue East, the Interstate car swings onto Superior Street behind a Woodland car headed for West Duluth. The first few passengers boarded while the car was sitting at its layover on the wye. As it passes through the downtown section of Superior Street, there are crowds of passengers waiting on every corner. They may select any of six different car lines, and three or four board the Interstate car at each stop.

At Lake Avenue, the rails of the short Aerial Bridge line join from the left. At 3rd Avenue West is the junction with the East 4th Street, East 8th Street, and Kenwood lines, which drop down a steep grade from the right. This is the busiest spot in the entire system, and a starter is stationed here all day to monitor on-time performance, sell tokens, and keep the lines on schedule. He occupies a small wooden booth on the sidewalk.

This is the heart of downtown, and your car waits at each corner for two ahead of it to finish loading. After passing the Union and Soo Line Depots, at 5th Avenue West and 7th Avenue West, the first passengers alight to transfer to the Incline. Its base station sits behind the sidewalk, and you can look straight up the hill at the Incline tracks. Superior Street passes the 8th Avenue West loop where streetcars stage; one is already waiting to

Rice's Point was gritty and industrial, with rail yards on the west side of Garfield Avenue. In two places rail industrial spurs crossed the streetcar line to serve grain elevators, and they were a periodic source of delay to the already delay-prone Interstate cars. Kathryn A. Martin Library, University of Minnesota Duluth, Archives and Special Collections.

leave for Lester Park. Your car swings left around the Point of Rocks. There is a wye at 12th Avenue West, the tail of which reaches around the corner so company work cars can access a rock quarry.

There is a complex junction at Garfield Avenue. The West Duluth, Grand Avenue, and Gary–New Duluth cars continue straight ahead on Superior Street, Piedmont cars angle uphill to the right, and the Interstate car turns left to head for Rice's Point and the Interstate Bridge. A long viaduct

This overview of Rice's Point in 1902 shows how the Interstate cars left Superior Street, crossed numerous railroad tracks on the viaduct (*lower center*), then traveled the length of the Point on Garfield Avenue, which was full of industry, grain terminals, and railroad facilities. The Interstate Bridge is visible in the distance.

Looking South on Garfield Ave. from about
300 at 9:15 A.M. Feb. 12, 1917. E.T.M.

The streetcars ran in the pair of one-way roadways that hung on each side of the bridge, while trains passed through the center spans. At each end they climbed or descended wooden ramps while the railroad continued on trestlework. That trestlework burned in 1918 and had not yet been replaced when this photograph looking across the harbor toward Superior was taken. The close-up of the Duluth off-ramp shows part of the turning loop that streetcars could use when the bridge was opened for ships. Opposite top: Kathryn A. Martin Library, University of Minnesota Duluth, Archives and Special Collections. Opposite below: Ca. 1905. Minnesota Historical Society. **This page:** Courtesy of the Douglas County Historical Society.

This aerial photograph was taken in 1954. The Interstate Bridge is the one closer to the camera and the fixed span on the Superior end has been replaced with a trestle. However, it still conveys the magnitude of the harbor crossing. Minneapolis and St. Paul Newspaper Negative Collection, Minnesota Historical Society.

The Superior end of the bridge emptied into Main Street on Connor's Point. The railroad approach to the bridge is at right. 1915. Courtesy of the Douglas County Historical Society.

carries the car over a maze of railroad tracks and down onto Garfield Avenue, which runs between rail yards on the right and docks and warehouses on the left, almost two miles of gritty industry. A pair of railroad spurs that access the Pittsburgh Coal Company dock and grain elevators are crossed at grade. Each time the car makes a safety stop, the conductor dismounts, walks ahead, flags the car across, and reboards. This happens six times during this trip.

A few passengers headed for work get off along Garfield Avenue, while others board for the trip to Superior. Just before the bridge, the track in the street swings left for two blocks to reach the Interstate Bridge. Your car makes an abrupt right turn alongside the railroad approach to the bridge, which is on a long trestle that comes in from the left. A loop track splits off to the left and circles under the bridge approach. Its purpose is to turn streetcars before they cross the bridge, useful for short-lining cars when the bridge isn't open. The railroad tracks occupy the center of the bridge. The wood plank roadway with the streetcar track in it rides an outrigger that hangs on the side of the bridge. There's a compulsory stop at the toll collector's booth, then a hollow rumble as the car slows to the required four miles per hour, and the wheels bang across the joints onto the bridge's swing span. Another safety stop to make sure the car hasn't derailed on the joint, and the car rumbles across the span and down the ramp to Connor's Point.

Although taken years after the streetcars and the Lamborn Avenue bridge were both gone (the center pier was still in place), the route of the streetcar down Connor's Point and across Howard's Pocket is highlighted. Courtesy of the Douglas County Historical Society.

The wood-decked Lamborn Avenue bridge swung on a center pier to let ships pass. 1932.

Looking N.W. from Cumming Ave.
35 paces south of southerly curb
on 3rd St.
3:20 P.M. 10-12-22
E.T.M.

3rd St. looking W. from John. Av.
10 a.m. 10.29.15. H.H. Brown.

After crossing yet another railroad track on Lamborn Avenue (now Grand Avenue), the Interstate line turned right onto 3rd Street, which was still part of the industrial area directly behind the waterfront. 1915 and 1922. Courtesy of the Douglas County Historical Society.

Now on the Superior side, the streetcar passes under the railroad's approach trestle and rejoins the other track in the center of Main Street for a couple of blocks. To the left fronting the bay are a coal dock and some warehouses. Park Point stretches along the far side of the bay and beyond that is the open lake. On the right is the Howard's Pocket ship channel leading to a shipyard and grain elevators. The car turns right onto Lamborn Avenue, pausing before banging over the Soo Line's track leading to its Superior freight house. Then it crosses the ship channel on another wood-decked swing bridge and passes the shipyard where numerous lakers are tied up. Angling left for two blocks, the car travels past elevators and docks before crossing the tracks of the Lake Superior Terminal and Transfer. Just beyond the tracks comes a right turn onto 3rd Street, lined with industrial and commercial buildings. At Ogden Street it passes the streetcar power house and the Superior carhouse.

A block later comes the left turn onto Tower Avenue, Superior's commercial spine. In two blocks the 6th Street loop, used by some Superior local cars, diverges to the left. A few blocks later the car crosses two more tracks next to the Soo Line and Omaha Road depots and enters the heart of downtown Superior. With two swing bridges and six railroad grade crossings, there's a good chance that something will delay the car, and as a regular rider you're relieved each time it doesn't happen. Soon the Broadway line diverges to the left, and the Union Depot is visible two blocks to the right. Now passengers get off at every corner. Belknap Street is the heart of the Superior system, with a starter based in a sidewalk booth to keep the cars on schedule. This is the main transfer point to the Broadway-Billings Park and East End-Allouez cars. Numerous passengers alight, and a small number get on. The East End–Allouez line, the heaviest local service in Superior, splits off to the left, and at 21st Street the Billings Park line turns

Superior. Wis. 1906

right. The South Superior line continues straight ahead. At various times in history, the South Superior line ran by itself, but much of the time it was through-routed with the Interstate line. After the East 21st Street line opened in 1922, Interstate cars on a 10-minute frequency alternated to serve the 21st Street and South Superior lines every 20 minutes.

On this trip, the Interstate car turns left for its short, one mile run east to the loop at 21st Street and Grand Avenue. This last stretch is lined with houses. The turn loop sits in an open field next to another set of railroad tracks. The Interstate car has traveled seven miles and carried 32 passengers.

From 3rd Street, Interstate and East End–Allouez cars, as well as all cars pulling out of the 4th Street and Ogden Avenue carbarn, turned onto Tower Avenue. This was the north end of the downtown commercial area in 1906. Courtesy of the Douglas County Historical Society.

TOWER AVENUE

YEARS OF OPERATION:
Horse car, 1889 to 1890; electrified in 1890; streetcars abandoned in 1935

Downtown Superior extended along Tower Avenue from 3rd Street to 21st Street. At the north end were the three railroad stations. Although the operation of the Superior lines changed over the years, most traveled some distance along Tower Avenue to access the heart of the commercial district. The intersection of Tower and Belknap Street was the primary transfer point between all the lines, and at one time featured a transfer station as well as a permanent starter who occupied a small booth on the sidewalk and supervised the entire Superior system.

The operational hub of the Superior system was the intersection of Tower Avenue and Belknap Street. All three lines passed through it, under the watchful eye of the starter in his booth on the northwest corner. Lights mounted on the booth told the motormen whether or not to hold for transfer connections. This photograph is one of the few showing the 1925-built lightweight cars in service. Kathryn A. Martin Library, University of Minnesota Duluth, Archives and Special Collections.

Although distorted by the camera, this panorama captures Tower Avenue at its most prosperous in the 1920s. At left center is the Broadway intersection, notable for the illuminated steel arches spanning it. Hibbard photograph, Library of Congress Prints and Photographs Division.

THE
COLUMBIA

TOWER AVENUE "THE WHITE WAY", SUPERIOR, WI

Street Scene, Superior, Wis.

Erected when electricity was still a novelty, the illuminated arch over the intersection of Tower Avenue and Broadway was a Superior landmark from 1902 to 1920. Collection of Peter Bonesteel.

PASSENGERS ENTERING DOWNTOWN SUPERIOR IN THE MORNING PEAK HOUR

PASSENGERS	LINE
180	INTERSTATE
35	BROADWAY
70	BILLINGS PARK
140	EAST END
50	21ST STREET
125	SOUTH SUPERIOR
600	**TOTAL**

COR. TOWER AVE. & BROADWAY, SUPERIOR. WIS.

Two views look down Tower Avenue toward Belknap Street from a block away. From the south at 16th Street, the turreted Hotel Superior commands the southeast corner. Courtesy of the Douglas County Historical Society.

19th St + Tower Av
4 PM. 6.23.14 H.

South of Belknap Street, Tower Avenue transitioned from commercial to residential. This is 19th Street in 1914. Courtesy of the Douglas County Historical Society.

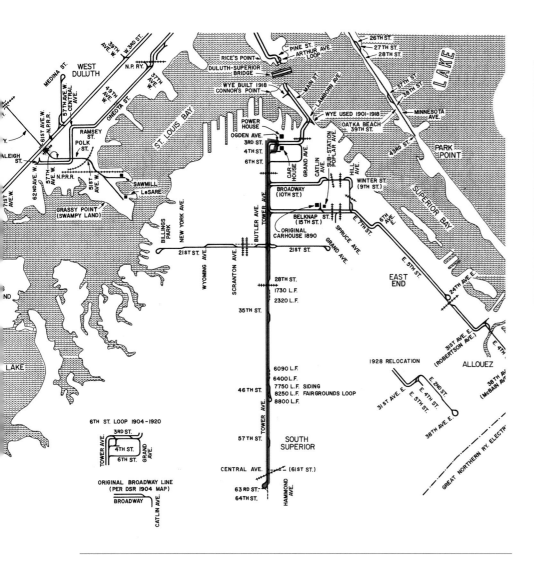

The only traffic generator before reaching South Superior was the Tri-State Fairgrounds at about 48th Street, and that was once a year. The bottom photograph looks south in 1930, and shows the fairgrounds at left and the double track to serve the extra streetcars during fair time.

SOUTH SUPERIOR

YEARS OF OPERATION:
1892 to 1931

SERVICE FREQUENCY:
20 minutes all day

South Superior is a rail junction at 61st Street and Tower Avenue surrounded by a modest cluster of homes and a small business district. To reach South Superior, the streetcars traversed about three miles of Tower Avenue that was completely devoid of development. The sole traffic generator along the line south of 28th Street was the annual Douglas County Fair at 46th Street. In 1924 the Great Northern Railway arranged to have its first locomotive, the 1862-vintage *William Crooks*, displayed at the fair, which it

reached via the streetcar tracks. That locomotive is displayed today at the Lake Superior Railroad Museum in the Duluth Union Depot.

The line was a clear case of boosterism outweighing business sense. One sign of this is that it was built as double track and was converted to single track with passing sidings in 1901. From 1926 to 1931 the South Superior line was through-routed with the Interstate line to reach downtown Duluth.

The extension down Tower Avenue to South Superior was one of the least productive segments of the DSR system. From about 28th Street to 55th Street there was nothing but open country. This is 30th Street in 1915. Courtesy of the Douglas County Historical Society.

This is the wye at 63rd Street, the end of the South Superior line in 1913.

S. Sup. Wye looking East.   Apl. 25. 13 at 3. P.M. By H.H.Brow.

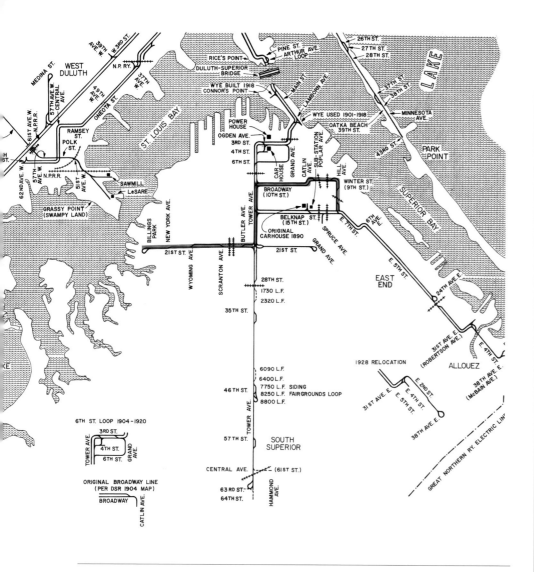

Map labels (reading roughly top to bottom, left to right):

WEST DULUTH
MEDINA ST.
W. 3RD ST.
W. 3RD ST.
N.P. RY.
57TH AVE. W.
CENTRAL AVE.
49 TH
AVE.
ONEOTA STREET
57TH AVE. W.
N.P.R.R.
RAMSEY ST.
POLK ST.
51 ST AVE. W.
62ND AVE. W.
61ST AVE. W. N.P.R.R.
SAWMILL LeSARE
GRASSY POINT (SWAMPY LAND)
BILLINGS PARK
NEW YORK AVE.
WYOMING AVE.
SCRANTON AVE.
BUTLER AVE.
TOWER AVE.
21ST ST.
21ST ST.
28TH ST.
1730 L.F.
2320 L.F.
35TH ST.
46TH ST.
6090 L.F.
6400 L.F.
7750 L.F. SIDING
8250 L.F. FAIRGROUNDS LOOP
8800 L.F.
TOWER AVE.
57TH ST.
CENTRAL AVE. (61ST ST.)
63RD ST.
64TH ST.
HAMMOND AVE.
SOUTH SUPERIOR

ST. LOUIS BAY
POWER HOUSE
OGDEN AVE.
3RD ST.
4TH ST.
6TH ST.
CAR HOUSE
CATLIN AVE.
GRAND AVE.
BROADWAY (10TH ST.)
BELKNAP ST. (15TH ST.)
ORIGINAL CARHOUSE 1890
SPRUCE AVE.
GRAND AVE.

RICE'S POINT
PINE ST. ARTHUR AVE.
DULUTH-SUPERIOR BRIDGE
WYE BUILT 1918
CONNOR'S POINT
MAIN ST.
LAMBORN AVE.
SUB. STATION POPLAR AVE.
HILL AVE.
WINTER ST. (9TH ST.)
E. 7TH ST.
6TH AVE. E.
EAST END
24TH AVE. E.
31ST AVE. E. (ROBERTSON AVE.)
1928 RELOCATION
31ST AVE. E.
E. 2ND ST.
E. 4TH ST.
E. 5TH ST.
38TH AVE. E.
E. 4TH AVE. E.
38TH AVE. E. (McBAIN AVE.)
ALLOUEZ
GREAT NORTHERN RY. ELECTRIC LINE

26TH ST.
27TH ST.
28TH ST.
37TH ST.
38TH ST.
MINNESOTA AVE.
OATKA BEACH 39TH ST.
43RD ST.
WYE USED 1901-1918
PARK POINT
LAKE
SUPERIOR BAY

6TH ST. LOOP 1904-1920
3RD ST.
TOWER AVE.
4TH ST.
6TH ST.
GRAND AVE.

ORIGINAL BROADWAY LINE (PER DSR 1904 MAP)
BROADWAY
CATLIN AVE.

BILLINGS PARK AND BROADWAY

BILLINGS PARK YEARS OF OPERATION:
1892 to 1935

BILLINGS PARK SERVICE FREQUENCY:
20 minutes all day

BROADWAY YEARS OF OPERATION:
1892 to 1931

BROADWAY SERVICE FREQUENCY:
20 minutes all day

The 21st Street viaduct over the railroad corridor that paralleled Tower Avenue at first only crossed some of the tracks. It was later lengthened to cross all of them. 1914. Courtesy of the Douglas County Historical Society.

These two lines, the most lightly patronized in Superior, were through-routed with each other for most of their existence. They branched east and west off the Tower Avenue commercial spine. The Billings Park line on West 21st Street crossed over the wide throat of rail yards to the west of Tower Avenue to access a residential neighborhood and a large city park. For a few years it was called the Steel Plant line, after the U.S. Cast Iron Pipe plant located a half-mile to the north. An actual extension to the steel plant was contemplated but never happened. Inbound cars turned north on Tower Avenue for a mile, made connections with the other Superior lines at Tower Avenue and Belknap Street, then turned east onto Broadway to serve two miles of a residential neighborhood as well as the city hall.

The Broadway line initially extended east on Broadway to Catlin Avenue, then south on Catlin to Belknap Street. There it met the East End line, terminating at the original carhouse. In 1900 all maintenance and repair work other than simple running repairs was transferred to the main DSR shop in Duluth. The original Superior carhouse was replaced in 1902 by a new facility at 4th Street and Ogden Avenue. In 1917, the Catlin Avenue track was removed. The Broadway line was extended east on Winter Street across the Omaha Road and Soo Line tracks to serve a rather isolated residential neighborhood. It then turned south on Hill Avenue, terminating at a junction with the East End line on Belknap. The only real traffic generators on the Broadway line were City Hall and St. Mary's Hospital at Clough Avenue.

Photographs of the Billings Park line are rare. This appears to be the loop at the west end of the line ca. 1905.

The Broadway line passed the old city hall at Hammond Avenue, ca. 1928.

Hill Ave. & 12th St. from point 57 paces north of roadway. 3:45 P.M. 8-14-22.

E.T.M.

The east end of the Broadway line followed the right-of-way of Hill Avenue, but there was no actual street when these photos were taken in 1923. The end of the line is three blocks ahead at Belknap Street, where passengers could transfer to the East End–Allouez line. Courtesy of the Douglas County Historical Society.

Looking north on Hill Ave. from
12th St. 3:45 P.M. 8-14-23
E.T.M.

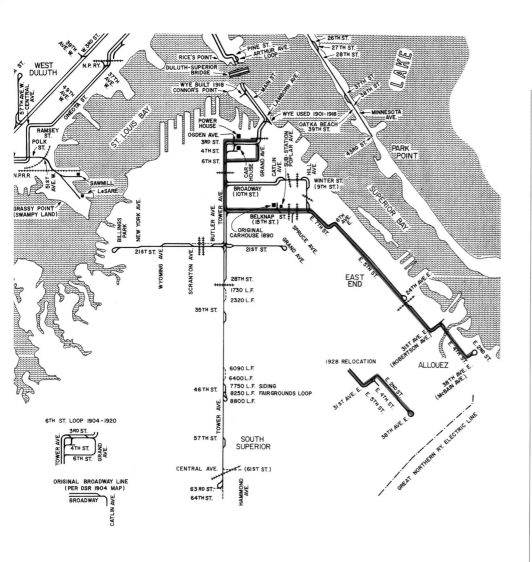

EAST END AND ALLOUEZ

YEARS OF OPERATION:
1892 to 1935

SERVICE FREQUENCY:
10 minutes all day, 20 minutes to Allouez.

The East End line was the longest and busiest of the Superior local lines. Like an outrigger, Superior's oblong East End neighborhood stretches along Superior Bay to the ore docks in the suburb of Allouez. This was where the city originated, before its downtown relocated to Tower Avenue. The ore docks stimulated reverse-commute ridership. Students rode the cars to Central High School on Belknap Street at Grand Avenue, and to East High School on 5th Street at 18th Avenue East. The State Normal School, later the State Teachers College, and today the University of Wis-

The north end of the line made a large one-way loop via 6th Street, Grand Avenue, 3rd Street, and Tower Avenue that was usually the north end of the East End–Allouez line. This is 6th Street between Hammond and Cummings Avenues. 1913. Courtesy of the Douglas County Historical Society.

ng E. bet. Hammond & Cummings Aves. 11 30/A.M. 11.13.13 H.H.Brown.

After running through downtown
on Tower Avenue, the East End and
Allouez cars turned east on Belknap
Street. This view looks east at Bax-
ter Avenue. Courtesy of the Douglas
County Historical Society.

consin–Superior, was located a block south of the line on Belknap Street. St. Francis Hospital was two blocks off the line at 23rd Avenue East.

The line was extended to Allouez in 1907 via a rather spindly bridge that carried 4th Street over the Nemadji River. In 1928, the bridge was condemned, and the line was relocated to a new bridge on 2nd Street, which became Highway 2.

From 1913 to 1927, at the loop in Allouez, passengers could transfer to the Itasca shuttle bus. Great Northern Railway employees, headed for the shops and rail yard that staged ore cars for the docks, transferred to a former Minneapolis streetcar operated by the railroad to reach the yard, over a mile away. It ran from 1913 to 1927, replacing a steam locomotive and coaches. It in turn was replaced by a gasoline-powered railcar.

In 1925 and again in 1931–32, the East End line was through-routed with the Interstate line to reach Duluth. However, this combination proved unreliable due to the swing bridges.

7th St looking N.W. from G. Av. 10:30 A.M. 11.11.15 H.H. Brown.

7 St looking St from
a point N. of 9. Ave.
10:35 A.M. H. H. E. M. Brown.

In 1915 the camera looks both ways on 7th Street from the 9th Avenue East intersection. Opposite: Looking northwest at the curve onto Belknap Street. Courtesy of the Douglas County Historical Society.

At 25th Avenue, East 5th Street crossed the Northern Pacific Railway, which had a depot at the intersection (*at right*). Because the railroad was there first, DSR had to maintain the crossing. To reduce maintenance costs, it was common practice to narrow to a single track. 1931.

To reach Allouez in 1907, the streetcar line followed 4th Street and crossed the Nemadji River on this long bridge. It eventually proved structurally inadequate, probably the reason for the pair of 1924 photos, and the line was relocated in 1928 to the Highway 2 bridge on 2nd Street. The trestle leading to the Northern Pacific ore dock is in the distance. Above: Courtesy of the Douglas County Historical Society.

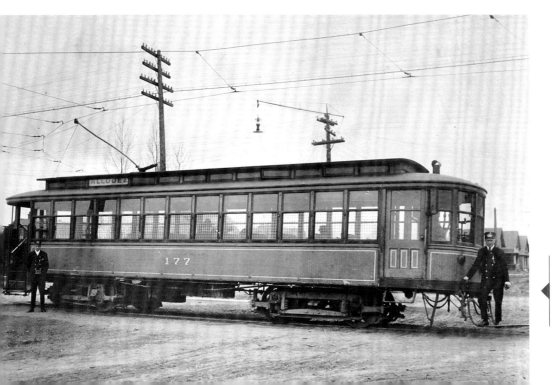

A crew lays over at the Allouez loop, ca 1912. Typically, every second car went to Allouez. Courtesy of the Douglas County Historical Society.

67 paces from 1 to 2
107 " " 1 " 3

Looking west on 4th St
107 paces east of Nemadji
River Bridge.
9:30 AM. 11/1/24
E.T.M.

Looking east on 4th St. 107 paces east
of Nemadji River Bridge.
9:30 AM. 11/1/24 E.T.M.

Franklin School (at left) and 37th Avenue are one block from the Allouez loop, directly behind the camera. This is the line that was relocated in 1928 onto 2nd Street, which is also Highway 2, when the old streetcar bridge on 4th Street was condemned. The Great Northern ore docks are behind the camera.

LINES NEVER BUILT

During the first two decades of the twentieth century, there was a frenzy of electric railway building, filling a short-distance transportation niche between the infrequent and dirty steam railroads and the horse-drawn carriage. Streetcar systems blossomed in most towns of any size, and inter-urbans—larger and faster electric cars—ran between cities that weren't too far apart. It proved to be a bubble that was punctured by the coming of the automobile.

Often examples of speculation at its worst, many proposals for electric railroads never went beyond the planning stage. Nonetheless, it is useful to recount the schemes that might have been.

San Francisco–style cable cars became widespread in the 1880s, during the horsecar era. They preceded electric cars as a viable technology by over ten years. As such, they seemed the perfect way to tackle Duluth's steep hills. In 1889, the city proposed the Highland Cable Company on Lake Avenue to serve the Central Hillside. Nothing came of it.

Once the East 9th Street line successfully climbed the eastern portion of the Central Hillside, the city proposed a West 7th Street line branching off from 6th Avenue East, with a possible connection to the Highland streetcar line at the top of the Incline. They also proposed extending the West 4th Street line through the steep neighborhood above Point of Rocks to 14th Avenue West. Before the Piedmont line was built, the city asked that it extend all the way to 13th Street, but the grades were too steep, and the line stopped at 10th Street. The highest neighborhoods located directly above downtown would remain without public transit until bus service arrived in 1929.

In 1909 a new company called the Duluth & Northern Traction was formed to serve the proposed Greysolon Farms development, to be located about two miles east of Woodland. Theirs was a somewhat unusual combination of housing and an actual farm that would supply food to the city. They proposed to build a four-mile connection and then use DSR tracks to bring both freight and passengers into Duluth. The DSR records contain a large file on the Greysolon proposal that runs until 1912. During that time D&NT tried multiple times to persuade city officials, but DSR was not interested, and the idea went nowhere. A 1911 newspaper story mentions the Greysolon Farms line and states that a second market garden line would extend from the north end of the Highland line.

Another extension of the Woodland Avenue line was proposed to the Homecroft neighborhood via Calvary Road. As with some of the other proposals, it was eventually accomplished with buses.

World War I brought a traffic boom to the new Morgan Park steel mill and the nearby McDougall-Duluth shipyard. A belt line was proposed to Morgan Park from Superior,crossing the St. Louis River. It never happened, but soon thereafter bus service from Superior to West Duluth was instituted over the Arrowhead Bridge.

Briefly in 1896 there was a scheme to connect Park Point to Wisconsin and to build on to Itasca, Wisconsin, thereby creating a shortcut to Duluth via the two points.

The Superior Steel Plant Traction Company was incorporated in 1912, when DSR refused to extend service directly to the West Superior steel plant. Nothing came of the new company.

It was proposed to extend the West Duluth 57th Avenue branch through Bay View Heights to the railroad town of Proctor. Bus service did the job beginning in 1937.

Superior Street through downtown was an operational bottleneck, as every downtown-bound streetcar in the system funneled through the same tracks between 12th Avenue West and 5th Avenue West. In 1919 an elevated single track was proposed above Michigan Street one block south of Superior Street. This would create a paired one-way loop with Superior Street, and streetcars would be freed from traffic congestion, at least in one direction.

Streetcars deadheading between the Duluth carhouse at Superior Street and 26th Avenue West and West Duluth, Morgan Park, or New Duluth had to backtrack east to 21st Avenue West to reach the main line. DSR contemplated a shortcut between Superior Street and Grand Avenue via Carlton Street. It would have saved a mile for each nonrevenue move, but it was never built.

Until 1925, the Northern Pacific ran a daily round-trip between Duluth and Fond du Lac with a self-powered gasoline-engine railcar. Apparently there was no freight service on the line, because the NP offered the tracks to DSR if they would continue passenger service. DSR turned to buses instead, providing a shuttle to the end of the streetcar line in New Duluth.

In 1928 the City of Duluth pushed hard for an extension off the Woodland line on 4th Street from Wallace Avenue to Ridgeland Road, just beyond Congdon Creek. DSR pointed out that only 24 homes had been built there. The primary traffic generator was East Junior High School, located two blocks east of Wallace. The compromise was to extend the East 4th Street line three blocks to a new turning loop at 4th and Wallace.

INTERURBANS

Between 1900 and 1915, electric interurban railways were all the rage. In the period before the automobile and paved roads changed transportation forever, the interurbans filled a need for frequent comfortable service over relatively short distances. Where steam railroads might offer one, two, or three trains a day, interurbans could deliver hourly service. They offered the greater convenience of multiple stops in the middle of town. Perhaps their most attractive characteristic was electric propulsion, a welcome relief from the usual soot and cinders.

Although common elsewhere in the Midwest, few interurbans established themselves in Minnesota. The Mesaba Railway ran the length of the Iron Range from Hibbing to Virginia and Gilbert. The Minneapolis, Anoka

& Cuyuna Range made it from Minneapolis to Anoka and no farther. The St. Paul Southern linked St. Paul with Hastings.

Several interurbans were planned for northern Minnesota and Wisconsin but were never built. The Superior–Cloquet Electric Railway incorporated in 1896. In 1902 the Superior Suburban Railway incorporated, intending to build south from Superior, maybe all the way to Black River Falls. In 1911, an extension of Superior streetcars was proposed from Allouez to Itasca, with the greater goal of building to Bayfield, Wisconsin. Allouez–Itasca became a shuttle bus line in 1925. As late as 1923, a line was proposed from Duluth to Thunder Bay.

The idea of a high-speed electric railway connecting the Twin Cities and Twin Ports first appeared in the form of the Minnesota Central, which organized in 1904. Nothing more was heard of the idea until the Twin City & Lake Superior incorporated in 1907 and came close to actually happening. It proposed a high-speed, double-track Arrow line. Instead of an overhead wire, power would be collected by shoes attached to the car trucks sliding along a third rail laid close to the track. This is the same technology used today by most city subway systems and some New York commuter railroads.

The route was an almost straight line of 129 miles, shorter than either the Great Northern or Northern Pacific routes, which measured 160 and 162 miles, respectively. Bypassing all intermediate towns, the nonstop trains of the new line would make the trip in two hours, compared to five for the steam railways. It was originally planned to terminate at Billings Park on 21st Street in Superior. Later the route was resurveyed, and the proposed terminus was shifted to 64th Street in South Superior.

Unlike the other interurban schemes, this one actually achieved some construction. According to a 1910 *Electric Railway Journal*, 50 miles of right-of-way was graded. In 1911 the Soo Line opened a third direct railroad between Minneapolis and Duluth through western Wisconsin, a distance of 166 miles. Travel times on expresses dropped to 3.5 hours. With the market saturated with faster service, the interurban venture appears to have ceased business in 1911.

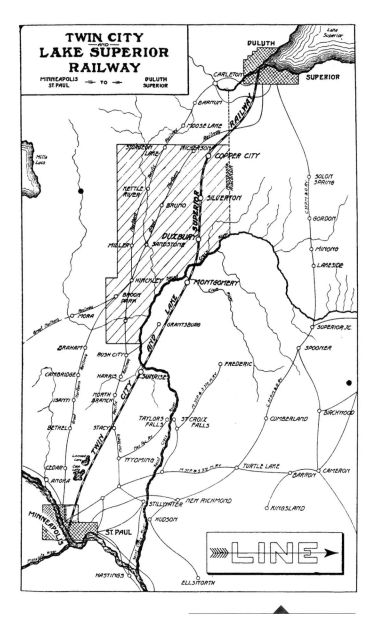

The Twin City & Lake Superior tried to build a high-speed, nonstop electric railroad between the Twin Cities and Twin Ports. This map appeared in a promotional flyer. Fifty miles of right-of-way were graded, then the money ran out.

6

INTRUDERS

 *Jitneys, Buses, and
the End of an Era*

With Lake Superior as a backdrop, trolley buses meet on Superior Street at 8th Avenue East. In the foreground is one of a pair delivered by Pullman in 1944. They were the largest in the fleet, seating 44. An older Brill heads the other way.

As automobiles evolved from a plaything for the wealthy to a production item for the mass-es, auto owners quickly realized there was money to be made by cruising streetcar routes and of-fering rides for a fare. They were called jitneys and quickly devel-oped into an irregular transit service, often scooping up pas-sengers just ahead of the sched-uled streetcars.

In February 1915, the *Duluth Herald* ran a truly prophetic quote from H. H. Franklin, president of the Franklin Automobile Company: "Even as the horse street railway service gave way to the electric car, so the electric cars will in a great measure give way to the automobile. As crude as may be the jitney automobile bus service which is taking the cities by storm, it is the beginning of a great and radical change in transportation."

On March 14, 1915, the first two jitneys appeared on the streets of Duluth. DSR sent out its load checkers to track this new competition, so we have actual statistics on their numbers. They counted 110 jitneys competing with the streetcars by midsummer. The *Duluth Herald* put the total number at 285, with an average of 150 running each day. It reported that DSR was losing $1,000 of daily farebox revenue and that taxi fares had dropped by 80 percent due to the competition.

By mid-August the jitney count had dropped to 20 (the newspaper said 80), as "jitneurs" found the business unprofitable. Jitney operations ceased during the winter months but resumed on a lesser scale in spring 1916, when 50 appeared on the streets. Fewer still appeared in spring 1917, and by that fall the jitney craze was practically over in Duluth. In spring 1918 only "a couple" appeared. However, jitneys resurfaced from time to time for several years thereafter.

The Duluth jitneys operated primarily on Superior Street between 26th Avenue West and 15th Avenue East, running just ahead of the streetcars and picking up the short-haul passengers.

This original DSR map shows all the bus routes as of January 1, 1929. All were short shuttles, except for the two interstate lines, one of which ran via West Duluth.

YEAR	DULUTH JITNEY PASSENGERS
1915	1,261,587
1916	461,787
1917	105,992
1918	6,996
1919	0
1920	0
1921	11,925
1922	228,917
1923	337,146

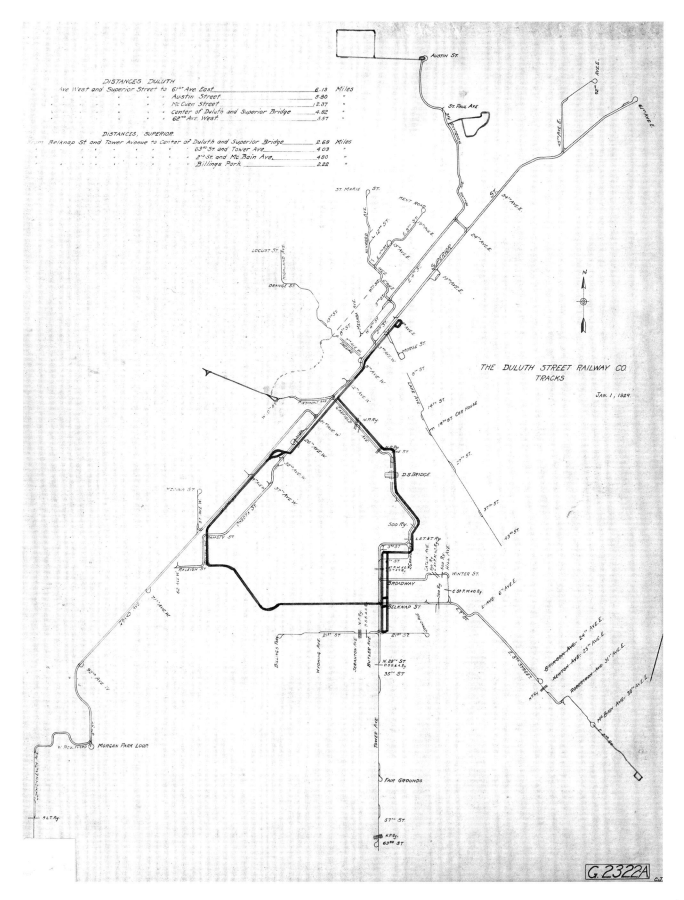

DISTANCES DULUTH
Ave West and Superior Street to 61st Ave East _____ 6.13 Miles
　　　"　　　　　"　　　　Austin Street _____ 5.80 "
　　　"　　　　　"　　　　McCuen Street _____ 12.37 "
　　　"　　　　　"　　　　Center of Duluth and Superior Bridge _____ 4.82 "
　　　"　　　　　"　　　　62nd Ave. West _____ 5.57 "

DISTANCES, SUPERIOR.
From Belknap St and Tower Avenue to Center of Duluth and Superior Bridge _____ 2.69 Miles
　　　"　　　　　"　　　　63rd St. and Tower Ave _____ 4.03 "
　　　"　　　　　"　　　　2nd St. and McBain Ave. _____ 4.80 "
　　　"　　　　　"　　　　Billings Park _____ 2.22 "

THE DULUTH STREET RAILWAY CO.
TRACKS

JAN. 1, 1929.

G.2322A

Gas buses were originally built on modified truck chassis. Hoods that projected out front were standard until the early 1930s. Kathryn A. Martin Library, University of Minnesota Duluth, Archives and Special Collections.

During their first year of operations in 1915, there were no restrictions on the jitneys, a case of technology outrunning regulation. They ran whenever and wherever they wished. Although the city seemed reluctant to control them, DSR complained loudly that this violated its franchise, and an ordinance eventually required a license and the furnishing of a bond. Jitney operators appealed this all the way to the State Supreme Court in 1916 and lost.

DSR estimated its revenue loss to the jitneys at about 20 percent during the summer months, approximately $150,000 in 1915, $40,000 in 1916, and $10,000 in 1917. The table on page 298 shows DSR's estimate of ridership loss.

Jitneys did not appear on the streets of Superior until April 24, 1921, when hourly service was provided. It was estimated that over 27,000 local passengers were carried that year. Their operations expanded considerably the following year when they carried over 300,000 passengers. This increased to 368,000 in 1923 and to 186,000 in the first five months of 1924. The Wisconsin Railroad Commission (WRC) chose not to regulate jitneys or buses, calling it a municipal responsibility.

In September 1923 DSR petitioned the WRC for assistance in getting the city to regulate jitneys. Although DSR was able to get council action, the city failed to enforce its new regulations. Even so, the chief jitney operator ceased service to the East End and Itasca in October 1924. At the height of their operations, it is estimated the jitneys carried almost 9 percent of Superior passengers. DSR purchased the Superior jitney operation in July 1925. Voters rejected repeal of the Duluth jitney bus ordinance in a 1931 referendum. Together with the declining novelty (auto ownership had become much more common) and the hard facts of economics, the jitney had had its day.

Early buses were really just overgrown jitneys, as more seats meant more revenue. Across the country, streetcar companies cried foul and fought what they viewed as unfair and unregulated competition.

Beginning about 1920, buses proliferated. The appeal was obvious. Here was a vehicle that could more readily compete in low ridership markets than streetcars. The major expenses of laying track and stringing overhead wire were completely avoided. A bus required no conductor—it could be run by a single employee—halving the usual staffing cost. The ability to run wherever a road existed permitted bus operators to experiment with routings to maximize ridership.

Small, unregulated buses began running on Superior Street in 1924. The city put the matter to the voters in a June 16 election. The result was 12,230 votes in favor and 9,483 against a bus regulatory ordinance. A temporary restraining order on June 23 allowed the buses to resume operations. However, the June 16 election was held valid in a further court hearing, and bus operations were halted on July 16.

To facilitate litigation on this and related matters, DSR established a subsidiary corporate unit, Duluth Coach Company, in June 1924. In August another competing bus service on East 9th Street was halted by the courts. A rival interstate operation by Superior White Company began running over the Interstate Bridge just before Christmas in 1924. DSR changed the name of its bus subsidiary in March 1925 to Duluth–Superior Coach Company and immediately acquired the Superior White Company and its interstate operation.

DSR's first venture into suburban bus operations was the Morley Heights shuttle in 1924, which connected with the Woodland line at Lewis Street. It was followed a few months later by the Calvary line, which met the Woodland streetcars at the Woodland loop and extended along Calvary Road to Calvary Cemetery. All bus operations thereafter, except trolley buses, were managed by DSR's wholly held subsidiary Duluth–Superior Coach Company.

More lines followed—from the end of the Allouez streetcar line to Itasca, and from the end of the New Duluth line to Fond du Lac. 1927 brought a second interstate bus from Duluth to Superior, this time via West Duluth and the Arrowhead Bridge. In two years, DSC established 29 miles of bus routes.

At the end of 1934, the company reported that streetcars carried 70 percent of its passengers, trolley buses 21 percent, and gas buses 9 percent. These numbers shifted in 1935 with the discontinuance of streetcars in Superior. By then, Duluth–Superior Coach Company was operating 39 buses, serving all former rail lines in Superior, two interstate lines, and four lines in Duluth. With the abandonment of the remaining Duluth rail lines, this increased to 127 buses and 29 trolley buses.

Until the late 1940s, internal combustion buses were too small to replace streetcars in heavy mainline service. Their first niche was as shuttles on the fringe of the city to feed the streetcar lines. A single bus would run a short route that cycled back to the streetcar transfer point every 20 minutes or however often the streetcar ran. Transfer connections were reliable. The Morley Heights and Calvary Road shuttles to the Woodland streetcar line were examples.

Diesel engines, with higher horsepower, began replacing gasoline engines in buses, permitting them to grow in size and capacity. By 1939 in Duluth, diesel and gas buses were large enough to replace streetcars on the lightly and moderately patronized lines, while the larger trolley buses handled the heavy lines. Kathryn A. Martin Library, University of Minnesota Duluth, Archives and Special Collections.

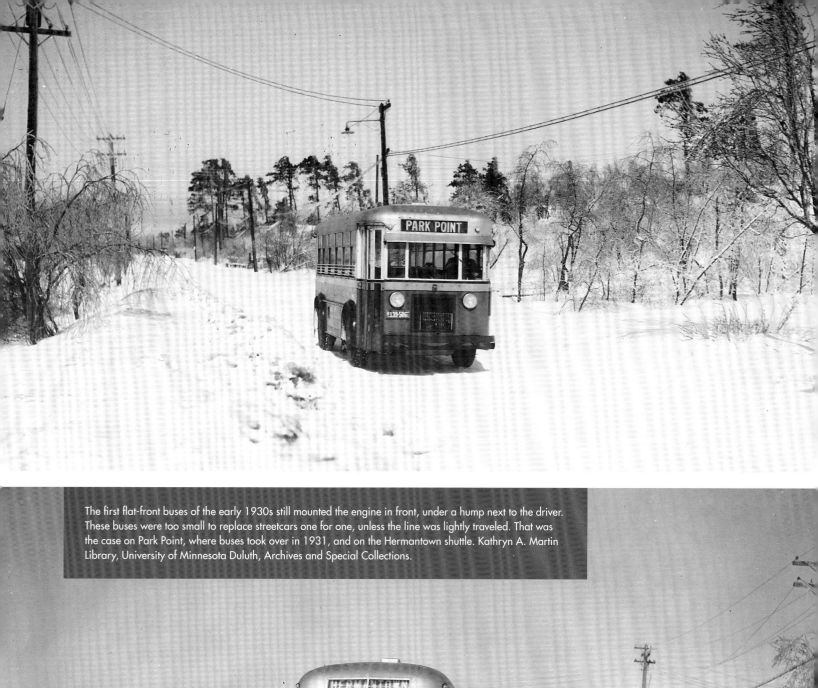

The first flat-front buses of the early 1930s still mounted the engine in front, under a hump next to the driver. These buses were too small to replace streetcars one for one, unless the line was lightly traveled. That was the case on Park Point, where buses took over in 1931, and on the Hermantown shuttle. Kathryn A. Martin Library, University of Minnesota Duluth, Archives and Special Collections.

The first trolley buses replaced streetcars on the outer end of the Lester Park line, from 45th Avenue to 61st Avenue. This is the first day of operation in 1931 at Superior Street and 45th Avenue East, where the buses transferred passengers to streetcars. Note the wire truck putting the finishing touches on the overhead. Kathryn A. Martin Library, University of Minnesota Duluth, Archives and Special Collections.

DSR soon used buses to reach destinations that were unlikely to ever be served by streetcars. These included many of the routes where streetcar lines had been proposed but never built, such as to Proctor, Fond du Lac, Itasca, and Duluth–Superior via West Duluth and the Arrowhead Bridge.

In the end, jitneys and buses weren't the real enemy. It was the private automobile. Streetcar advocates tried to persuade the public with arguments that were logical: It was cheaper to use transit than to own a car. It was certainly safer. A 1925 *Duluth Herald* article pointed out that DSR had carried 25 million passengers without killing anyone, while auto deaths were piling up rapidly. It didn't matter. The auto represented convenience and personal freedom, and that was enough. The streetcar was doomed.

Superior Street at 10th Avenue East.

ELECTRIC TROLLEY BUSES

Electric trolley buses were a niche player in the history of North American public transit. Developed in the early 1920s, by the 1930s the trolley bus offered the reliability, passenger capacity, and power of electric streetcars without the expense and inflexibility of tracks. They could pull over to the curb, removing the obstacle of a vehicle boarding and alighting passengers in the middle of the street.

Most trolley bus lines nationally were former streetcar lines. The electric generating and transmission infrastructure was already in place. A second overhead wire had to be installed as the negative return to the powerhouse. Streetcar rails had served that function. Because trolley bus poles have a swiveling harp that tracks the overhead wire even though the bus has pulled to the curb, the hardware at turns and junctions had to be replaced with a different design. After some experience, DSR also changed to a different shape of overhead wire.

Because they were electrically powered, trolley buses featured extremely rapid acceleration that diesel buses even today can't match. They could climb hills that would render a diesel asthmatic, a plus for a city like Duluth.

Trolley buses had two additional advantages—no exhaust fumes and greater capacity. Until World War II, gas and diesel buses were too small to replace streetcars one for one, but trolley buses could. Because of their greater horsepower-to-weight ratio, higher-capacity trolley buses appeared years before their diesel counterparts.

Twin City Rapid Transit experimented with a short trolley bus line on Bloomington Avenue in south Minneapolis in 1922. DSR showed some interest at the time, but the technology was not fully developed, and the Minneapolis experiment was canceled that same year.

In 1929 DSR did a study to determine where trolley buses should replace streetcars. The primary criterion was track condition. Streetcar tracks were assumed to have a 30-year life, so the best candidates were those lines due for rail replacement. Park Point was the leading candidate, but it was the east end of the Lester Park line, from 45th Avenue to 61st Avenue, that was chosen in 1931. The track on East Superior Street was at the end of its useful life, so the rest of the Lester Park line from 3rd Avenue West to 45th Avenue East was converted in 1934. Despite being only 21 percent of the fleet after the streetcars were gone, the Duluth trolley buses in 1945 carried 33 percent of all revenue passengers.

One of the great advantages of all buses, including trolley buses, is that they could pull to the curb to load. It kept transit riders out of the middle of the street and greatly reduced delays to automobiles. This is Superior Street at 2nd Avenue East ca. 1955.

Trolley bus roster.

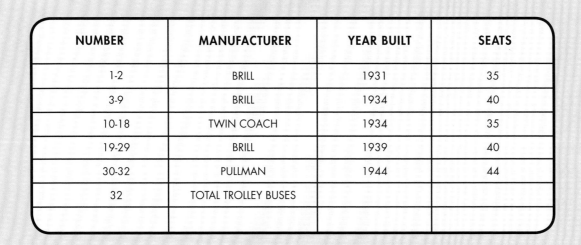

NUMBER	MANUFACTURER	YEAR BUILT	SEATS
1-2	BRILL	1931	35
3-9	BRILL	1934	40
10-18	TWIN COACH	1934	35
19-29	BRILL	1939	40
30-32	PULLMAN	1944	44
32	TOTAL TROLLEY BUSES		

RIDER'S DIGEST

Compliments of
DULUTH - SUPERIOR TRANSIT CO.

Vol. 9   **June 7, 1947**   **No. 9**

WHAT A DIFFERENCE!
See "TRANSIT'S CONTRIBUTION TO QUIETNESS", page 2

This cartoon from the Rider's Digest pamphlet distributed on the buses mocks the noisiness of the old streetcars compared to their modern replacements.

At their apex, trolley buses ran in 73 North American cities. Today they remain in only seven. After the streetcars were gone, it became clear that the over-head-wire power system made trolley buses about 15 percent more expensive to run than diesel buses, which by 1950 had grown to 50-passenger capacity. Trolley bus replacement cost was higher, even though they lasted longer than diesels. The absence of exhaust fumes and the ability to easily climb any hill wasn't enough. Transit operators were for-profit enterprises, beset with falling ridership and farebox revenue. Public transit subsidies were years in the future. As the trolley buses wore out, conversion to motor buses was the only feasible choice for most operators. Most of them disappeared during the 1950s and early 1960s.

Although spartan by today's standards, the trolley bus interiors were modern to the eyes of riders accustomed to 30-year-old streetcars. This is one of the two Pullmans built in 1944.

Trolley buses had other disadvantages beside cost. They couldn't operate away from the overhead wire. They couldn't be through-routed with gasoline shuttle buses, which required the continued operation of shuttles on Crosley Avenue and to Morgan Park, Hermantown, New Duluth, and Fond du Lac and duplicative gas bus service to Proctor. Converting to diesel buses permitted through-routing that reduced expenses and eliminated the inconvenience of transferring to and from the shuttles. Their replacement was hastened by the conversion of some downtown streets to one way that would have required an expensive realignment of the overhead wire. The reconfiguring of Mesaba Avenue on the west end of downtown also played a role.

With the exception of the Piedmont line, which was converted to gas buses in 1949, Duluth's trolley buses lasted until 1957, within a few years of their demise in other smaller cities. The onslaught of the automobile continued to drive down transit ridership, and making a profit became ever more difficult. Transit operators lowered their cost structure by eliminating the streetcars, then the trolley buses. In 1958 DST began selling surplus company-owned real estate to generate cash. The company's financial situation continued to deteriorate. A work stoppage in 1967 pushed the company to the edge, and it announced a deadline to end all service.

WARNING
LOOK OUT FOR PITS

The Duluth carhouse was modified with concrete floors and double overhead wire to serve the trolley buses. Kathryn A. Martin Library, University of Minnesota Duluth, Archives and Special Collections.

HERE ARE 5 REASONS WHY

TROLLEY COACHES

ARE POPULAR   IN DULUTH...

Since making their initial appearance in Duluth in 1931, trolley coaches have been a huge success in that city. Fifteen years' experience with these vehicles has proved to the management of the Duluth Superior Transit Company that trolley coaches are ...

1st - GOOD "SALESMEN"

Trolley coaches have met with a high degree of public acceptance in Duluth. With an average seating capacity of 39, the system's 32 coaches carried a total of 8,700,000 revenue passengers in 1945.

2nd - MONEY MAKERS

Trolley coaches are economical to operate and require very little maintenance. During 1945 they returned a net operating revenue of .2738¢ per seat mile.

3rd - LONG LIVED

The original coaches, purchased in 1931, are still in excellent condition. Each coach has traveled approximately 360,000 miles and is still averaging 25,000 miles annually.

4th - HILL CLIMBERS

The territory served is hilly and trolley coaches are operated on lines with grades up to 7 per cent. Fully loaded, they easily climb the steepest hills and are not even "winded" when they reach the top.

5th - COLD WEATHER VEHICLES

Long periods of sub-zero weather are not uncommon to Duluth. Despite severe cold spells the system's trolley coaches stay right on the job. They are even stored outdoors in temperatures which, at times, reach 25° below zero.

2761-T

Ohio Brass

MANSFIELD, OHIO
Canadian Ohio Brass Co., Ltd., Niagara Falls, Ontario

This advertisement from a post-war transit trade magazine promotes the virtues of electric trolley buses, with Duluth as the example. Ohio Brass was the primary supplier of overhead wire components. Their business was rapidly disappearing as buses replaced streetcars after World War II. Trolley buses were the only bright prospect for the future.

Service didn't end immediately, but the wheels were set in motion for a public takeover of the system, mirroring a national trend. The Duluth Transit Authority was formed in 1968. The state legislature gave it the power to levy revenue bonds. On February 1, 1970, the DTA succeeded Duluth–Superior Transit Company and has run the transit system ever since.

Three decades of fleet evolution in the storage yard: streetcars only in the 1920s, shared with trolley buses and gas buses in the 1930s, and then buses only in the 1940s. Kathryn A. Martin Library, University of Minnesota Duluth, Archives and Special Collections

No. 7

SURVIVORS AND REMNANTS

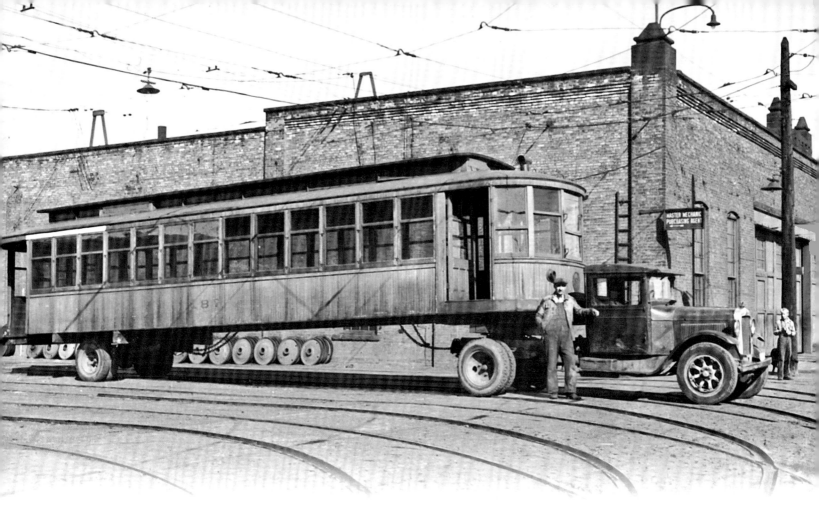

Even after the streetcar system was abandoned in 1939, pieces of it survived, and remnants remain to this day. The most obvious are the lines themselves. Although different in detail and run by buses, most follow the same streets as their electric predecessors, often carrying the same names.

Streetcar and railroad car bodies made excellent and inexpensive small buildings. As its system shrank in the 1930s, DSR began selling them and trucking them to new homes.

FOR SALE
Old Streetcars
Slightly used!

CHEAP
Cost $8,000
to $14,000.
Make us an offer

They're not much good if you figure on using them for transportation, but a lot of people have made good use of them in a variety of other ways. They're ideal for summer cabins sun porches, playhouses, greenhouses, roadside stands and many other purposes. One of our amatuer photographer friends is considering one for his yard to be used as a projection theatre for his home movies. We hear of new uses every day. There are a few left which will be sold for a reasonable price. Delivery is easily arranged at low cost. Call Mr. H. HANSEN Purchasing Agent, Melrose 260 for full particulars.

The Duluth, Missabe & Iron Range Railroad purchased car 268 and rebuilt it with a diesel engine to shuttle employees between the Proctor roundhouse and yard office. It remained in that service until about 1961.

Streetcar bodies made good cabins. This one was located near Gooseberry Falls.

The Duluth and Superior carhouses were converted to bus use until replaced in the 1970s. The DSR office building at 28th and Superior is still there, across the street from the new public transit garage. An electrical substation remains on Grand Avenue at 92nd Avenue West as part of a road maintenance garage. The Lester Park waiting station still stands, as does the Glen Avon waiting station on Woodland Avenue. Long buried tracks protrude from the pavement on 57th Avenue West and are still hidden beneath miles of other streets in both Duluth and Superior. There is virtually no physical sign of the 7th Avenue West Incline, although portions of the parallel sidewalk and stairway still exist. The sign on a namesake bar a block away on Superior Street is the only obvious indication that it ever existed.

Two car bodies became the Trolley Café in Cromwell, Minnesota.

The company's corporate records survive in the collection of the North-east Minnesota Historical Center at the University of Minnesota Duluth.

Upon abandonment in 1939, streetcar 268 was purchased by the Duluth, Missabe & Iron Range Railroad. A diesel engine was installed, and the car began a second career, shuttling railroad workers the mile between the roundhouse and yard office of the sprawling Proctor terminal until 1961. It was the last DSR streetcar to operate.

Stripped of their trucks, motors, and electrical gear, numerous car bodies were sold for use as buildings. They were cheap and weatherproof, becoming cabins, sheds, chicken coops, and, in Cromwell, Minnesota, the Trolley Café. Some are probably still out there. The body of lightweight car 303 survives as a cabin in Solon Springs, Wisconsin.

Against all odds, two Duluth streetcars run today at the Minnesota Streetcar Museum in the Twin Cities. Single trucker 78 was built in 1892 and ran until 1911. Its body became a shed in Duluth. Car 265, built at Twin City Rapid Transit's Snelling Shops in 1915, became a cabin, also in Solon Springs, Wisconsin, in 1939. Both have been restored and operate for the public every summer.

Streetcar 78 was built for DSR by the Laclede Car Company of St. Louis, Missouri, in 1892 and was typical of the first generation of electric streetcars. It served until 1911, and its body survived as a shed. Acquired by the Minnesota Streetcar Museum, it was restored to operation in 1991 and now runs on their demonstration railway in Excelsior, Minnesota.

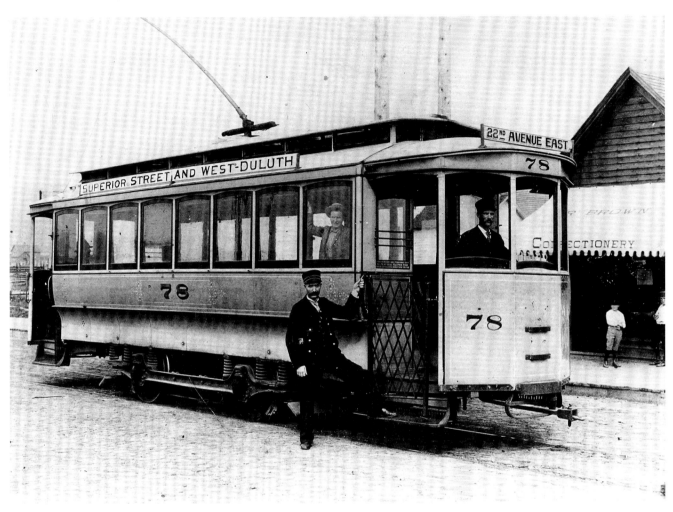

APPENDIXES

APPENDIX A: DULUTH STREET RAILWAY SYSTEM RIDERSHIP BY YEAR AND MODE

YEAR	DULUTH				SUPERIOR			SYSTEM TOTALS			
	STREETCAR	GAS BUS	TROLLEY BUS	SUBTOTAL	STREETCAR	GAS BUS	SUBTOTAL	STREETCAR	GAS BUS	TROLLEY BUS	SUBTOTAL
1901	7,318,207			7,318,207	3,585,642		3,585,642	10,903,849			10,903,849
1902	8,815,734			8,815,734	3,640,571		3,640,571	12,456,305			12,456,305
1903	10,068,043			10,068,043	3,900,556		3,900,556	13,968,599			13,968,599
1904	10,487,791			10,487,791	3,547,037		3,547,037	14,034,828			14,034,828
1905	11,376,292			11,376,292	3,828,353		3,828,353	15,204,645			15,204,645
1906	13,224,399			13,224,399	4,830,053		4,830,053	18,054,452			18,054,452
1907	15,226,121			15,226,121	5,436,707		5,436,707	20,662,828			20,662,828
1908	16,673,962			16,673,962	5,395,873		5,395,873	22,069,835			22,069,835
1909	17,838,604			17,838,604	5,479,016		5,479,016	23,317,620			23,317,620
1910	19,621,673			19,621,673	6,145,977		6,145,977	25,767,650			25,767,650
1911	20,244,173			20,244,173	5,849,888		5,849,888	26,094,061			26,094,061
1912	19,320,775			19,320,775	5,725,345		5,725,345	25,046,120			25,046,120
1913	22,794,559			22,794,559	6,959,269		6,959,269	29,753,828			29,753,828
1914	23,624,306			23,624,306	6,782,705		6,782,705	30,407,011			30,407,011
1915	21,629,220			21,629,220	5,706,238		5,706,238	27,335,458			27,335,458
1916	25,759,691			25,759,691	7,043,271		7,043,271	32,802,962			32,802,962
1917	29,420,624			29,420,624	8,181,825		8,181,825	37,602,449			37,602,449
1918	30,143,796			30,143,796	8,985,702		8,985,702	39,129,498			39,129,498
1919	35,033,472			35,033,472	10,225,655		10,225,655	45,259,127			45,259,127
1920	35,077,568			35,077,568	9,704,035		9,704,035	44,781,603			44,781,603
1921	32,393,458			32,393,458	8,335,191		8,335,191	40,728,649			40,728,649
1922	30,404,734			30,404,734	7,356,207		7,356,207	37,760,941			37,760,941
1923	29,900,207			29,900,207	7,163,244		7,163,244	37,063,451			37,063,451
1924	23,575,229	2,894		23,578,123	5,631,045		5,631,045	29,206,274	2,894		29,209,168
1925	25,149,212	256,824		25,406,036	5,488,880	149,075	5,637,955	30,638,092	405,899		31,043,991
1926	23,899,226	336,122		24,235,348	5,355,282	245,325	5,600,607	29,254,508	581,447		29,835,955
1927	21,394,672	362,583		21,757,255	4,982,296	286,927	5,269,223	26,376,968	649,510		27,026,478
1928	20,195,505	367,415		20,562,920	4,532,028	275,278	4,807,306	24,727,533	642,693		25,370,226
1929	18,305,194	362,281		18,667,475	3,916,853	352,480	4,269,333	22,222,047	714,761		22,936,808
1930	15,521,869	299,455		15,821,324	3,083,260	252,054	3,335,314	18,605,129	551,509		19,156,638
1931	12,445,484	432,185	59,451	12,937,120	1,885,139	446,042	2,331,181	14,330,623	878,227	59,451	15,268,301
1932	10,566,400	541,564	245,274	11,353,238	1,434,276	672,068	2,106,344	12,000,676	1,213,632	245,274	13,459,582
1933	9,788,414	499,913	207,192	10,495,519	1,341,387	646,429	1,987,816	11,129,801	1,146,342	207,192	12,483,335
1934	9,361,366	593,745	1,187,107	11,142,218	1,463,234	699,319	2,162,553	10,824,600	1,293,064	1,187,107	13,304,771
1935	7,780,184	1,008,643	2,719,581	11,508,508	672,609	1,695,400	2,368,009	8,452,793	2,704,043	2,719,581	13,876,471
1936	8,182,916	1,377,656	2,869,510	12,430,082		2,758,907	2,758,907	8,182,916	4,136,563	2,869,510	15,188,989
1937	8,059,267	1,704,714	2,826,066	12,590,047		2,821,514	2,821,514	8,059,267	4,526,228	2,826,066	15,411,561
1938	7,058,702	1,980,990	2,648,956	11,688,648		2,515,645	2,515,645	7,058,702	4,496,635	2,648,956	14,204,293
1939	3,534,661	4,496,478	3,632,090	11,688,229		2,531,185	2,531,185	3,534,661	7,027,663	3,632,090	14,194,414
1940		6,412,768	5,189,591	11,602,359		2,394,920	2,394,920		8,807,688	5,189,591	13,997,279
1941		6,394,058	5,322,621	11,716,679		2,457,721	2,457,721		4,915,442	5,322,621	14,174,400
1942		8,358,124	6,196,247	14,554,371		3,029,411	3,029,411		6,058,822	6,196,247	17,583,782
1943		11,388,360	7,649,279	19,037,639		4,384,048	4,384,048		8,768,096	7,649,279	23,421,687
1944		12,584,333	8,421,162	21,005,495		5,208,742	5,208,742		10,417,484	8,421,162	26,214,237
1945		12,469,897	8,700,347	21,170,244		5,286,598	5,286,598		10,573,196	8,700,347	26,456,842
1946		12,244,651	8,749,911	20,994,562		4,764,775	4,764,775		9,529,550	8,749,911	25,759,337
1947		12,604,781	8,419,272	21,024,053		4,701,965	4,701,965		9,403,930	8,419,272	25,726,018
1948		12,673,481	8,347,180	21,020,661		4,649,369	4,649,369		9,298,738	8,347,180	25,670,030
1949		10,840,737	7,420,887	18,261,624		3,784,537	3,784,537		7,569,074	7,420,887	22,046,161
1950		10,691,884	7,193,703	17,885,587		3,582,738	3,582,738		7,165,476	7,193,703	21,468,325
1951		8,291,745	5,546,245	13,837,990		2,578,246	2,578,246		5,156,492	5,546,245	16,416,236
1952		7,408,709	5,883,397	13,292,106		2,324,948	2,324,948		4,649,896	5,883,397	15,617,054
1953		6,787,266	5,441,760	12,229,026		2,080,055	2,080,055		4,160,110	5,441,760	14,309,081
1954		5,973,799	4,914,948	10,888,747		1,747,634	1,747,634		3,495,268	4,914,948	12,636,381
1955		5,222,925	4,168,312	9,391,237		1,373,093	1,373,093		2,746,186	4,168,312	10,764,330
1956		5,814,844	3,000,188	8,815,032		1,221,801	1,221,801		2,443,602	3,000,188	10,036,833
1957		7,367,371	917,500	8,284,871		1,113,448	1,113,448		2,226,896	917,500	9,398,319
1958		7,034,557		7,034,557		998,625	998,625		1,997,250		8,033,182
1959		5,276,044		5,276,044		766,888	766,888		1,533,776		6,042,932

APPENDIX B: NUMBER OF CARS IN OPERATION 1922

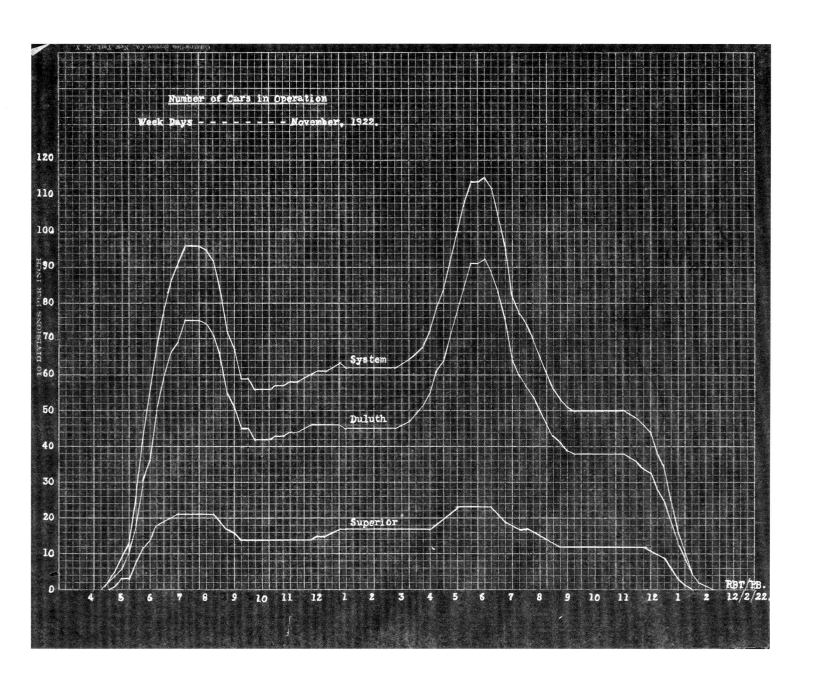

APPENDIX C: DULUTH STREET RAILWAY TRACK MILES

YEAR	DULUTH	SUPERIOR	TOTAL	COMMENTS
1882	1.00		1.00	
1883	1.00		1.00	
1884	1.23		1.23	
1885	1.67		1.67	
1886	2.99		2.99	
1887	3.25		3.25	FIRST HORSECARS IN SUPERIOR
1888	4.22		4.22	
1889	4.22		4.22	
1890	19.40		19.40	HORSECARS IN BOTH CITIES ELECTRIFIED
1891	20.53		20.53	
1892	28.93		28.93	
1893	28.93		28.93	
1894	30.60		30.60	
1895	30.60		30.60	
1896	36.10		36.10	
1897	36.10		36.10	
1898	36.10		36.10	
1899	36.10		36.10	
1900	48.80	26.00	74.80	SUPERIOR RAPID TRANSIT ACQUIRED
1901	48.80	23.40	72.20	
1902	49.51	21.55	71.06	
1903	49.51	21.55	71.06	
1904	49.50	21.55	71.05	
1905	50.93	21.55	72.48	
1906	51.70	21.57	73.27	

This table shows the number of miles of track operated by Duluth Street Railway. Track miles owned by other companies are not shown until DSR took ownership.

APPENDIX C: DULUTH STREET RAILWAY TRACK MILES (CONT.)

YEAR	DULUTH	SUPERIOR	TOTAL	COMMENTS
1907	53.47	21.57	75.04	
1908	54.47	22.67	77.14	
1909	55.24	22.75	77.99	
1910	54.96	23.53	78.49	
1911	56.89	23.54	80.43	
1912	58.88	23.54	82.42	
1913	58.93	23.54	82.47	
1914	58.96	23.54	82.50	
1915	60.22	23.54	83.76	
1916	65.47	23.72	89.19	
1917	76.56	27.32	103.88	INTERSTATE TRACTION (PARK POINT) ACQUIRED
1918	76.70	27.32	104.02	
1919	76.77	27.32	104.09	
1920	76.77	27.51	104.28	
1921	76.96	28.61	105.57	
1922	77.20	28.63	105.83	
1923	79.01	28.63	107.64	
1924	81.04	28.63	109.67	
1925	81.04	28.69	109.73	
1926	83.67	28.69	112.36	
1927	83.92	28.69	112.61	
1928	85.57	28.69	114.26	HIGHEST SYSTEM MILEAGE
1929	84.84	28.80	113.64	
1931	84.84	28.80	113.64	
1935	65.98		65.98	SUPERIOR ABANDONED
1936	63.71		63.71	
1937	61.15		61.15	
1938	60.58		60.58	

APPENDIX D: TRIPS BY STREET 1925

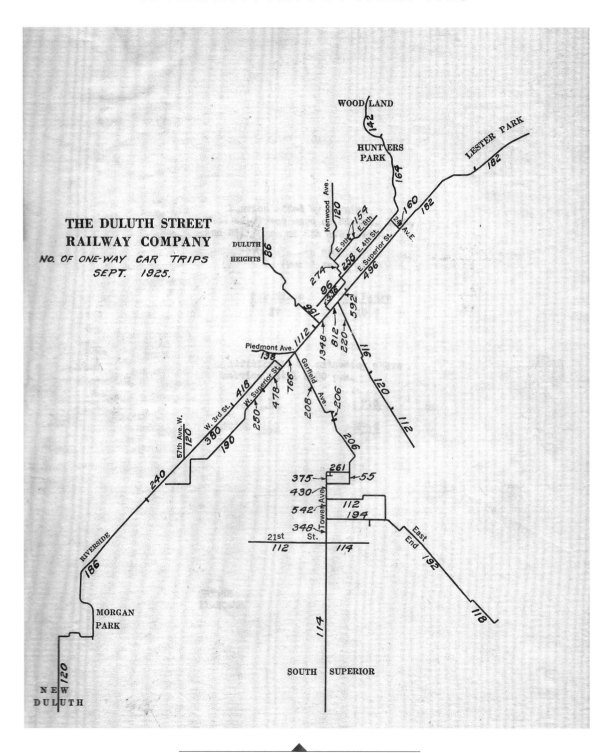

This map, created by DSR, shows the number of week-day streetcar trips on each line segment in 1925.

APPENDIX E: STREETCAR RIDERSHIP BY HOUR AND DAY OF WEEK, 1925

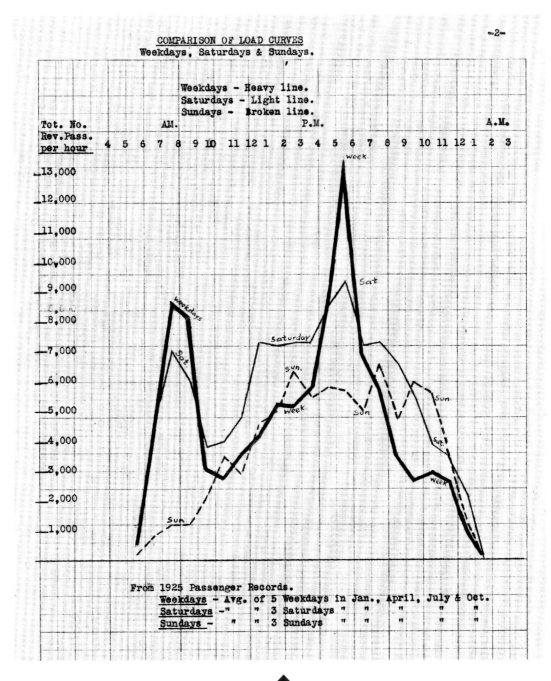

This original DJR chart compares weekday and weekend ridership patterns. These curves are familiar to all transit professionals and persist largely unchanged in most large city systems to this day. For example, the afternoon rush hour is usually heavier than the morning because it also includes nonwork trips that don't happen in the morning. Also typical is the quiet period between 9 a.m. and noon.

APPENDIX F: PASSENGERS CARRIED BETWEEN DULUTH AND SUPERIOR

DULUTH–SUPERIOR BRIDGE

YEAR	STREETCAR	BUSES	SUBTOTAL
1900	351,546		351,546
1901	962,561		962,561
1902	1,157,214		1,157,214
1903	1,326,927		1,326,927
1904	1,207,724		1,207,724
1905	1,272,660		1,272,660
1906	1,524,869		1,524,869
1907	1,217,812		1,217,812
1908	1,267,862		1,267,862
1909	1,606,869		1,606,869
1910	1,776,591		1,776,591
1911	1,705,532		1,705,532
1912	1,552,698		1,552,698
1913	1,948,525		1,948,525
1914	1,969,309		1,969,309
1915	1,671,869		1,671,869
1916	2,021,655		2,021,655
1917	2,711,757		2,711,757
1918	2,611,108		2,611,108
1919	2,674,035		2,674,035
1920	2,421,129		2,421,129
1921	2,135,999		2,135,999
1922	1,909,368		1,909,368
1923	1,944,835		1,944,835
1924	1,621,832		1,621,832
1925	1,664,635	222,807	1,887,442
1926	1,588,327	319,221	1,907,548
1927	1,349,687	288,625	1,638,312
1928	1,260,164	167,185	1,427,349
1929	1,083,035	161,436	1,244,471
1930	687,830	249,117	936,947
1931	369,911	290,183	660,094
1932	378,926	312,983	691,909
1933	356,022	254,214	610,236

Streetcars, later joined by competing buses, transported passengers between Duluth and Superior via the Interstate Bridge and later the Blatnik Bridge that replaced it. From 1927 to 1956 there were also interstate buses between Superior and West Duluth. Because the data extends all the way to 1964, the decline of transit at the hands of the automobile is evident.

APPENDIX F: PASSENGERS CARRIED BETWEEN DULUTH AND SUPERIOR (CONT.)

DULUTH–SUPERIOR BRIDGE

YEAR	STREETCAR	BUSES	SUBTOTAL
1934	361,942	275,751	637,693
1935	141,825	481,480	623,305
1936		675,714	675,714
1937		706,512	706,512
1938		626,793	626,793
1939		618,414	618,414
1940		616,579	616,579
1941		622,417	622,417
1942		747,965	747,965
1943		1,055,929	1,055,929
1944		1,233,302	1,233,302
1945		1,222,662	1,222,662
1946		1,123,783	1,123,783
1947		1,108,968	1,108,968
1948		1,104,917	1,104,917
1949		940,049	940,049
1950		848,972	848,972
1951		629,731	629,731
1952		621,706	621,706
1953		568,728	568,728
1954		473,306	473,306
1955		367,661	367,661
1956		364,667	364,667
1957		323,911	323,911
1958		298,546	298,546
1959		242,710	242,710
1960		284,930	284,930
1961		266,142	266,142
1962		248,887	248,887
1963		219,035	219,035
1964		212,687	212,687

No. (See Map)	Name of Line	Base Headway	No. Cars Basic Schedule	Rush Hour Headways A.M.	Midday	P.M.	Additional Cars – Rush Hours A.M. Summer	Winter	Midday Summer	Winter	P.M. Summer	Winter	Length of Line (Round trip miles)	Schedule Speed Miles Per Hour With Layover	Without Layover	Duration of Layover	Running Time (Mins. Round trip Midday – Excl. Layover)
	Main Lines																
1	Lester Park	20		10	20	10							12.30*	10.98	12.72#	9#	58
2	Crosley Ave.	20		10	20	10							12.48	11.52	12.90	7	58
3	Woodland	20	23	10	20	10							11.64	10.74	11.64	5	60
4	East 8th St.	20		10	20	7½	19	29	6	6	32	36	5.78	7.50	8.88	7	39
	-to-																
5	New Duluth	20		20	20	20							24.69	12.42	13.68	11	108
6	57W. & Medina St.	20		20	20	20							10.86	8.22	11.40	22	57
7	71st W. & Grand	-		10	10	10							12.05	10.50	12.05	8½	60
8	Aerial Bridge	20		10	10	10											
9	to 32nd Ave. W.	-	4	10	10	10	4	4	4	4	5	5	6.83	8.16	10.74	4-8	38
10	& West Duluth	20		10	20	10							12.71	10.86	11.88	6	64
	Hill Lines																
11-12	Kenwood to 8W.	20	3	20	20	20	0	0	0	0	1	1	7.24	7.24	10.08	9-8	43
13-12	East 4th St. to 8W	10	6	10	10	7½							6.30	7.56	9.90	8-4	38
14	& Piedmont Ave.	20		10	20	10	1	2	0	0	2	3	9.69	8.28	9.69	6-4	60
15-16	W4th (5E. to 5W.)	20	1	20	20	20	0	0	0	0	0	0	1.87	5.61	8.20	4-5	11
17	Incline	15	2	15	15	15	0	0	0	0	0	0	1.12	4.44	8.40	7	8
18	Highland	30	1	15	30	15	1	1	0	0	1	1	3.72	7.44	11.70	10-1	19
19	Park Point	20	2	20	20	20	0	0	0	0	0	0	6.61	9.90	11.64	3-3	34
	Interstate																
20-21	Armory Loop to S.Sup.	20	9	10	20	10	4	4	0	0	4	4	22.91	10.56	12.00	10-6	114
22	" " 21st & Gd												17.99	9.72	12.00	10-10	90
23-24	Billings Pk.& Bdw.	20	3	20	20	20	0	0	0	0	0	1	8.96	8.96	11.16	8-4	48
25-26 27	Allouez, E.End to 6th St. Loop	20	4	10	10	10	3	4	3	3	3	6	12.56	9.42	11.50	14	66
	Total -		58				32	44	13	13	48	57		9.56-(1st 8 Mos. 1929)			

* As the lines under "Main Lines" are all operated together by through-routing, distance and speed on each is figured to 3rd Ave. West, the business center.

Under winter conditions more running time is allowed and less layover is left.

RBT-9/18/29.
PG.

APPENDIX H: STREETCAR RIDERSHIP VERSUS AUTOMOBILE REGISTRATION

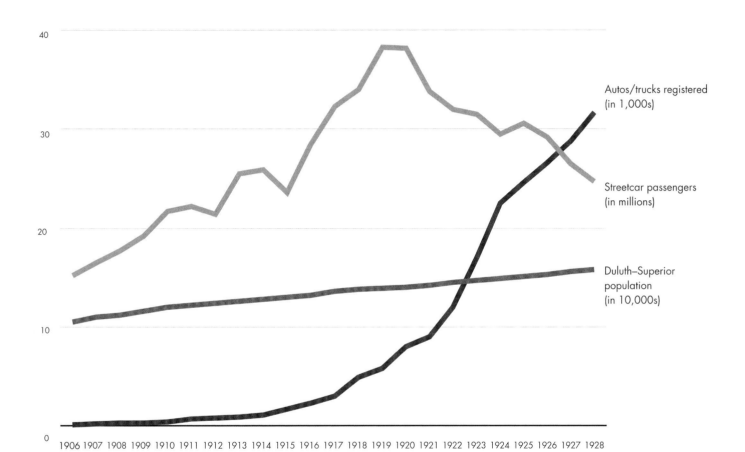

Drawn from an original DSR chart, this graph shows transit system ridership against combined Duluth–Superior population and auto and truck ownership. It should be noted that miles of paved roads increased rapidly along with auto ownership.

APPENDIX I: PASSENGERS BY ROUTE SEGMENT, 1925

ROUTE SEGMENT	DAILY PASSENGERS
SUPERIOR STREET, DOWNTOWN TO 24TH AVENUE EAST	12,009
WEST END ON 3RD STREET (21ST TO 40TH AVENUE WEST)	11,744
WEST DULUTH ON GRAND AVENUE (74TH TO 40TH AVENUE WEST)	8,080
GARFIELD AVENUE	6,919
WEST END ON SUPERIOR STREET, DOWNTOWN TO 40TH AVENUE WEST	5,998
CONNOR POINT AND TOWER AVENUE TO 21ST STREET	5,497
EAST 4TH STREET	5,291
EAST END–SUPERIOR	4,734
EAST 9TH STREET TO 14TH AVENUE EAST	4,337
LESTER PARK (SUPERIOR STREET EAST OF 24TH AVENUE EAST)	4,152
MORGAN PARK TO 74TH AVENUE WEST	4,091
WEST DULUTH VIA ONEOTA STREET TO 40TH AVENUE WEST	2,812
PIEDMONT AVENUE	2,426
SOUTH SUPERIOR	2,186
INCLINE	2,170
1949 KENWOOD AVENUE SOUTH OF 14TH STREET	2,158
LAKE AVENUE	2,146
BILLINGS PARK	1,781
WOODLAND AVENUE NORTH OF MINNEAPOLIS AVENUE	1,724
NEW DULUTH TO MORGAN PARK	1,483
PARK POINT	1,481
HUNTER'S PARK (24TH AVENUE EAST TO MINNEAPOLIS)	1,384
EAST 8TH STREET	1,221
HIGHLAND AVENUE	1,114
ALLOUEZ	1,009
BROADWAY	729
21ST STREET (TOWER AVENUE TO GRAND AVENUE)	712
KENWOOD AVENUE NORTH OF 14TH STREET	543
6TH STREET LOOP IN SUPERIOR	491
WEST 4TH STREET	303

This table, taken from a DSR report, ranks the line segments from highest to lowest weekday ridership.

APPENDIX J: ROLLING STOCK ROSTER

DULUTH STREET RAILWAY EARLY STREETCARS

QUANTITY	CAR NUMBER	TYPE	BUILDER	YEAR BUILT	COMMENTS
3	1–3	HORSECAR		1883	NARROW GAUGE. ONE SOLD TO MINNESOTA POINT STREET RAILWAY.
12	4–15	HORSECAR		1886	NARROW GAUGE. SIX SOLD TO MINNESOTA POINT STREET RAILWAY.
3	16–18	HORSECAR		1888	NARROW GAUGE.
12	19–30	SINGLE TRUCK CLOSED	LA CLEDE CAR CO.	1890	TWO SOLD TO DULUTH BELT LINE.
7	31–37	SINGLE TRUCK CLOSED	LA CLEDE CAR CO.	1891	
6	38–43	SINGLE TRUCK CLOSED	LA CLEDE CAR CO.	1891	TWO SOLD TO DULUTH BELT LINE. CAR 42 LATER CONVERTED TO PRIVATE CAR "ST. LOUIS" IN 1896.
3	44–46	SINGLE TRUCK CLOSED	NORTHERN CAR CO.	1891	
20	47–66	SINGLE TRUCK CLOSED	LA CLEDE CAR CO.	1892	FOUR SOLD TO INTERSTATE TRACTION (PARK POINT).
1	67	DOUBLE TRUCK OPEN	NORTHERN CAR CO.	1892	ORIGINALLY TCRT #548.
20	68–87	SINGLE TRUCK CLOSED	LA CLEDE CAR CO.	1893	
1	88	SINGLE TRUCK CLOSED		1894	
2	89–90	SINGLE TRUCK CLOSED	BROWNELL	1890	ORIGINALLY BUILT FOR MOTOR LINE IMPROVEMENT CO. (WOODLAND LINE).
4	91–94	SINGLE TRUCK OPEN TRAILER	BROWNELL	1891	ORIGINALLY BUILT FOR MOTOR LINE IMPROVEMENT CO. (WOODLAND LINE). SOLD TO INTERSTATE TRACTION (PARK POINT).

APPENDIX J: ROLLING STOCK ROSTER (CONT.)

SUPERIOR RAPID TRANSIT COMPANY EARLY STREETCARS (ALL NARROW GAUGE)

QUANTITY	CAR NUMBER	TYPE	BUILDER	YEAR BUILT	COMMENTS
3	1–3	HORSECAR		1884	CONVERTED TO TRAILER BEHIND ELECTRIC CARS.
3	4–6	SINGLE TRUCK CLOSED TRAILER	PULLMAN	1890	
2	101–102	SINGLE TRUCK CLOSED	STEPHENSON	1888	
5	103–107	SINGLE TRUCK CLOSED	PULLMAN	1890	
2	108–109	SINGLE TRUCK CLOSED	PULLMAN	1891	
10	110–119	SINGLE TRUCK CLOSED	NORTHERN CAR CO.	1891	TWO SOLD TO INTERSTATE TRACTION (PARK POINT).
5	120–124	SINGLE TRUCK CLOSED	ST. LOUIS CAR CO.	1892	ONE SOLD TO INTERSTATE TRACTION (PARK POINT).
6	125–130	SINGLE TRUCK CLOSED	LA CLEDE CAR CO.	1893	
6	131–136	SINGLE TRUCK CLOSED	AMERICAN	1894	

APPENDIX J: ROLLING STOCK ROSTER (CONT.)

STREETCARS ACQUIRED THROUGH PURCHASE OF PARK POINT TRACTION COMPANY 1917

DSR NUMBER	PARK POINT NUMBER	BUILDER	YEAR BUILT	COMMENTS
N/A	4	LA CLEDE CAR CO.	1899	
285-286	10–11	ST. LOUIS CAR CO.	1905	
287-288	101–102	DANVILLE CAR CO.	1911	

APPENDIX J: ROLLING STOCK ROSTER (CONT.)

STREETCARS BUILT FOR DSR BY TWIN CITY RAPID TRANSIT COMPANY

QUANTITY	NUMBERS	BUILT AT SHOP	YEAR BUILT	SOLD TO DSR (IF FIRST OWNED BY TCRT)	CLASS	COMMENTS
12	151–162	31ST STREET	1900		B-3	
1	63	31ST STREET	1901		INCLINE	REPLACED BY 220 AND 221 IN 1911.
15	163–177	31ST STREET	1904		D-7	163 CONVERTED TO DOUBLE-ENDED CROSLEY SHUTTLE CAR IN 1934.
5	178–182	31ST STREET	1905	1905	E-4	
15	183–197	31ST STREET	1906		G-6	
6	198–203	SNELLING	1908		I-1	
11	204–214	SNELLING	1909		K-2	
5	215–219	SNELLING	1910		K-8	
2	220–221	SNELLING	1911		INCLINE	
16	222–237	SNELLING	1911		K-8	
4	238–241	SNELLING	1911	1911	L-8	
10	242–251	SNELLING	1912		L-8	
3	252–254	SNELLING	1912	1912	L-8	
2	255–256	31ST STREET	1901	1913	C-3	ASSIGNED TO HIGHLAND LINE.
6	257–262	SNELLING	1914		L-8	
4	263–266	SNELLING	1915	1916	L-8	
4	267–270	SNELLING	1914	1916	L-8	
8	271–278	SNELLING	1917		L-8	
4	280–283	31ST STREET	1903		D-7	LEASED TO DSR 1917–1920.
2	279, 284	SNELLING	1914		L-8	
6	289–294	31ST STREET	1906-7		G-6, H-6	
6	295–300		1919		SINGLE TRUCK BIRNEY	BUILT BY AMERICAN CAR CO.
5	301–305	SNELLING	1925		LIGHT-WEIGHT	BUILT BY LICENSEE LIGHT-WEIGHT NOISELESS STREET-CAR COMPANY.

APPENDIX J: ROLLING STOCK ROSTER (CONT.)

SERVICE CARS

CAR NUMBER	BUILDER	YEAR BUILT	TYPE	COMMENTS
51	LA CLEDE CAR CO.	1892	TOWER CAR	CONVERTED TO TRAILER BEHIND ELECTRIC CARS.
1/39	DSR	1898	SNOW PLOW	
1/64	DSR	1901	FLAT CAR	
2/65	DSR	1902	FLAT CAR	
2/66	SDSR	1903	SNOW PLOW	
1/67	DSR	1904	TOWER CAR	TWO SOLD TO INTERSTATE TRACTION (PARK POINT).
3/140	DSR	1906	SNOW PLOW	ONE SOLD TO INTERSTATE TRACTION (PARK POINT).
3/96	DSR	1907	FLAT CAR	
1/141	TWIN CITY RAPID TRANSIT	1911	WRECKER-CRANE	
4/97	DSR	1912	FLAT CAR	
	DSR	ABOUT 1915	GONDOLA TRAILER	
	DSR	ABOUT 1915	FLAT TRAILER	
	DSR	ABOUT 1915	FLAT TRAILER	
62	LA CLEDE CAR CO.	1892	SUPPLY TRAILER	
5/142	DSR	1917	FLAT CAR	

APPENDIX J: ROLLING STOCK ROSTER (CONT.)

SERVICE CARS

CAR NUMBER	BUILDER	YEAR BUILT	TYPE	COMMENTS
6/143	DSR	1917	FLAT CAR	
7/144	DSR	1917	FLAT CAR	
1/145	DSR	1917	FLAT CAR	
4/146	TWIN CITY RAPID TRANSIT	1917	SNOW PLOW	
131	AMERICAN CAR CO.	1894	SUPPLY CAR	
	THEW CO.	1922	ELECTRIC SHOVEL	
	DSR	1923	GONDOLA TRAILER	
	DSR	1923	GONDOLA TRAILER	
	DSR	1923	GONDOLA TRAILER	
GOLIATH	DSR	1928	ICE BREAKER	
5/147	LA CLEDE CAR CO.	1899	SNOW PLOW	
3/148	LA CLEDE CAR CO.	1899	TOWER CAR	

APPENDIX K: BUS ROUTE ADDITIONS AND SERVICE CHANGES, 1924–1939

MORLEY HEIGHTS BUS LINE STARTED, OPERATED BY DULUTH COACH COMPANY BETWEEN MORLEY HEIGHTS AND WOODLAND STREETCAR LINE AT LEWIS STREET.	DECEMBER 18,1924
CALVARY LINE STARTED FROM END OF WOODLAND STREETCAR LINE AT AUSTIN STREET TO CALVARY CEMETERY.	JANUARY 28,1925
DULUTH–SUPERIOR INTERCITY LINE ACQUIRED BY DSR FROM SUPERIOR WHITE COMPANY.	APRIL 12,1925
ITASCA LINE STARTED, FROM END OF ALLOUEZ STREETCAR LINE TO ITASCA.	JULY 13,1925
FOND DU LAC LINE STARTED FROM END OF NEW DULUTH STREETCAR LINE, FOLLOWING ABANDONMENT OF NORTHERN PACIFIC RAILWAY DULUTH–FOND DU LAC PASSENGER TRAIN.	JANUARY 1,1926
CALVARY LINE EXTENDED THROUGH ARNOLD DISTRICT.	MAY 20,1926
DOWNTOWN DULUTH–DOWNTOWN SUPERIOR LINE VIA ARROWHEAD BRIDGE STARTED.	JULY 20, 1927
SKYLINE BOULEVARD LINE STARTED FROM 6TH AVENUE EAST AND 7TH STREET STREETCAR CONNECTION TO HERMANTOWN VIA SKYLINE BOULEVARD AND HERMANTOWN ROAD.	JUNE 15,1928
REMAINDER OF SKYLINE BOULEVARD LINE ABANDONED.	NOVEMBER 1,1929
ARROWHEAD BRIDGE LINE SHORTENED TO SUPERIOR–WEST DULUTH.	APRIL 1,1930
PARK POINT STREETCAR LINE CONVERTED TO BUS.	JUNE 16,1931
SOUTH SUPERIOR AND BROADWAY STREETCAR LINES CONVERTED TO BUS.	JUNE 26,1931
LESTER PARK STREETCAR LINE FROM 45TH AVENUE EAST TO 61ST AVENUE EAST CONVERTED TO TROLLEY BUS.	OCTOBER 4,1931

DSR began running buses in 1924, and by the mid-1930s buses carried more than half the system ridership. Without the expense of laying tracks and stringing overhead wire, DSR could experiment with bus routings, and so it did.

APPENDIX K: BUS ROUTE ADDITIONS AND SERVICE CHANGES, 1924–1939 (CONT.)

REMAINDER OF LESTER PARK STREETCAR LINE FROM DOWNTOWN TO 45TH AVENUE EAST CONVERTED TO TROLLEY BUS. PIEDMONT STREETCAR LINE CONVERTED TO TROLLEY BUS.	AUGUST 5, 1934
ALLOUEZ PORTION OF EAST END STREETCAR LINE CONVERTED TO BUS FOLLOWING ICE STORM DAMAGE.	MARCH 5, 1935
INTERSTATE AND BILLINGS PARK STREETCAR LINES CONVERTED TO BUS	JUNE 6, 1935
EAST END STREETCAR LINE CONVERTED TO BUS, ENDING ALL SUPERIOR STREETCAR SERVICE.	JUNE 24, 1935
KENWOOD STREETCAR LINE CONVERTED TO BUS.	AUGUST 31, 1936
LONDON ROAD BUS LINE STARTED.	JANUARY 4, 1937
GARY–NEW DULUTH PORTION OF STREETCAR LINE CONVERTED TO BUS.	MAY 5, 1937
WEST 8TH STREET LINE STARTED CONNECTING STREETCAR AT 39TH AND GRAND TO STREETCAR AT 57TH AVENUE WEST AND 8TH STREET VIA 40TH AVENUE WEST AND 8TH STREET.	JUNE 1, 1937
BAY VIEW HEIGHTS–PROCTOR LINE STARTED, CONNECTING TO STREETCAR IN WEST DULUTH.	JULY 12, 1937
HERMANTOWN LINE EXTENDED TO HAINES ROAD.	NOVEMBER 1, 1937
BUSES SUBSTITUTED FOR WEST DULUTH VIA ONEOTA STREETCARS EVENINGS AND SUNDAYS.	JUNE 21, 1938
WEST DULUTH VIA ONEOTA STREETCAR LINE REPLACED BY BUS.	MARCH 13, 1939
WOODLAND, CROSLEY, EAST 4TH STREET, EAST 8TH STREET, GRAND AVENUE–MORGAN PARK STREETCAR LINES REPLACED BY BUS.	JULY 9, 1939
INCLINE AND HIGHLAND STREETCAR LINE, LAST RAIL SERVICES IN DULUTH, REPLACED BY BUS.	SEPTEMBER 4, 1939

APPENDIX L: DULUTH STREET RAILWAY COMPANY ORGANIZATION CHART

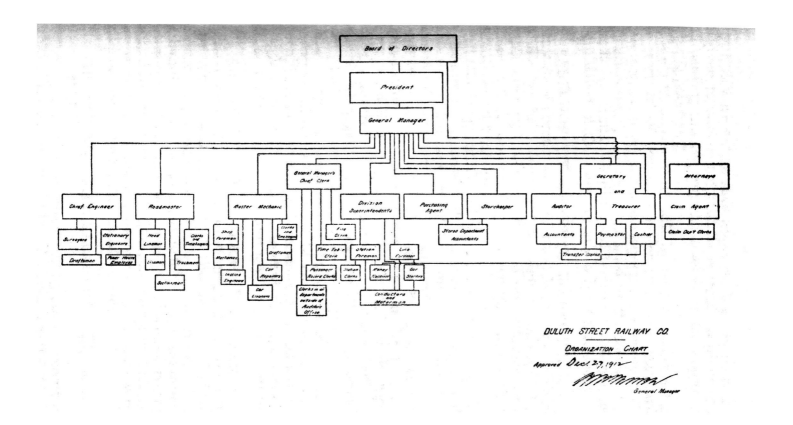

FURTHER READING

Alanen, Arnold R. *Morgan Park: Duluth, U.S. Steel, and the Forging of a Company Town*. Minneapolis: University of Minnesota Press, 2007.

Beck, Bill, and C. Patrick Labadie. *Pride of the Inland Seas: An Illustrated History of the Port of Duluth–Superior*. Afton, Minn.: Afton Historical Society Press, 2004.

Badger Traction. Central Electric Railfans' Association, 1969.

"Buses of Duluth–Superior," *Motor Coach Age*, March 1985.

Dierkins, Tony. Zenith: *A Postcard Perspective of Historic Duluth*. Duluth: X-Communication, 2006.

Dierkins, Tony, and Maryanne C. Norton. Lost Duluth. Duluth: Zenith City Press, 2012.

Hudelson, Richard, and Carl Ross. *By the Ore Docks: A Working People's History of Duluth*. Minneapolis: University of Minnesota Press, 2006.

Kreuzberger, James. Unpublished manuscript, research, and notes on Duluth–Superior streetcars.

Lydecker, Richard, and Lawrence J. Sommer, eds. *Duluth: Sketches of the Past*. American Revolution Bicentennial Commission, 1976.

Moran, Ken, and Neil Storch. *UMD Comes of Age*: *The First One Hundred Years*. Virginia Beach, Va.: Donning Co., 1996.

Olson, Russell. *Electric Railways of Minnesota*. H. M. Smyth Company, 1976.

Sebree, Mac, and Paul Ward. *The Trolley Coach in North America*. Interurbans Press, 1974.

INDEX

Aaron Isaacs worked for Metro Transit for thirty-three years. He has been active in the Minnesota Streetcar Museum for forty years, serving on its board and as its magazine editor and archivist. He is author of *Trackside around the Twin Cities and the Como–Harriet Streetcar Line* and coauthor of *Twin Cities by Trolley: The Streetcar Era in Minneapolis and St. Paul*. He edits *Tourist Railroads and Railway Museums* magazine.